SHANGHAI POLICEMAN

E.W. PETERS

FOREWORD BY ROBERT BICKERS

First published in 1937

SHANGHAI POLICEMAN
By E. W. Peters

ISBN-13: 978-988-19983-8-5

Shanghai Policeman was first published in 1937.
Edition copyright © 2011 Earnshaw Books.
Foreword copyright © 2011 Robert Bickers.

Published by Earnshaw Books Ltd. (Hong Kong).

For Sumiko

LIST OF ILLUSTRATIONS

FOREWORD

IN A CITY of myths, the Shanghai policeman is an enduring symbol. All the routine problems of urban policing were exacerbated by the challenges facing a city governed by three different municipal administrations and run by at least two other police forces. He faced a powerful underworld threat—the Shanghai Green Gang, waves of kidnapping and armed robbery, intermittent civil warfare and foreign invasion, espionage and violent political terrorism. The force was well armed, and it needed to be: armed criminals had everything to lose under Chinese law, so they shot to kill. Unarmed thugs attacked the police to steal their weapons, and left no witnesses if they could help it. The numbers on the annual roll call of the dead of the Shanghai Municipal Police (SMP), which patrolled the foreign-controlled International Settlement in the city, rose steeply in the 1930s. Over 120 Sikh, Chinese, Japanese and European men were killed on duty between 1914 and 1942. So the force's memory lives on not least because it was forced to pioneer modern riot control methods, and the unarmed combat and firearms training programmes that influenced developments internationally in the middle of the twentieth century. It had to be as modern as the threats it faced.

The Shanghai connection remained a villainous one. The assumed story of the foreign recruits of the 1920s and 1930s is often that they were all ex-Black & Tans—paramilitaries who served during the Irish revolt—or Palestine Police, forces with a reputation for violence, or else that they were all former soldiers. But although there were many ex-servicemen in the force, the truth was more prosaic, and those who had earlier served in the colonial police were tiny in number. One reason the myths grew, was that very little was known about these men and the history of the force before the Shanghai archives began to open in the mid-1990s, as well as a sense that in a tough city the policeman must have been tough himself.

The SMP lives on in the European popular imagination through Hergé's 1933 Tintin story, *Le Lotus Bleu*, set in a vividly realised Shanghai, while the racist and corrupt chief of the force in that volume appeared in two further instalments of the Belgian *bande dessinée* hero's story. Although the odd contemporary article about the policing of the city can be found in such publications as the *Police Journal*, only one man, E.W. Peters, ever published his story of life on the Shanghai beat while the force was extant. And Ernie Peters had his particular reasons for doing so, as you shall see.

An unemployed ex-army motor mechanic, Ernest William Peters, arrived in Shanghai in late November 1929, having a month earlier in London been sworn into the service of the Shanghai Municipal Council as a Probationary Sergeant. It was a routine appointment, and there was little unusual about either his background or past experience. Peters had left school at 16, worked on a troop ship and then as a colliery pony driver, before spending seven years in the Royal Tank Corps, five of them in India. A taste for service overseas probably steered him to apply to the SMP. In April 1936, after six and a half years in China, he was back in Britain, and providing interviews to the popular press about his Shanghai years: 'Ruined by Fight for His Honour', announced the *News of the World*, 'He won, but was left nearly penniless'.

Peters announced he would be writing a book, and it is that volume, 'edited' by Hugh Barnes and published in 1937, that you have in your hands. It is at once a memoir of the life and work of a foreign policeman in the International settlement at Shanghai, an expose, as the dust cover blurb noted, of 'armed gangs, drug traffic, opium smoking and Chinese methods of justice, punishments and executions' — the seconds before one of which were caught on the cover itself — and the inside tale of one of Shanghai's 'most sensational cases of recent years, when the author was charged with the murder of a Chinese beggar'. This singular memoir exemplifies, both in its tale of ordinary policing and in its account of that 'sensational' case, the politically explosive position in which the Shanghai Municipal Police always operated.

The Shanghai Municipal Police (SMP) had been established in 1854, and had grown with the settlement from an initial complement of a score of men recruited from Hong Kong, to a force that in 1935 was almost 5,000 strong. Peters was one of 489 'Foreign Branch' staff, mostly Britons, leavened with White Russians, who policed the city with 583 Sikhs, 251 Japanese, and 3,574 Chinese. It was a sophisticated organisation, dealing with all the problems generated by a settled population in 1935 of 1,160,000 Chinese and foreign nationals, and those tens of thousands who came through its porous borders from the wider city of Shanghai every day. Most of the work of men like Peters was routine urban policing, but it also had an important political section, the Special Branch, which in liaison with Chinese and foreign agencies fought to break communist activism and Soviet espionage, and an innovative, world-leading riot squad, the Reserve Unit, in which Peters spent a part of his Shanghai police career.

The SMP had by 1935 recovered from its greatest disaster, the May 30th incident in 1925, when a panicking station commander, Edward Everson, fearing that political demonstrators would over-run his station just off Nanjing Road, ordered his mixed complement of mainly Sikh and Chinese constables to open fire. Everson had fired the first of the shots, and 12 Chinese died, his actions catapulting the International Settlement at Shanghai into a national and international storm. More than any other single event in the 1920s, May 30th radicalised large numbers of younger Chinese to struggle against the foreign presence in China. Anti-British boycotts were launched, and further bloody incidents in Canton and at Wuhan deepened the crisis. The Settlement survived these events, but in the aftermath its police force was augmented, professionalised under a new command, and it developed its new crowd-control strategies and enhanced its intelligence and political policing.

Ernie Peters joined as a result of this major bid by the force to boost numbers. He was one of 118 men recruited in 1929, mostly coming out from Britain in relatively small batches (partly to lessen the danger of their being subverted *en route* by communist agents). Like him many of those recruited in 1929 were ex-army, but they came from all walks of life. They were ex-miners, postmen, salesmen, farm-workers and railway workers, or they had been serving in British police forces. Many of those who served in the army left their regiments in Shanghai to join the SMP because they enjoyed life in the city. They generally did not make very good policemen, liking life in the city rather too much. Its entertainment culture was attractive, and even a low-ranking foreign policeman led a more comfortable life than he would have at home. They complained unfailingly, and often with reason, about the poor treatment by their self-anointed foreign social betters, but they shared many of the perks of the Shanghai life nonetheless. Some of these benefits included the bars and the nightlife they escorted their Russian or Japanese girlfriends to, and the houseboat holidays out west into the countryside for hunting game. Former servicemen were deemed good recruits by the police hierarchy, as it was assumed that they would be more amenable to discipline, but in fact most of them swapped army for police life to get into what they intended to be a more relaxed and flexible civilian job. The resulting conflicts fill the police files and disciplinary records.

Peters was a nondescript policeman: 'usual ex-soldier type', an annual appraisal noted, 'not too reliable, but not a bad officer under supervision'. He boozed a bit more obviously than most, and bent the rules where he could. Peters' record shows him swearing at a superior, staying out of police quarters without permission, 'soliciting drink on duty', and disobeying orders. 'Inclines to take chances' notes another appraisal. As was required, he took classes in Shanghainese, although by early 1935 he was failing to keep this up adequately and his career was likely to stall as a result. Peters took seven months' leave in October 1934, sailing via Japan to Canada, then heading overland to take ship to Britain, probably back to Dover, his hometown. He sailed back to Shanghai via the Suez Canal in the spring of 1935, and according to his account here, was planning by the end of 1935 to resign his position, and move back to Britain with his Japanese girlfriend, Sumiko, to whom *Shanghai Policeman* is dedicated. But then in the early morning of 1 December 1935 Peters and a subordinate, Sergeant W.A. Judd, were alerted to the plight of an indigent Chinese man, Mao Debiao, lying seriously ill by the side of a Shanghai roadside. The events that followed would lead to a murder charge and a sensational trial, the narrative climax of this book.

Shanghai Policeman is a memoir—ghost written, I think it is fair to conclude—and an apologia, but it also sits firmly within a wider popular literature about China that focused on cruelties and torture, making use of still fairly new printing technology which allowed the inexpensive reproduction of photographs, and of changing notions of what was acceptable to show in those photographs. As reviews noted, and as you can see, some of the plates show hideous scenes. Accounts in word or image of Chinese executions and cruelties had long been a standard feature of foreign representations of the country, but in the 1930s a new genre of shocker exposé appeared, exemplified in particular by the works of 'Bok', among them *Vampires of the China Coast* (1932) and *Corsairs of the China Seas* (1936). These books, and others like them, primarily existed to package the photographs, while others focused on a limited repertoire of salacious themes: gambling, torture, executions, opium smoking or other narcotic use or addiction, prostitution, and especially European prostitution in Asia. Henri Champly's *The Road to Shanghai* (1934), and Hendrik de Leeuw's *Cities of Sin* (1934) were two of the best known of the latter. Of course, the worlds such writers 'exposed' existed at least in some form. White Russian prostitution was an obvious feature of 1930s Shanghai life. Narcotics were a social and political reality in city life. The men of the Shanghai Municipal Police lived with these realities on Shanghai's streets. They were also the body which formally witnessed executions arising from sentences passed down by the local Chinese courts for offences committed in the International Settlement. Photographs were taken, and the private papers of former policemen contain many of these, very much like the ones reproduced in the book.

In the book Peters quickly skates through his recruitment into the force, and then runs through the obvious subjects of reader appeal that shaped the Shanghai exposé. The personal vignettes have a ring of truth to them, although occasionally the prose parrots gobbets of other works outlining aspects of the situation at Shanghai. It gains corroboration too from the sorts of personal materials of policemen that have survived, such as Lancastrian Maurice Tinkler's letters home in the 1920s, which formed the core of *Empire Made Me*, my account of his life in the city and in the Municipal Police. There are expensive encounters with Russian bar girls and fake champagne, the hurly-burly on the streets, complaints about the stuffed-short snobberies of the British establishment, and accounts of the violence of Shanghai gun crime.

'We recruits', Peters notes, 'felt that it was not a very encouraging beginning to our life in the Force to be paraded and marched to the Public Mortuary twice a week', from where police funeral processions set out. This was an exaggeration, but four men, all Chinese, were killed in 1930, his first year of service, and 13 were wounded, in 40 different armed encounters. The police shot dead 15 criminals. Incidents like these are narrated here, but Peters himself had a luckily quieter life, although like all serving in 1932 he had to deal with the vicious horrors of the Sino-Japanese War that ravaged the northern suburbs of the city.

You may ask yourself as you read where Shanghai fact stops and fiction begins. But with Shanghai it is always difficult to tell. The private letters home of another officer, mild-mannered Dubliner, Barney Wall, sometimes reads like a hard-boiled thriller. Tinkler, a better writer than Peters or his 'editor', Hugh Barnes, was more conscious of himself as a tough guy, but the Shanghai life could be tough for these men. Still, as Peters also shows, policing could have its direct benefits. Servants were issued to the recruits, and they had the run of the city, while gambling joints made useful payments to augment salaries: 'there are times when a policeman's lot *is* a happy one' he concluded. Peters served as a beat officer, and then for a while in the riot squad, the Reserve Unit, established by the famous W.E. Fairbairn, a former Royal Marine, who pioneered many of the tactical and training innovations that became SMP norms. The account of his police career is a little formless, although it is broadly chronological, but then for its last 100 pages the book shifts gear to focus on the events of 1 December 1935 and its aftermath.

I will leave discussion of Mao Debiao's tragedy to Peters, and you can find some additional material in the appendix, but I will say that Peters and Judd were lucky. No jury of British Shanghai residents was likely to find them guilty of murder, although a lesser charge might well have stuck. But even though both men stood far outside the social circles which ran the city, and which provided the jury, the policemen were white and their hapless victim was an entirely marginal Chinese man. Their rank and file SMP colleagues more clearly felt themselves on trial over the case, and were not happy that the force hierarchy had swiftly moved to have formal charges brought against the pair. But the politics of Shanghai in late 1935 were different from even those of the year Peters arrived, and Chinese and overseas public opinion were increasingly powerful political factors. The SMP was always effectively on trial, as pressure mounted for the return to Chinese control of the heart of the country's largest city, and its policies and the actions of its men were scrutinised closely.

It was on paper an odd incident. His SMP personnel file shows, as this book does, that Peters had little sympathy for the Chinese, beggars or otherwise. He faced a serious disciplinary charge in mid-1930 largely resulting from his racist disdain for Chinese. Private firms could hire SMP armed police to protect cash deliveries, and the charge arose on one such occasion when the Chinese cashier at the Luna Park greyhound stadium employed them. Peters apparently 'objected to being told by a Chinaman to wait . . . and to take orders from him', one witness stated. In his own words the man 'adopted an overbearing and offensive attitude to them which they objected to as the bystanders laughed at them and they lost face'. Being laughed at by the Chinese was a recurrent Shanghai British nightmare, and a common justification in court testimony or written statement for minor acts of violence. Britons and other foreigners felt on guard, looked for slight, and lashed out if they thought they saw it. So there is little sympathy for the Chinese of Shanghai in Peters' book, and little sympathy shown during his six-years of service. His racism is persistent, and sullen, although no more so than many of his time (and understanding it is also complicated a little by his relationship with Sumiko). But it does not stand out from the record, and it does not seem to foreshadow the treatment of Mao Debiao. However, Peters was a man inclined 'to take chances', and possibly not entirely sober on the night of 1 December 1935. And that everyday callous racism—taking offence at the laughing bystander, for example—was often enough to tip the scales into violence or cruelty. Knowing all this, and knowing his world, I find I do not personally believe Peter's version of the Mao Debiao incident.

Peters, or probably Hugh Barnes, opted to strike a strong sentimental note in the book, arguing that the events that led to the policeman's departure from Shanghai ruined the plans of two young lovers to leave China and make a new life together back in Britain. That's an old, old story of course, but information from the family certainly suggests that the relationship was a real one — I had my doubts when I first read the book, thinking it was worked up to make Peters seem a more sympathetic character. Sumiko maintained contact with the family for some time after our Shanghai policeman's return to Britain. But Ernie Peters never went back out east, and Sumiko never came west. He kept a photograph of the pair of them; but during the war he married a British woman. Peters had found work in a factory in London, and after the war as a publican in his native Dover. What Shanghai stories he told over the bar at the King Lear, the sea-front pub he managed from 1949 to 1970, we probably will not ever know, nor those he glossed over. We are left instead with this book, and with the court records and the testimony of the records that survive of this Shanghai policeman's life.

One of the last entries on the Peters file in the police archive in Shanghai is a clipping of a review of this book in a local newspaper, *The China Press*. It 'gives the reader the "low-down" on how Sergeant Peters fought the Shanghai underworld' the notice sarcastically concludes. Scrawled across the bottom of the clipping is the instruction 'Don't buy it', but you should, for the book is more revealing than Peters ever realised, or his disdainful colleagues back in Shanghai ever understood.

Robert Bickers,
July 2011

SHANGHAI POLICEMAN

I

I JOINED THE Shanghai Municipal Police Force in October 1929.

I do not really quite know now why I did so, unless it was that it seemed a good job with good pay, good prospects and a moderate amount of excitement and adventure. Above all, it was abroad. After serving for five years in the Royal Tank Corps in India, I found it difficult to settle down in England, or rather there seemed nothing for me to do at home. The slump was just beginning and jobs were becoming scarce. So when I saw an advertisement for recruits for the Shanghai Municipal Police, I jumped at the idea. I knew little or nothing about Shanghai or the conditions of police work out there, but, besides being a chance of employment at last, I was thrilled with the idea of travelling again—at my employer's expense. So I decided to try my luck.

I sent my qualifications to the agents of the Police Force, and was soon asked to go to their offices in Fenchurch Street for examination. It was fairly easy, except the physical test, which was much stiffer than I had expected. But the kindly old doctor proclaimed me physically fit, and I was accepted. Probably my good Army record was taken into account, and the fact that I was a first-class motor-mechanic, knew how to use a revolver, and had considerable experience of the management of natives from my time in the Tank Corps.

We—that is to say, about thirty other new recruits and myself—had an interview with an ex-Assistant Commissioner of the Police in Shanghai, who gave us a rough idea of the work and conditions out there, explained what our future duties would be, and told us how they differed from those in the Home Police Forces.

I remember one of his remarks that seems strangely inadequate now, when I think of my actual experiences in the Force:

"In general, the duties of the Force consist of routine work of a modern business centre, modified as necessary to suit local requirements. Inquiries into crime are of a special nature, as the criminal classes are chiefly Chinese, accentuated by the fact that the territory bordering the Foreign Settlement is not under the control of the Shanghai Municipal Council."

As a definition of the work of the Force, it is rather sketchy. Of course it was impossible for him to go into minute details, but if his statement is the considered opinion of the authorities, then most of my actual work in Shanghai during the last six years must come under the heading of "modifications to suit local requirements."

He certainly warned us of the dangers, mentioned that most of the crime in Shanghai was of a major kind, spoke of the armed robberies, kidnappings, drug traffic and other problems that we would encounter, such as the traffic, which is terribly congested in the city owing to the streets being crowded with old and modern forms of transport, cars running at a furious speed alongside rickshaws, one-wheeled hand-carts, and even wheelbarrows. I was led to imagine that being a policeman in Shanghai would not be very different from being one in London, even taking into account the modifications necessary to suit local requirements. Looking for a little adventure, this rather damped my spirits; but they rose again when he said that armed robberies occurred daily, and gave us a brief lecture on opium-smoking and the drug traffic in general. I began to think that the life would not be so bad, after all, and to expect a bit of excitement. I was not mistaken.

On October 16th I set sail for Shanghai with twelve other recruits.

As I knew from what I had been told in London, Shanghai is the largest shipping and commercial centre in the Far East, but I did not know that it is an absolutely unique city, that there is no other city in existence with such remarkably complicated conditions, and no other city in which the customs of one of the oldest civilizations in the world are to be found alongside the most modern inventions of twentieth-century science. Ports are often said to be meeting-places for the East and the West, but it is literally true of Shanghai, and true in the sense that many nations do not only meet there—they live there alongside one another. It has been called a League of Nations in itself, and if ever there were an example of the impossibility of that ideal in reality, it is to be found in Shanghai, where so many different nations are trying to come to mutual understanding and to live peacefully with one another.

As the complex and anomalous conditions in Shanghai have great effect on almost every aspect of police work in the city, and as they were probably the reason why my career in the Shanghai Police Force was recently brought to such a sudden and dramatic end, I must now give a brief description of them. In no other big city is police work so interesting, so highly developed, or faced with such formidable difficulties. The whole work of the police is complicated by the peculiar conditions of Shanghai, and I must therefore describe them before speaking of the actual work itself.

Shanghai consists of the Foreign Settlement, the French Concession and Chinese Territory (Chapei and Nantao).

About eighty years ago it was nothing more than a small town. Its development has been so rapid, it seems almost unbelievable when looking at its towering modern buildings, trying to find one's way through its maze of streets crowded with a seething and tumultuous population, dodging in or out between the congested traffic or visiting its fine docks full of the world's shipping. In all this tremendous commercial and industrial activity, the simple life of less than a century ago seems to have been left centuries behind.

When my ship approached Shanghai, I half expected to see a sky-line dotted with Chinese pagodas and temples, and I felt rather disappointed and almost cheated of an experience when I saw the long line of modern industrial buildings with nothing Chinese about them.

Not so many years ago the site of the International Settlement was a mud flat, now it has a population of many nationalities. It covers an area of about nine square miles, and its population consists of a majority of Chinese, and also a foreign community (*i.e.* non-Chinese), principally represented by Japanese, British, Russians and Americans, the Japanese predominating.

The Foreign Settlement is controlled by the Shanghai Municipal Council, which is paid for and elected by the ratepayers, and not appointed by the British Government, as some people imagine. It is this Council that employs the Police Force of w hich I became a member.

With regard to the Settlement and the Council, I cannot do better than quote a Chinese author, Ching-Lin Hsia; for although an examination of the whole subject is quite outside my scope, besides probably making somewhat dry reading, something is required to explain what follows.

> The status of the different foreign nationals in the Settlement is never defined, the relationship between the Settlement and the various governments is not at all clear and the position of the Municipal Council of the Settlement in relation to the Chinese Government is decidedly anomalous. Consequently the International Settlement of Shanghai is hard to describe in a word or a phrase.
>
> It is unique among the cities of the world. It is almost indescribable, though it has been variously and wrongly called a "free city," a "republic" and a "principality."[1]

Another writer says: —

> In fact, the Municipal Council is independent of the consuls and of the Diplomatic Body, and is almost independent of the home governments.
>
> In a word, the Government of the International Settlement is complex, anomalous and indescribable.*

---

* *China, Where It is To-day, and Why*, by Millard.

In face of the opinion of these authors, I will only attempt to explain those aspects of the situation that concern police work in general and that affected my personal experiences.

From the police point of view, the first complication arises from these three distinct areas—the Foreign Settlement, French Concession and Chinese Territory, each controlled by a separate authority and with a separate police force.

The French Concession has nothing to do with the Settlement. It employs its own police force, consisting of French and Chinese, with a few Russians.

In Chinese Territory the Chinese Government employs its own police, consisting, of course, entirely of Chinese.

Both these areas adjoin the International Settlement at various points, and are separated from it by boundary stones and gates.

Many of the difficulties and problems that arise are due, in my opinion, to the very little mutual understanding between the different governing bodies. This does not apply so much to the French Concession as to the Chinese authorities, with whom there is always a certain amount of trouble.

For instance, take Chapei—that is to say, Chinese Territory. Unless a policeman of the International Settlement is in actual pursuit of a criminal, he is not allowed to cross the boundaries. For a uniformed member of the Force to trail a Chinese suspect near the Chinese Territory is thus quite hopeless. In any case, he runs the risk of being himself arrested by the Chinese Police for entering the territory bearing arms. Moreover, by the time you have found a member of their force and asked him to assist and co-operate in apprehending the suspect, the latter has disappeared for ever in the maze of alley-ways that line the boundary. Chinese Territory thus becomes a safe haven for a large majority of Shanghai's criminals.

Besides these boundaries, there are also roads extending past them, called extra-settlement roads. Whatever repairs become necessary to these roads they are done by the Shanghai Municipal Council, but the Chinese authorities expect to have some say in the policing of them. The parties came to the understanding that they should both control these roads, but a lot of dissension and ill-feeling has arisen at various times, mainly, I think, because the Chinese resent our being there at all. They use any sort of bluff if it enables them to exercise their authority, as appears in the following incident.

A telephone message was received at a certain police station that a tenant living alongside one of these extra-settlement roads was in trouble with a Chinese Territory policeman. This person paid Settlement rates and taxes, and was therefore entitled to our police protection. So we sent a police officer to settle the matter. On arrival at the house in question, he found the Chinese policeman inside ordering the tenants to quit in a manner that threatened strong action if they did not. It was actually a matter calling for investigation by our officer—a Scotchman, by the way—but the Chinese policeman refused to answer any questions, and promptly ordered him to leave the premises, enforcing his remarks by drawing his pistol and threatening to shoot. Our Scotch officer refused to stand this bluff, immediately drew his own pistol and fired at the Chinese. By good luck, or perhaps excellent marksmanship, he struck his wrist, that of the hand holding his gun, and the man ran for his life.

Inquiries were made later, and the whole affair was thrashed out. It ended in the Scotchman being transferred to the other side of the International Settlement and his police number being changed, for reasons of personal safety.

On another occasion a police officer on patrol duty in a district adjoining Chinese Territory had reason to reprimand a Chinese rickshaw coolie for a small breach of regulations. The coolie made some rude retort, and the officer attempted to arrest him. In doing so he made the mistake of entering Chinese Territory. Without any questioning whatsoever, he was soon in the hands of three Chinese policemen, who roughly bundled him off to one of their stations, where he had to wait until a deputation arrived from our Force. An apology was then made on both sides, and

Top: THE BUND, SHANGHAI

Bottom: A TYPICAL STREET IN THE INTERNATIONAL SETTLEMENT

there the matter ended, except that the officer was verbally reprimanded by our officials for his conduct.

Another case arising from these extra-settlement roads involved many residents in Shanghai, and was repeated not once,
but hundreds of times. As far as I know, it is still happening.
There was a certain cinema in a road running parallel with
Chinese Territory. On leaving, the audience would get into their
cars ranked outside, and persons who wanted to turn their cars
found a small side road branching off the main road in which the
cinema was, very convenient. So they usually drove two or three
yards up this road and then reversed. But woe betide anyone
who drove over the boundary line. He was immediately turned
out of his car and fined fifty dollars on the spot. If unable to pay,
his car was detained until the money was produced. But anyone
who knew the ropes could get off scot free by offering the policeman five or ten dollars. The matter was finally reported to the
police in the Settlement, and an official was sent to complain to
the police station concerned in Chinese Territory. Once again an
apology was offered, and nothing more was done.

But these territorial questions are not the only difficulties
connected with police work in Shanghai. The very nature of the
Municipal Police Force itself causes many complications, for outside the French Foreign Legion I can hardly believe there is a
more cosmopolitan body.

It consists of British, Japanese, Indians (Sikhs) and Chinese, a
total of about 5463 officers and men. The British are the controlling element, but the Chinese predominate numerically. There
are also some Russians, who make up for their paucity of numbers and their incapacity as policemen by causing more trouble
than anyone else.

The sole supervision of the Chinese Branch of the Force is in
our hands, with the help of Chinese inspectors and sergeants.
This means first and foremost that we must have some knowledge of the Chinese language. It is so essential that promotion,
and even one's position in the Force, depend on it. In the midst

of routine police duties it is no easy task to learn that notoriously difficult language, but it has to be managed somehow. Then we are expected to study the Chinese themselves and to extend our knowledge of their ways and customs as much as possible. As far as I am concerned, they remain a baffling but ever-intriguing mystery, for the more I thought I understood them at one moment, the less I found that I knew about them later.

Some of their cunning is soon discovered. It does not take you long to notice that the smart Chinese policeman as turned out of the Police Depot soon develops into a man who will shirk his everyday patrol or traffic duty if a very sharp watch is not kept upon him. They have reduced this shirking to a fine art. The crime is so prevalent in Shanghai that at night there are always two policemen patrolling a beat together.

I was supervising a particular section accompanied by a Chinese police sergeant one summer a few years ago at about two o'clock in the morning. Now, at this period of the year most of the Chinese sleep out of doors on the pavements, in the alleyways, or anywhere that seems at all cool. We stopped at a point where we knew two constables should be at that time, and waited several minutes, expecting them to turn up. As they did not do so, we decided to walk on and see if anything was amiss. Something certainly was. We found them lying on the pavement using their uniform hats as pillows, both fast asleep. Imagine such a thing happening in England. Why, *The Times* would be full of indignant letters from all the public if a City policeman so much as took off his helmet when on duty. But the Chinese love their sleep so much that there seems nothing wrong to them in the sight of policemen sleeping on the pavement.

One of these men had decided to have a little nap and asked the other one to keep watch; but, unfortunately for him, the latter could not resist the temptation of having a little snooze himself, so both were caught in the act.

But in any emergency, such as an armed robbery or a kidnapping, or any crime involving quick action and shooting, I take off my hat to the Chinese. He is a first-class policeman then, and in that respect can stand comparison with the police in Europe and America. The trouble is that his spurt of energy and enthusiasm for his job does not last. He is a slacker at routine work, and you can really only trust him when there is a shoot-up—but that is saying something for a man.

Taking the good with the bad, the conditions under which he works and his very small pay (about twenty-eight shillings a month when he first joins), he is not such a bad policeman, after all.

Then comes the Japanese branch. They are unofficially supervised by their own officials. Although we are also supposed to supervise them, little is done in reality for we know that we should soon be told to mind our own business if we attempted to do so. As far as their own nationals are concerned, they are certainly good policemen; but in other respects I have nothing much to say for them, except I have met some fine fellows among them and had some good times with them.

The Indians, the Sikhs, generally act as traffic policemen. Big, impressive, simple men, they must be led. But with a man capable of leading them, they are hard nuts to crack. The Chinese usually complain that the Sikhs give them rougher treatment than the rest of the police during the riots that are always occurring in Shanghai.

Last of all come the Russians. They work under the same conditions as we do, and they get the same pay. There is a large Russian community in Shanghai, which is the reason for their employment. On gaining promotion they are sometimes placed on charge-room duty, but ninety per cent. of them are incapable of doing the work. If a Russian is put on patrol duty, a younger man, a Britisher, really has to do his job, for he is not efficient enough to do it himself. In my opinion, the Russian is quite useless as a policeman. At the best of times on patrol, he merely works conscientiously and automatically. He usually seems afraid of his own shadow. Worst of all, he seldom shrinks from doing anyone a bad turn if he thereby clears himself.

The cosmopolitan nature of the Force fully represents the character of the city itself, for Shanghai must be one of the most cosmopolitan cities in the world. It is one of the largest treaty ports in existence — that is to say, a port in which many different nations enjoy extraterritorial rights to exploit trade and business, and in law are exempted from interference by the local authorities, in this case the Chinese. In Shanghai more than twenty nations enjoy these rights.

They have their own consulates, and several have their own law courts. Thus, if one of their nationals is charged with any crime whatsoever, he (or she) has the right to be tried in his own courts and to have a fair trial according to the laws of his own country. So if a British subject is charged by the Chinese for any offence, be it murder or even the most trivial traffic irregularity, he is accorded all the rights of a British citizen and trial by his own countrymen.

But there are also a few nations not endowed with extra-territorial rights. The people of these countries are termed "unrecognized foreigners." They are allowed to trade and to carry on their business in Shanghai, but have no right to be tried for any offence under their own national law.

Germany is such a country, and Germans in Shanghai are tried in a Chinese Court presided over by a Chinese judge.

Then there are thousands of "White Russians" — the people who fled from Russia after the revolution and form a community by themselves. They are also "unrecognized foreigners," and are considered people without any country at all. Exiled from Russia, to which it would mean death for them to return, it is quite a common occurrence for Russian girls to marry foreigners with extra-territorial rights for the express purpose of obtaining those rights themselves.

I have already mentioned the strange fact that some of these Russians are employed as police officers by the Shanghai Municipal Council. A few years ago they were rather an isolated branch of the Force, with a reduced scale of pay which always seemed to me quite sufficient for them considering their notorious inefficiency. But now they have been placed on the same footing as the other branches, and enjoy the same pay and privileges—in fact, they have more privileges than the rest of us. I was not allowed to marry until I had served six years with the Force, yet Russians already married are often admitted. Perhaps because of this, or for other reasons of which I will speak later, they are generally very unpopular in the Force.

Although the Police Force is represented by a Commissioner (a Britisher), who is in sole charge of the various nationalities working alongside one another in it, the Japanese and Chinese branches have their own Commissioners and junior ranks. Strict co-operation is essential between the various branches, but there is usually some unrest and ill-feeling going on, especially between the Chinese and Japanese.

The great difference in their pay forms a never-ending source of dispute, and it seems to me that the Chinese have some grounds for complaint. On joining the Force, a Chinese constable receives the equivalent in English money of under one pound ten shillings a month, while a Japanese constable receives about eight pounds a month. It is a difficult question, however, and there are some justifiable reasons for this tremendous difference. The Japanese has by far the greater sense of class distinction, his social life is on a much higher level than that of the Chinese, and his living expenses are therefore much larger. Whatever may be said against the Japanese, as a man to live with and to work with I would choose him every time rather than a Chinaman. At least his race has a code of cleanliness which he maintains at a very high standard.

Roughly speaking, the lower ranks of the various branches work quite separately under the control of their own officers according to their nationality, while as much mutual understanding and liaison as possible exists between the various sergeants, inspectors and commissioners in the higher ranks. For instance, the welfare of the Chinese branch rests with their Commissioner, but he discusses any complaints or suggestions with the Commissioner of the whole Force before taking action.

Now a few general remarks about the work itself, which differs as much from ordinary police work in any other big city in the world as the Force itself differs from, say, the City Police in London. The problems which we have to face in Shanghai are unique, and to say that our work consists of keeping order in a modern business centre is a most inadequate description of what we have to do.

Think of all you have read of the gangsters in New York, then transfer that civil war between organized society and ruthless criminals to the complicated cosmopolitan city I have tried to describe above, and you will have some faint conception of the work of the Shanghai Municipal Police. Even then it leaves out the eternal problem of the Chinese character (as I have said, the criminals with whom we have to deal are mostly Chinese), and the fact that we are trying to preserve order among one of the most mysterious and enigmatic peoples in the world—at least, to the Western mind.

Nothing is easy in Shanghai for the police. We have most of the problems to be found in other cities, only usually intensified. For instance, the traffic problem of greater London would be somewhat complicated if there were nine thousand nine hundred and ninety rickshaws running along the streets and dashing between the motors and other vehicles.

This traffic problem is one of the first things that strikes a visitor to Shanghai. He may well be appalled at the difficulties arising from the congestion, the narrow streets, ancient and modern modes of transport, and the complete lack of road sense of the average Chinese.

The only modern traffic regulations existing in Shanghai at the present time are traffic lights. They are not automatically controlled, as in large cities at home, but are worked by the police themselves. One man stands on a small raised platform to operate the lights, while another stands in the middle of the crossing and blows a whistle which takes the place of the precautionary light elsewhere.

Traffic policemen have to be posted in positions where they would not be required at home, and the result is that a large section of the Force has to be reserved for point duty. If we had to deal only with modern traffic, the trouble would not be so bad; but the situation is complicated by the fatalistic attitude of the Chinese, the innumerable rickshaws, the hundreds and hundreds of old-fashioned one-wheeled barrows, hand-carts and trolleys, as well as a kind of horse-drawn brougham, and, worst of all, the crowds of uneducated Chinese farmers and farm labourers who are always drifting into Shanghai in the hope of making their fortunes.

If automatic traffic controls were erected, they would be quite useless, for it would be far too much to expect the Chinese to obey or even to notice their indications.

As it is, the hundreds of offences of disregarding signals actually given by the police dealt with at Court each week are nothing compared with those bailed at police stations. Petty traffic offences are bailed on payment of from ten to fifty cents, and these cases never go to court. The offenders seem to like the arrangement. It is quite common to find a rickshaw coolie with over twenty of these bail receipts which he proudly shows to the police, not understanding what they are for.

Surrounded by such half-wits, the traffic policeman has a nerve-racking job. For instance, he stops one line of traffic at a cross-roads to allow the other to pass. Someone shouts for a rickshaw. Immediately, disregarding the traffic signal, twenty or more rickshaws dash across from every side, with all the coolies shouting and cursing. The result is probably a civil action in court arising from the damage, all caused by a rickshaw coolie wanting to earn maybe ten coppers. As there are three hundred coppers to a shilling, his scanty earnings produce a quite disproportionate amount of trouble.

Most of the accidents to pedestrians are their own fault. They stroll quite unconcernedly across the busiest streets, paying no attention to the traffic. The people from the country outside Shanghai are some of the worst offenders. They behave as if they were still strolling over their ploughed fields.

Then there are the superstitious Chinese. A stream of traffic will be proceeding along a road at a moderate rate—say twenty miles an hour. Suddenly a Chinese is seen to run across the road and cut in between two motor-cars. He is highly elated on reaching the other side—if he is lucky enough to do so. He believes that if he, can pass anything running swiftly, it will carry with it the evil spirits that are always dogging his footsteps.

Considering all this, perhaps the policeman on point duty in a busy street in Shanghai may be excused if he sometimes uses his traffic stick—a wooden stick about three feet long painted in black and white sections—to teach the coolies a little road sense. This quite unofficial method has often saved many lives, and a blow and a curse are better than a street accident, anyhow.

Improvements in traffic control are gradually being made, but I think it will be many years before anything like the order of a European city reigns in the streets of Shanghai.

But traffic control is one of the lighter aspects of a policeman's work in the city. It has a much more serious and far more dangerous side—the work of trailing and apprehending Shanghai's criminals. As it forms the subject of much of what follows and of many of my personal experiences and adventures, I will only emphasize now that the major part of the crime there is heavy stuff. In England a policeman seldom meets an armed burglar, and is pretty safe in expecting to be able to make an arrest without himself going under fire. We, on the other hand, always have to deal with armed robbers, and their arrest often means a pistol duel.

We are, of course, armed ourselves. Before going on duty a man receives his pistol and ammunition. Quite apart from the possibility of a shoot-up, this has its dangerous or amusing side—it depends how you look at it. The Chinese police in the Force are, of course, also supplied with pistols. Now, the Chinaman is naturally curious and inquisitive; he loves playing with everything that comes handy. Good shot as he is when the occasion demands, he cannot leave his gun alone, but is always taking it out of its case and proudly examining it for no reason at all. We are not expected to load unless it seems necessary, but the Chinaman almost unconsciously slips a cartridge into the breach, raises the safety-catch, and there he is with a loaded weapon without being aware of it himself, for he soon forgets what he has done.

On returning to the station, all weapons and ammunition have to be handed back again, with astonishing and often alarming results; for the Chinese, thinking their pistols are empty, unconcernedly pull the trigger to make sure, and the charge-room echoes to a fusillade of shots, while the other police duck and run in all directions.

A person entering a charge-room at home in England will probably see a police sergeant sitting behind his desk. If things are not very busy, no one will be in attendance, except perhaps a plain-clothes man.

In Shanghai it is all quite different. On entering a charge-room there, you will first of all see the sergeant as before, but then you will notice two or three Chinese constables in uniform, but not carrying pistols. These men are on duty in the charge-room solely for the purpose of taking finger-prints, searching prisoners and checking their property. Next you will notice several Chinese in mufti. One is a Chinese clerk who acts as interpreter to the sergeant on duty. Another is known as the official interpreter, and deals with all the cases brought to the station that cannot be interpreted by the clerk. The latter is probably a native of Shanghai, and thus does not understand other Chinese dialects. The third man is probably the telephone clerk, who receives and sends out all general messages. It is his duty also to check all messages received from the central control room, which distributes anything very important to all stations.

These messages are sent by the teleprinting system, whereby each station has a teleprinter or electrical typewriter, and the messages are simultaneously received from the central control room in every station in Shanghai.

In cases of very important messages — say, for instance — "Motor Car, licence no. 1234, stolen from the Bund and used by kidnappers last seen speeding in a northerly direction. All duties to be warned to keep a sharp look out" — the telephone clerk immediately switches through to all the street telephone-boxes in his section. These boxes are just containers holding the telephone, and they are generally fixed to telegraph poles. A bell rings, and a red light will show until the policeman on patrol answers it. He notes the information and informs his sergeant, who sees that everyone in his section receives the message.

But to return to the personnel in the charge-room. In some stations there are also Japanese and Russian interpreters, who translate cases in those languages. Then you will see a Sikh standing on guard outside the station cells.

That is about all, but it is enough to show how different a charge-room in Shanghai is from one at home.

Then each station is allotted a radio-van for probably four hours a day. This consists of a van that resembles, only on a smaller scale, those used for removals in England. A radio receiving set is installed in it with a foreigner (*i.e.* non-Chinese) in charge, and a Japanese and four other constables working under him.

They set out to patrol the roads in their district, stopping at various points and dismounting. Having given the driver instructions to meet them at an agreed time at a certain cross-roads, the party, all wearing bullet-proof vests, will proceed on foot. It will probably split up, the foreigner and two Chinese walking on one pavement and the Japanese and the other Chinese on the other.

They will then stop anyone or anything that looks suspicious, from pedestrians to rickshaws, motor-cars and even motor-omnibuses, and make a thorough search for arms and drugs.

The searching will be done by the Chinese constables, while the foreigner and the Japanese stand by with drawn pistols, ready to fire if the person being searched is found with a pistol that he shows signs of using. Although I have often been on this duty, I have never had the luck to arrest a person with a pistol, or rather I should say a person with an unlicensed pistol. Whilst searching Chinese I have frequently found pistols on their persons, concealed more or less from sight, but they always produced a licence issued by the police giving them the privilege of carrying a gun. They are generally rich Chinese or Court officials who have obtained permission to carry arms for self-preservation against armed robbers or kidnappers.

Every hour the broadcasting centre sends out a test call to all the radio-vans operating in the Settlement, which enables the receiving-set to be tuned in to perfection. All reports of armed robberies, armed kidnappings, murders, large fires or any events requiring police action are broadcast to the radio vans as they occur in their various areas. The vans then proceed at full speed to the specified spot, the men ready for action, wearing their bullet-proof vests and carrying bullet-proof shields.

As Shanghai lies on the Yangtse River, the innumerable creeks and waterways play an important part in the work of the police. They are classed as Chinese Territory, which adds a further complication to our many difficulties, and they affect, or rather hamper our work in many ways. Used for transporting goods from Shanghai to the outlying districts, they are often crowded with every type of Chinese boat, usually sailing-boats. If there is no wind, the boats are propelled by the aid of a large single oar, much in the same way as sculling. In Shanghai it is called *yaluing*. It looks quite simple until you try, then you find that it is almost impossible to keep the oar from slipping off the wooden strut in the stern on which it rests. Its manipulation is really an art acquired by the Chinese born and bred on these boats.

The waterways seem conveniently provided for anyone who wants to commit suicide — at least, that is their frequent use. It is far too much trouble for the Chinese River Police to remove the bodies, so we of the Municipal Police have to do so. It is also our duty to keep the creeks clear of obstructions, but, on the other hand, the Chapei Police take charge if anything is stolen from one of the boats in a creek. These arrangements complicate still further an already anomalous situation, and the only person who benefits from them, perhaps, is the criminal.

At night the creeks are infested with beggar boats. The police near the waterways go off duty at sunset, and the beggars seize the opportunity to bring their boats close to the shore, tying them along the embankments even in the most central parts of the city, and then going off to do their begging. With this class of people it is an absolute profession performed by the whole family in unison, including the children, who usually manage to excite more sympathy than their parents. Like the beggars in Elizabethan England, they will injure themselves and rub filth into the wounds to move the emotions of the public. They think that the more ghastly their wounds and the more sickly their appearance, the greater chance they have of gaining the public's sympathy and money. This makes them walking carriers of disease, and they are forbidden to enter the International Settlement, but it is impossible to keep them out, and it is part of our routine chasing them into Chinese Territory.

They hide themselves in the alley-ways and lie down, first of all in a strong and healthy condition. After a few days of this in every sort of weather, they are unable to move, and eventually die of exposure. The hospitals refuse to receive them unless they are in a very serious condition. This may seem rather callous, but if there were not some restrictions of this kind, the hospitals would be crowded out by them, and there would be no room for the regular patients.

Begging is one of the old customs of China, and it is impossible to stop it. All we can do is periodically to round up the beggars in the International Settlement, bundle them into police vans, take them to the boundaries and there kick them out, leaving them to their own resources. The only trouble is that two or three days later they are all having another ride in the police van. And so it goes on.

In face of such conditions, you require some of the China-man's own fatalism. The ordinary workman in Shanghai is the most matter-of-fact, easy-going person I know. He somehow seems to think that his fate is ordained for him, and so it is no use his worrying about anything.

Everyone has heard of the Chinaman's cunning, silence and inscrutability. After spending several years in close contact with them, those three brief words seem to me to describe them better than any others. I can think of none better, in spite of all my experiences of their ways. You are always encountering these aspects of the Chinese character.

Take a crowd of builders. They will swarm about the scaffolding like a lot of ants hundreds of feet up in the air, walking along very narrow planks and sitting down on odd corners with complete unconcern, quite oblivious of the great danger which they all run. Serious accidents are quite common, but that fact does nothing to stop them. They believe that they won't fall until it is their fate to do so, and that if it is their fate to fall, nothing can prevent them from doing so. Even then, it must take some nerve to behave as they do.

When they do fall from a great height, unless a policeman is near, the Chinese have a curious custom. The victim is seized by his companions, who hang on to his arms and legs and continuously bump him up and down on the ground. The often unconscious man is supposed to be brought to his senses by the shock of the bumps. Considering that he may have already fallen several hundred feet, he seldom survives such rough treatment, which effectively knocks out of him what few senses he may still possess.

I remember once seeing two Chinese working on the side wall of one of the police stations. They were sitting on a wooden plank suspended by two ropes from the top of the building, in the same way as sailors are lowered in a cradle down the side of a ship to paint it. They were dangling at the height of about a hundred feet from the ground. I wondered what the ropes supporting the plank could be tied to above as I knew that the roof was flat, and could think of nothing there sufficiently strong to hold such a weight. So up I went to investigate. On arriving on the roof I was amazed to see that the rope was simply tied round a large wooden tub holding a fern. This was jammed against the ledge that ran round the top of the building. It was certainly fate and nothing but fate that was preventing the men from falling to certain death. A sudden movement, or even, I thought, a squall of wind, and the old tub would have toppled over the edge and hurtled down on top of them to the ground.

On the other hand, I remember once when on duty in the charge-room a Chinese came to the station at about one o'clock in the afternoon and reported that a friend of his was lying dead in an alley-way close by. I immediately sent a detective to the spot to investigate. He returned about five minutes later accompanied by the "dead" man, who was none the worse for his mid-day siesta. Some Chinese sleep very soundly, and when the friend could not wake this fellow up with a gentle shove he thought he must be dead, and hurried in great concern to report the matter to the police.

Strange are the minds of the Chinese, and almost impossible to understand. They face the risk of death in its most unpleasant form without turning a hair, but once it has taken place there is an awful fuss, as will be seen when I describe some of the funerals I have attended.

A policeman in Shanghai is in an excellent position to observe the manners and customs of the Chinese at close quarters: as a matter of fact it is part of his job to do so. We in the Police Force are brought in much closer contact with them than the other foreign residents, who seem to avoid them as much as possible. In fact, one of the most curious things about China's greatest treaty port is the way the various nationalities keep to themselves. Each nationality forms a community, and there is little social intercourse between the various groups of foreigners, except by way of business. I have often been astonished at the ignorance of Chinese life among the majority of the foreign residents in Shanghai, especially my own countrymen. I have met English business men in Shanghai who have spent ten or twenty years there and know less about the city and the Chinese than I did in six months. The business man of every nationality goes there to make money quickly, and this seems to entail having as little to do with the Chinese as possible.

The large English community in Shanghai consists mainly of these business men. Perhaps it is quite natural that they should be more interested in their own affairs than in the ways and customs of the Chinese. Be that as it may, I feel quite justified in claiming to know more about the Chinese than most of them do.

I began exploring Shanghai as soon as I arrived. After an interview with a high official of the Force, we were taken to our quarters and given a little money and two days in which to settle down before starting our regular training. We obtained our Chinese *tsee tsai*, or servants, who soon had our kit ship-shape, and a couple of friends and I decided to explore Shanghai.

Before sallying out on our tour of inspection, we had all been much amused by the preparations which one of our fellow-recruits was making for his debut in Shanghai. A big, red-headed fellow, a typical Scotchman from the Highlands, he had previously been employed as a gamekeeper on some big estate up there. He had lived simply and well, but entirely in that little sphere, and his thoughts had centred chiefly on his gamekeeping.

Tom — as I shall call him — had spent much time taking various articles of clothing out of his trunk, and at last declared that he was ready to explore Shanghai. He was dressed in a gamekeeper's suit — plus-fours with a jacket buttoned high at the neck and typical poaching pockets. A pair of white spats adorned his ankles, and then Tom produced a bowler hat, brushed it very carefully, as if setting out for the local Kirk, and solemnly placed it on his head. It was of the George Robey type — a hat with a very narrow brim that rested somewhat high on Tom's head. Then he asked us very seriously if we thought he was fit to make his entry into Shanghai society. He seemed a little dubious at first, thinking perhaps that he ought to have brought his kilt; but on receiving encouragement from us, he boldly sallied forth. We followed at a respectful distance.

Passing down a few streets, we came to the Bund, where some of Shanghai's largest commercial buildings are situated, and thus a very busy and crowded spot. We thought it was time to abandon Tom here, as by then he had quite a large part of the Chinese community following him, no doubt wondering who the strange celebrity was.

Later on, when he had learned more of Eastern, or perhaps I should say Western ways, Tom enjoyed the joke of his first appearance in Shanghai as much as anyone, and will not mind the incident being mentioned again.

Leaving our Scotch gamekeeper in the midst of his admiring and amazed crowd, we began our little tour of inspection, but were soon in difficulties. We found ourselves lost in a very narrow side street, and felt rather uncomfortable, as it seemed to us that everyone was staring at us, and all eyes were Chinese. We saw nothing but Chinese shuffling to and fro, rickshaw coolies touting for hire and coolies pushing heavily laden wheelbarrows along. Without saying anything to one another, we retraced our steps, and, to our relief, at last found ourselves back on the Bund again. Our first attempt to explore the city left us with a somewhat unpleasant impression.

It was only later that I became aware of the enthralling interest of this vortex in which so many nationalities are struggling for expression. Being the largest city in the Republic of China, Shanghai is the centre of politics and culture. It has been greatly developed, however, under British influence, and this has had a considerable effect on local manners and customs. Two influences seem to be at work. On the one hand, our Western civilization penetrates into China more through this city than anywhere else; on the other, Chinese statesmen and wealthy Chinese who want to avoid the misery of internal strife and the attacks of bandits seek refuge in Shanghai, bringing with them various customs from their native places. Thus Oriental and Occidental civilizations, new and old, meet and conflict continually in Shanghai.

The society woman adopts Western fashions in public, and manages them with much good taste, but this does not prevent her from clinging to her own customs at home. Of recent years women have escaped from the oppression of some of their strict old conventionalities, such as the tight binding of their feet from birth. This is now absolutely forbidden.

The men, however, seem to behave differently. They do not lead the same double life, so to speak. They either follow as much as possible Western ideas and culture, or adhere to their old Chinese customs but they do not try to combine the two completely different modes of life.

Tea-drinking amongst the Chinese is more than a social habit, it is a rite. Tea-shops are to be found everywhere and people of all classes go to them to transact their business over cups of tea. There are also tea-shops for the merchants of special trades, such as those for the cotton dealers and coal merchants. Even the criminal classes have their special tea-shops in which they meet to confer over their important business — crime. These shops are often of great assistance in the arrest of criminals, as police informers frequent them to collect useful information.

Tea is always sold on a large scale in the streets. Chinese push trolleys bearing a charcoal-heated copper up and down the streets day and night, selling tea to the coolies and labourers. They do the same with food, and besides shouting their wares, they use a variety of gongs to advertise their goods. Then there is the bookseller, who spreads out his double-folded shelf on any road and sings his way to fortune. Stalls containing toys, sweet potatoes, wheat, vermicelli and other foods are arranged along the pavements. They are all licensed by the Shanghai Municipal Council, and a fine job it is to get these dealers to renew their licences at the beginning of each month. One will say that he has got a new licence but has left it at home; another will produce a

Top: THE DRAWER IN THE WALL FOR UNWANTED BABIES
Bottom: AN INTERNATIONAL POLICEMAN ON PATROL IN THE CHINESE
PART OF THE SETTLEMENT

licence which he has just borrowed from a friend who is selling goods in the next street. This all means a few more little problems for the police.

Then there are the sew-sew or seamstresses, who walk the streets looking for needlework to do. They also frequent the docks and wharves, where they do various work for the foreign sailors and merchant-men. In reality this forms a cloak for prostitution, and policemen are posted at the docks to put a stop to it.

Funerals in Shanghai are often an awe-inspiring sight. A dozen or more coolies are to be seen carrying a carved dragon that stretches sometimes for twenty to thirty feet and is decorated with wonderful gold brocades. This actually covers the coffin, and the chief mourner and other relatives follow immediately behind, to be followed in their turn by what are called professional mourners, who weep and wail to save the chief mourner the job.

The most filthy coolies and beggars, anxious to earn a few cents, bear large beautifully decorated banners on which the meritorious deeds of the deceased are written. Old-fashioned Chinese bands and modern foreign ones are — or rather were, for this custom is fast dying out — attached to the funeral processions of the rich. It was thought that the noise they made gave the dead more "face" and proclaimed his lofty status in life.

As I have said, begging is a recognized profession in Shanghai. This has curious results. When a beggar outside a shop is told to move on by the police and to cease interfering with the shop's business, he always replies that he is also doing business, and asks why his should not be considered as much as that of the shop's. Their strangest reply, perhaps, is when told not to beg outside a foreigner's house. They say that they contend that human nature is the same throughout the world.

These beggars will sell their children as slave-girls for a few dollars, or as prostitutes in the brothels. This practice is also common enough among the poorer classes who accuse famines, floods and internal strife as being responsible for their action.

None of the poorer classes have ever heard of birth control. It is quite a common sight whilst walking on night patrol to see a dozen small bundles lying at various places—in alley-ways, on the pavements or on waste land. These bundles, generally of cloth or matting, contain the bodies of dead or dying newly born children. They are either children born out of wedlock or children still-born whose parents cannot afford to bury them. As for the children abandoned alive, their parents' poverty has led them to adopt this means of ridding themselves of the responsibility of keeping them.

If this happened at home, there would naturally be an intensive inquiry until the culprits were found and a charge of infanticide preferred against them. Not so in Shanghai. As soon as the report concerning a case of this description is made at a station, a Chinese detective is sent along to investigate. He usually returns and reports that there has been no foul play. Because there are no marks of assault on the baby, no foul play is considered to have taken place. The grim comedy of the situation does not seem to strike the authorities. The foul play of leaving the baby there in the first place is not officially recognized. But so much of this abandonment of babies occurs that it has become just police routine to record the case without further comment.

When the detective has reported—no foul play—the charge-room sergeant telephones to the Shanghai Public Benevolent Society, who place the baby's body in a motor-van used for the purpose and take charge of it for burial.

One of my friends in the Force in Shanghai was an ex-marine. When some of our ships were stationed there, he took several of his old pals (at about 3 a.m., after a night out) to a large piece of ground at the rear of the Chinese Court and proudly showed them ten to twenty bodies of abandoned Chinese children. This seems rather a favourite spot to leave them, and in fact on any morning at about 3 or 4 a.m. this terrible sight can be seen there.

This is not the only method of disposing of babies in Shanghai, however. You will be walking along a certain street in the centre of the city when you will see a Chinese woman take a young baby from a bundle under her arm. Then she will pull open a drawer which is let into a brick wall like the night safes outside a bank in England. She puts the child in the drawer, closes it and rings a small bell. That is the last that she will ever see of her baby. The drawer will be opened on the other side of the wall, which is an orphanage, where the child will be brought up.

Of all the memories that I have taken away with me from Shanghai, none seems more strange, more terrible or more pitiful than these: the little dead bodies of the babies that are collected from the streets of the city every morning as regularly as the dustbins are cleared elsewhere, and the babies whose mothers post them, as it were, into an orphanage wall.

It could happen nowhere except in Shanghai.

II

SOON AFTER OUR arrival in Shanghai, we began our training in the Police Depot to which we had been drafted, spending three months there before doing any work in an actual police station. After finishing school every evening at about five o'clock, I was free until physical training started at six-thirty the following morning. With several friends I usually explored Shanghai and slowly began to differentiate between the countenance of one Chinese and that of another, which I was quite unable to do at first.

Besides visiting the modern business centres, we went to the Chinese quarters of the city. It was a strange experience, passing all the quaint shops and houses and mingling with the Chinese crowds, at first with a sense of danger, but slowly gaining confidence. I remember being shown what I was told was a poultry shop with dozens of ducks hanging up outside. For a moment I refused to believe it, for the objects suspended in long lines were all painted a gaudy red colour. But on closer inspection I found that they really were ducks painted thus to comply with an old Chinese custom. The Chinese consider them a great delicacy, although they have ceased to have any resemblance to a duck at all and look as if they have been rolled as flat as a pancake by a steamroller.

Then you might come to a shop selling eggs. You notice that they are painted in many different colours, blue, red and black predominating. They have probably been buried in mud for several months, according to Chinese taste the longer the better. The fish in the fish shops looks like pieces of old rag. It is also buried by the Chinese, and then classed as a great delicacy.

I remember the first Chinese market I saw. All kinds of food are to be found there, and it is an education in itself to watch the Chinese buying and selling.

For instance, a Chinese woman comes to market with her bag of coppers. She probably has about two hundred of them. It must be remembered that three hundred coppers equal a shilling in English money. She goes to a meat stall, where she wants to buy some pork. The butcher slices off a piece, and she asks the price. He will certainly put the actual price up about twenty-five per cent., and then begins a battle of wits. The woman finally states the highest price that she will pay for the pork, the butcher refuses and she walks away, perhaps about twenty yards or so. Then the butcher calls her back and the deal is concluded. This is how every purchase is made in the different markets.

As I have said, we began the day at six-thirty in the morning with physical training. This consisted of a good three-miles run in the vicinity of the depot, finished off by Swedish exercises. Twice a week we were let off the run, and the following routine was carried out.

As armed robberies and kidnappings are so prevalent in Shanghai, the police have to undergo a special physical training under conditions similar to those which they will encounter when they are trailing these robbers. I believe this intensive physical training is peculiar to the Shanghai Police Force, and that there is no other Force in the world that undergoes it. But so abnormal are the conditions of crime in Shanghai, and so favourable are they often to the criminal, that exceptional steps have to be taken by the police to meet them. I sometimes thought the method used was rather like the intensive training of fowls in a poultry yard, the modern method that keeps them continually on the run and hopping over the perches in search of food; but when I came to be chasing an armed robber myself and jumping over the roofs from one house to another, I realized its usefulness.

For competition and efficiency, three of us would begin this training together. Off we would go, our first obstacle being a hurdle. Jumping over this, we encountered a large concrete tank filled with water, spanned by a wooden pole. We had to run across this narrow pole, which represented a pole or plank hurriedly placed between two roofs in an actual pursuit. There were usually many casualites and many fell into the water. Those lucky enough to survive this test carried on. The next obstacle was a rope suspended from a wooden bar held by two posts ten feet from the ground. This we had to climb and, throwing ourselves over the top, drop to the ground on the other side. We then proceeded to crawl through a barrel suspended about two feet from the ground so that it swung to and fro as soon as we touched it. Our next test was to run along a steeply sloping plank that ended in a barrel at about fifteen feet from the ground. This we had to crawl through and then climb rung by rung down a sloping ladder on the other side. This meant that we had practially to turn a somersault at the top of the ladder, for of course we came through the barrel head first. Then we seized the top rung of the ladder and swung ourselves over to climb down. We then had to clamber over a six-foot wall and run a hundred yards to the pistol range, draw our pistols and fire six rapid rounds at a small head-target. By that time we were fairly exhausted. With shaking hands and knocking knees we raised our pistols, to the terror of the spectators, who scattered in all directions at some particularly wide shot.

Then we hurried back to our quarters, jumped into a bath, had breakfast and attended school at nine o'clock. Our courses there consisted of Police Law, Elementary Mathematics, Geography and General Knowledge.

At that time there was a big epidemic of heavy crime, especially armed robberies, and quite a number of our Chinese policemen were being killed by the robbers. It lasted throughout my training period. Although I knew well enough that a policeman's life in Shanghai was a bit more exciting than that of a man patrolling a quiet London suburb, it gave me rather a shock when I was expected to attend the funeral procession of

a Chinese policeman killed in the execution of his duties sometimes twice a week.

These funerals are carried out with great pomp and splen-
dour, which means that the deceased gains much "face" in the
eyes of his relatives.

The funeral procession starts from the public mortuary where
the body has been taken for the inquest. The ceremony is attended by representatives of every branch of the Force, and in some
cases probably more than a thousand of the personnel are there
to escort the deceased to his last resting-place. The coffin comes
first, draped with the flag of the Shanghai Municipal Council,
and carried by about eight coolies. It is followed by the chief
mourners, all dressed in white, the funereal dress in Shanghai.
They are screened in front and on either side by white cloths.
The wife walks behind this screen, and shows her grief by giving
vent to the most blood-curdling wails and groans imaginable.
Periodically she casts herself on the ground in an hysterical par-
oxysm, completely overwhelmed by her emotions.

Whether this is simply an old Chinese custom or the sincere
expression of a widow's grief, I don't know, because apart from
the tears of children I cannot remember having seen the Chinese
cry except under physical force.

The chief mourners, who are on foot, are followed by several cabs—old-fashioned four-wheelers—in which sit relatives
and professional weepers. The latter are people paid to weep
and wail in case sufficient noise has not been made by the others. Their efforts blending with those of the widow set up a
most infernal din that seems sufficient to wake the dead, if that
were possible.

But still more noise is wanted, so the procession is completed
by a couple of Chinese bands, generally about twenty strong.
The members are all dressed in uniforms resembling those worn
by military bands in England, with this difference, that they are
decorated all over with brightly covered braid, and most of the
men wear a sergeant's stripes on their tunics.

They are equipped with quite modern instruments, and have often learned various Western tunes and airs; but unfortunately they usually play them at the wrong time, seldom choosing, even by accident, the right tune for the right occasion. We would be marching solemnly along in the procession when suddenly one of these bands would strike up "It's a long way to Tipperary" or "Annie Laurie," while farther in the rear another band would be gaily playing "Pack up your troubles in your old kit-bag."

On the other hand, we got a little of the atmosphere of a Western funeral at Chinese weddings by hearing the police band playing the "Dead March" in *Saul*.

Behind the Chinese bands in the funeral procession come the Chinese branches of the Force, both uniform and C.I.D., and then detachments of the Japanese, Sikh and Foreign police. A curious custom is observed. All the police attending the funeral are given a yellow flower to wear in the buttonhole while walking in the procession.

It slowly wends its way through the Settlement, special traffic arrangements having to be made to cope with the situation. The burial-ground is in Chinese Territory. On reaching the boundary the procession halts and breaks up, the relatives being the only people who proceed farther. The actual burial will take place according to the usual custom of the Chinese—that is to say, the coffin will be left lying on the top of the ground, to be removed months or even years later by the widow and taken to the deceased's particular village or home town.

We recruits felt that it was not a very encouraging beginning to our life in the Force to be paraded and marched to the Public Mortuary twice a week, and there lined up with hundreds of policemen of all nationalities, Chinese, Japanese, Russians and Sikhs, to take part in one of these funeral processions.

One of the interesting places to which I went in those early days was what is known as a Sing Song House. One evening I was out seeing the sights with a Chinese with whom I had become friendly. I had heard about these Sing Song Houses, and, being inquisitive, I suggested that he should take me to one. He smiled and took me to a decent-class Chinese hotel. We were conducted to a private room by a Chinese boy or servant, and we ordered beer and tea, the latter, of course, for my Chinese friend. He then spoke to the servant in Chinese, and in a few moments was brought a long strip of paper folded up like those views that one buys at the seaside — those that pull out like a concertina. On this were written in Chinese the names of the Chinese girls and their addresses (the Sing Song Houses).

My friend selected four of these, and after we had been drinking and talking for about a quarter of an hour, four girls arrived. Having seen quite a lot of the girls on the streets of Shanghai, I was given rather a shock when I saw these. They were very well dressed in native costume, certainly very pretty and some might say almost beautiful, and their mannerisms were delightfully attractive. My friend ordered food and drink for the party, and the girls joined us at table. He then quoted a few songs from a book he had with him, and the girls sang them in turn. I must confess that I could have done without this part of the entertainment. I cannot describe the tunes or the music now, although I know at least two Chinese songs; but at that time it seemed horrible to me. We endured this agony for about an hour, and then decided to go, and the girls returned to their Sing Song House to await their next call.

I also went to a cabaret at about this time. I had heard so much of the night life of Shanghai, with its night clubs and cabarets, that I had become intrigued. So on Christmas Eve 1929 some of my friends and I set off for our first introduction to high life. We arrived at the famous Black Cat Cabaret at about half-past ten. I had never seen a place more brilliantly lighted. Everyone was making merry — British, Americans, Chinese and Russians — and on one side of the dance-floor sat the Russian dancing-girls.

We sat on the other side, and after dancing with a certain girl for three dances you paid her a dollar or the equivalent in dance tickets, which were bought from a young Russian woman selling them near the entrance.

I remember dancing with a very pretty Russian girl who told me all her troubles in attractive broken English. (Most of these girls are gold-diggers, but I only found this out later by experience.) I felt so sorry for her that I invited her and her friend to our table, and when she told me that she liked to drink to forget, I ordered a bottle of champagne. Another soon followed, and my friend told me that I gave her another when she left our table. My pocket told me the same story next morning. I learned my lesson, and the next time I saw that girl I returned smile for smile, and there were no more invitations to my table.

At last the time came for us to sit for our examinations. The night before, I and another man decided to forget about the morrow and, leaving the remainder of our class swatting hard, went out for the evening. The next day we both felt very sorry for ourselves, and hardly in a fit state to set down what knowledge we had acquired during the previous three months in the depot. Imagine our amazement when, after a couple of days, we learned that my friend was first and I was second in the class. This gave us the privilege of selecting our own stations, as far as could be arranged.

We chose a small station, as we thought that we should be able to learn our work more easily there than in a large one. So we were both posted to Dixwell Road Police Station, a very quiet place in a district adjoining Chinese Territory.

I was sent out on patrol accompanied by an experienced policeman, and was taught how to sign the Chinese patrol and traffic policemen's books, and how to keep a check on them throughout their beats.

Whilst going round the district, I noticed many Chinese policemen standing at the corners of some of the alley-ways in uniforms quite different from those of our own Chinese police. My fellow-officer told me that they were Chinese Territory (or Chapei) police, and warned me to leave them well alone.

I found out the wisdom of his advice two days later. I was still being shown round the district by this same officer, and we were walking along a private road just behind the police station. It belonged to a Land Investment Company, and was patrolled by both the International Settlement and Chapei police, this dual control having been mutually agreed upon by both Forces. The houses on one side were in Chinese Territory, and there had recently been a big argument because an International Settlement firm were building on a boundary road.

Suddenly three Chinese (Chapei) policemen approached us with pointed rifles and fixed bayonets and ordered us off the road. We tried to explain that we had as much right to be there as they had, but this only seemed to enrage them, and they shoved their bayonets into our stomachs and simply walked us off the road. We both thought that discretion was the better part of valour, and, swallowing our pride, returned to the station and reported the matter. It was too big a thing for our inspector to tackle, so he handed it over to the Divisional Superintendent. It finally reached the Commissioner, and after a lengthy debate with the Chinese authorities, we found ourselves in the same position as before in regard to the dual control of the road, except for the fact that in the meantime we had been humiliated. It was in all the morning papers the day following the incident "*Foreign Police Officers Pushed Off Road by Chapei Police.*" We had to put up with many grins and sneers from many quarters for some time, but we had done the best thing, even at the cost of our pride, which a Shanghai policeman finds he often has to sacrifice for the sake of keeping the peace.

Just after this I went on patrol duty on my own, and began to think that I was a policeman at last. At that time, early in 1930, there was a big Communistic movement in Shanghai, especially amongst the student classes. It was developing into a very serious situation, and we were all warned to keep special watch on any gatherings and demonstrations. There is, of course, no free speech in the city.

One day, after I had been at the station about ten days, I was on patrol, when I noticed a crowd of Chinese walking in front of me shouting and singing. They were carrying huge banners covered with Chinese characters. The farther they walked, the larger the crowd became. Being a green-horn, I was uncertain for a moment whether it was not a funeral procession, but something seemed to be wrong, so I swiftly made towards the crowd. At that moment a Japanese sergeant and constable came up and explained to me that they were Communists.

Seeing us approach, the crowd dispersed, but not before several arrests had been made — about a dozen in all, as several Chinese police had by this time arrived on the scene. I gave orders for the arrested men to be taken to the station while I remained behind to collect various pamphlets and other communistic literature which had been dropped by the mob. I took them back with me to the station, where I found the Japanese giving information about the affair to the charge-room sergeant. I thought no more about the matter, and went back on patrol. I ought to mention that every policeman has what is known as a work-sheet. Every case and arrest in which he is involved is noted on this sheet, which is checked over four times a year, and the chances are that good cases are rewarded by several months' seniority.

The Communists were sent for trial next day. I was not called to give evidence, but both the Japanese policemen were. The Communists received eighteen months' imprisonment and the Japanese police three months' seniority. The latter, of course, had not mentioned my name to the charge-room sergeant, and I was too much of a green-horn then to know that I ought to have done so myself and made my own report. It was my own fault, but I never let the Japanese steal a march on me again, which is something of a feat in Shanghai, where they are some of the smartest and slickest people in the city.

Many raids were then being made by the detective branch on different schools in the district where students were suspected of concealing Communistic literature. A uniform policeman must attend when these raids take place, and I have frequently gone out with a raiding-party and been told by the officer in charge to wait outside and arrest anyone leaving. And many times have I sneaked in and done a bit of searching on my own account, often finding hoards of Communistic papers in the most unexpected places.

One day a friend and I were sitting in our quarters, which were next door to the police station. We were off duty, but suddenly the alarm bell began to ring outside our door. This meant that something serious was taking place—perhaps an armed robbery. We both rushed to the station full of excitement, for we had never before had an alarm call. There we found the station car loaded with policemen and waiting to move off. We were told to put on bulletproof vests and jump in.

These vests are made of thin steel laths covered with strong fabric which fits over the head and rests on the shoulders. They cover a man back and front from the neck to just below the hips. They are completely bullet-proof except against Mauser pistols. For these there are special Mauser-proof vests, but of course they are much heavier and clumsier.

Having put on our vests, we jumped on to the running-board of the car. With one hand I grasped the hood, in the other I clutched my .45 automatic Colt pistol.

Turning a sharp corner I nearly fell off, and had to take a fresh grip, at the same time swinging my gun-hand rather freely inside the car. The inspector in charge wanted to know if I thought he was the robber. We arrived at last somehow, and all dismounted. A pedestrian told us that the armed robbers had entered a house about fifty yards down an alleyway off the main road. On hearing this, my friend and I dashed up this alley-way at breakneck speed, to be brought to a sudden halt by the quiet remark of our inspector that we could walk to our death as easily as run to it. He advised us to use a little more strategy and less foolhardiness, which made us feel rather foolish. Proceeding more warily, we reached the house in question, surrounded it, and several of us searched it thoroughly from top to bottom, but without finding a trace of a robber. As usual, they had got wind that we were on our way, and had slipped into Chinese Territory. Perhaps it was as well for us, for I'm afraid our exuberance would not have helped our aim if we had had an actual pistol duel with them.

As I gained experience in my work, I was allowed to go out on patrol more and more alone, unaccompanied by another police-man. One early morning I was thus passing an alley-way in my section when I heard cries of "*Jang dau,*" which means "robber."

I immediately ran up to investigate, and found an old Chi-nese, who addressed me volubly in his own language, of which I knew very little at that time. He seemed to be trying to tell me something, but when he pointed to the cellar of a small Chinese tenement, and cried "*Jang dau,*" I knew what he meant, for that was one of the first Chinese words I had learnt.

I drew and loaded my pistol, expecting to find a desperate armed criminal in the cellar; but when I had broken down a small wooden barrier that led to it from the street and shone my elec-tric torch into the darkness, keeping my body well away from the opening, I saw nothing but a rather scared-looking Chinese huddled up in one corner. Covering him well with my pistol, I beckoned him to come out. He wisely obeyed, and I dragged him into the alleyway. I searched him, but found no weapons concealed on his person, so I went into the house with him, and saw that he had stolen some clothing and a few odd trinkets, which he had stowed away in a basket and had been on the point of carrying away when the old man had raised the alarm. He was finally charged with burglary, and received a sentence of six months in gaol. And that was the end of my first rather inglorious arrest of an unarmed robber.

Some weeks later I was sitting in my quarters off duty one evening when the alarm bells rang. I dashed to the station, and was told to proceed at once to a certain road where a large house was on fire. When we arrived we found that the fire brigade was there already, and had got the outbreak under control. We made a cordon round the area to keep the inquisitive Chinese from hampering the firemen. The latter finally left, leaving several of us still on duty to prevent any looting on the part of the mob.

Our inspector now made a safe return to the station, telling us to keep clear of the fire area, where every few minutes a rather large explosion was taking place; but two other officers and myself decided to investigate.

On entering the building, we found one of the largest wireless sets that I have ever seen—I think it must have been a broadcasting set. A further tour of the house revealed hundreds of bottles of chemicals, which were bursting one after another from the heat. These were not the actual explosions that we had heard, however, the latter being caused by the chemicals themselves as they streamed all over the place and came in contact with one another. The mystery was soon solved when we discovered that the occupants of the house were Japanese who had been manufacturing narcotics on a large scale, and had probably been in communication with Japan or their depot by means of the powerful broadcasting set. Some accident had occurred during the work. In such an inflammable place once the fire had caught hold it spread quickly, and the Japanese had to run for their lives, and even jump from some of the windows. Two of them were severely injured. We made a few arrests, and confiscated what narcotics remained. The culprits were handed over to the Japanese authorities, and we never heard what happened to them. They quite possibly remained unpunished, as the Japanese are always furious whenever any of their countrymen are arrested by the Foreign police, whose work they hamper whenever they can.

About this time I caused rather an uproar in the station myself. I was on night charge-room duty one morning at about 1 a.m. when a Chinese constable brought in a dog with both its back legs broken. It had been run over by a motor-car, a type of accident that is always happening in Shanghai, where there are innumerable stray dogs about the streets.

I decided that the only thing to do was to destroy this dog at once, and thought of using a pistol. Then someone had a brain-wave, and suggested the station shot-gun, which is kept at every station to shoot rabid dogs on the streets.

I took the dog to the rear of the station, found a suitable plot of grass, laid the poor chap down on it, and put him out of his misery. At that early hour in the morning the sound of the shot aroused the whole station. In a few minutes the fellows had all turned out wearing their steel vests and ready for an attack on the station which they felt sure was being made by armed robbers.

Our quiet little station had its first trunk murder case while I was there. Although no arrests were made, the case has its important side. For it illustrates the difficulty of arresting criminals in those parts of the Settlement that adjoin Chinese Territory. In our district it was quite easy for them to commit a crime on one side of a road under the jurisdiction of the Municipal Council, and then run over to the other side that was controlled by the Chinese authorities, and where we had no power. Thus, owing to the lack of co-operation between the Council and the Chinese, and sometimes I thought because of intentional difficulties raised by the latter, the criminals often escaped scot free.

On this occasion a Chinese constable was walking along his beat when he came across a trunk and a large bundle that looked like clothing. As it all seemed to have been abandoned, the policeman had a peep into the bundle, and discovered the decapitated head of a Chinese. He immediately reported his gruesome discovery, and it was taken straight to the station.

The usual formalities having been observed—that is to say, both trunk and bundle were carefully examined by the Finger-Print Bureau and then photographed by the police photographers—the ghastly contents were laid out on the same lovely little green lawn on which I had dispatched the poor dog. The coolie who took them out of the trunk had a grim sense of humour. Seizing the head by the hair, he calmly placed it on the lawn, and proceeded to arrange the body and legs neatly beside it. Then, coming to the arms, which had been cut off at the shoulder, he took them by the hands and put them down also, highly amusing the spectators by "shaking hands" with them and each of the limbs in turn. Horrible as it may sound when described like that, so grim are many of our police experiences in Shanghai that the only way of putting up with them is to smile when we have half a chance. And the impassive face of the Chinese as he thus saluted the dismembered body was irresistibly comic.

For some time how it had been possible for the trunk and bundle to be left on the pavement only about a hundred yards from the police station itself remained a complete mystery. Then, when questioned by some of our detectives, a Chinese who lived just opposite the spot where it had been found explained what had happened. From an upstairs window he had seen a rickshaw loaded with the "goods" come from Chinese Territory, accompanied by a Chinese who walked beside it. He had seen him and the rickshaw coolie deposit the trunk and bundle on the pavement, and watched the latter being paid his fare and then the Chinese slipping back into Chapei.

Although this was rather an unusual occurrence, he had been afraid to report the matter to the police, and it was only after intensive inquiries by our detectives that this scanty information was obtained. With these inadequate clues nothing more could be done, and the murderer was never captured. Once again Chapei had afforded safe haven to an escaping criminal.

Another case at Dixwell Road Police Station involved me to some extent. I was on patrol in charge of a section one day when a Chinese sergeant came up to me and said that he had been obliged to reprimand a Chinese constable on traffic duty for idling and talking. It appeared that both the sergeant and the constable came from the same province, which was why he had reported the matter to me instead of to the inspector in charge of the station, who would have given the constable about five extra drills, a punishment consisting of going to the Police Depot and being drilled for an hour five days in succession in the square.

Strong words had passed between them, and finally the constable had lost "face" in view of the public. To "lose face" is what the Chinese call being humiliated to the lowest degree, while to "gain face" means an increase in public honour and prestige. That is as near as I can get in a few words to a description of this strange feature of the Chinese character; but it is much more complicated than that in practice. It is easier to give instances of "face" than to describe it, easier to tell stories about it than to say precisely what it is. It is something more than Western honour and prestige, something so inherent in the race that it governs much of their life and conduct. Everyone, and especially the police, in China has to take "face" into account in his dealings with the Chinese.

I remember telling this constable to "*tong sing*," — to take care — but I noticed that he treated my words rather casually. Anyhow, it seemed such a trivial affair that I soon forgot all about it.

The next day I attended the Traffic Court as a witness in a case, and on returning I saw a large gathering of Chinese about thirty yards from the Police Station. I noticed some pools of blood on the ground and some smashed shop-windows, and I thought there had been a free fight; but this is what had really happened.

A detachment of Chinese police had marched from the station at 11 a.m. to take up their duties, in charge of the sergeant referred to above. The constable I have mentioned was in the rear rank, just in front of the sergeant. Apparently when they were about thirty yards from the station the constable had turned round, drawn his pistol and said to the sergeant, "*Veh iau doong*" (Don't move). Then, without another word, he shot him through the chest. The sergeant staggered forward and collapsed on the pavement. As he lay there, the constable fired another four shots at him, but missed, and they had gone through some neighbouring shop-windows. With the last round in his magazine, the constable had shot himself.

They were both lying dead when I arrived — all as a result of losing a little "face."

I had to transfer their bodies afterwards from the Hospital Mortuary, where they were immediately taken to be pronounced officially dead, to the Public Mortuary to await the inquest there. I commandeered two coolies used for odd jobs at the station and the hand ambulance.

Arriving at the Hospital Mortuary, we stripped the dead policemen and tied identification labels on their arms. They were lying on stone slabs about five feet high. One of the coolies had been employed by the police for over thirty years, so he was a fairly old man. The other was quite a young chap. They proceeded to remove the sergeant first. The old coolie took the head and shoulders, the youngster the feet, and they tried to lift him. They should have been in reversed positions, for the old man was at the far heavier end, and it was too much for him. Unable to stand the strain, he dropped the deceased sergeant's body to the ground, the other still holding on to the feet. I shall never forget the hollow sound the head made as it struck the concrete floor.

But the Chinese have none of the Western respect for the dead, or rather their respect shows itself in an entirely different way, as in their pompous funerals and strange burial customs. For a few minutes the coolies did nothing but laugh, and one of them said, "If he wasn't dead before, he should be now."

As for me, I felt a little sick, which the Chinese would say was a mark of a decadent race, for so they consider many of the expressions of Western emotion.

I had been about five weeks at this station in Dixwell Road when I saw a notice in the charge-room that had just arrived from Headquarters and was being circulated to all stations.

It said that a test would be held on a certain date to select a driver for the Riot Squad Van. Having had a long and varied experience of all types of car, including a Rolls Royce Armoured Car, which I had driven for several years in India, I decided to have a shot at the job, and submitted my name. The idea of being attached to the Riot Squad had long been my ambition.

SOME MEMBERS OF THE RESERVE UNIT, WITH THE RIOT SQUAD VAN IN THE BACK-
GROUND

Attending the Reserve Unit which was the headquarters of the Riot Squads, I found that about a dozen police officers besides myself had presented themselves for the test.

The Riot Van is about the largest thing in motor vehicles I think I have ever seen. I doubt whether any other police force in the world use such a thing, but conditions in Shanghai demand such a car to transport a special squad of police to the centre of any trouble as soon as it occurs in any part of the city. There is only one of these large vans in Shanghai, and it was for this that they were requiring a new driver.

It resembles a pantechnicon of immense proportions. There are two sirens in front and a large bell, which are sounded and rung continuously to clear the traffic from its path. It can hold fifty men quite comfortably inside, besides hammers, shovels and crowbars used for breaking into buildings and clearing away debris. There are also bullet-proof vests, steel shields, handcuffs and the long sticks or *lathis* used by the Sikhs in riots or strikes, as well as the ropes and chains that are stretched out to keep crowds back from fires and demonstrations.

From the inside a few steps lead up on to the roof, where the officer in charge stands on a small platform with his deputy beside him (a post of honour, and frequently of considerable danger). Here there is another large bell which is rung intermittently by him as occasion demands. A Thompson machine-gun is also mounted on this sort of platform-turret, and another gun for firing tear-gas at unmanageable crowds.

The van equipment is completed by two large banners covered with large-sized Chinese characters. These are kept in readiness to be flown in full view of the mob when required. One states the grave offence of rioting and contains the warning that tear-gas will be used. If this is of no avail, the other is flown, and this states that if the crowd does not disperse, it will be fired upon.

On that critical morning the Riot Van stood in a large garage in a compound that had a semi-circular drive on to the roadway that ended in rather a narrow tunnel near the exit. The first man clambered into the driver's seat and with a clashing of gears managed to get the van moving. He proceeded cautiously across the compound and turned a sharp left into the drive to the roadway. But in making this turn, he must have forgotten the immense size of the van, because the rear wheels mounted the narrow pavement of the drive. I thought he was going to smash into the Reserve Unit building itself. He was told to stop, however, before any real damage had been done. But to avoid further risk to municipal buildings, the Transport Officer in charge himself drove the van out on to the road.

Another man jumped in and, engaging in first gear, drove off up the road. All we could hear were several tunes being played in the gear-box, and when he at last returned we gathered that the driver had been unable to change into second gear.

By this time I think the Transport Officer was becoming fed up, for the remainder of us were taken out in a private motor-car belonging to the Transport Section. I was one of the last to be tested. He told me to drive along several streets congested with rickshaws, barrows and carts, questioned me about my experience and asked me road signs and what I would do in various emergencies. During this test I was strictly military. On turning corners to the left, I would ask the inspector to put his hand out to indicate the direction, and at times I refused to speak to him when he asked me too many questions, so as to give him the impression that my mind was on my driving, and not on my conversation with him.

After a half-hour of this, he told me to return, and I received orders to report back for duty at my station. I thought I had failed to pass the test, but imagine my joy when a couple of days later my name appeared in Police Orders as transferred to the Reserve Unit as a reserve driver for the Riot Squad Van. The next day I packed my trunks and started work in a special branch of the Police Force where there is none of the usual routine.

The Reserve Unit is used solely in connection with riots, strikes, large fires, armed robberies in the vicinity, gambling raids on a large scale and any general disturbance or unusual happening in Shanghai. Its headquarters are in a very large building which is divided into sections for foreigners, Sikhs and Chinese. Attached to it is the Police Armoury. Everyone belonging to the unit lives on the premises under the orders of an Assistant Commissioner.

I settled into my new and very comfortable quarters, and was then introduced to the Foreign personnel, who numbered about thirty. Then I was shown round the building itself, and noticed that there were alarm bells installed in the most convenient places outside our quarters. There could be no excuse for not hearing them.

I had an interview with the officer in charge, who explained the very important character of the unit's work, the need for strategy and calmness in executing any duty allotted to me and wished me luck in my new job. Then I was handed over to the Riot Van driver.

He was a Russian, one of the very few whom I have ever admired or liked. I am sorry to say he is dead now, having killed himself in rather a sad incident. He had been the official driver for some years, and there was very little that he did not know about the old "Red Van," as we used to call it.

My first attempt to drive it was not very successful. He had told me the various little peculiarities of the van, and explained the special technique required to drive it, and I made quite good progress until I tried to reverse.

I was reversing through the drive from the roadway into the compound. At first I found that I needed a neck like a swan to enable me to look to the rears and perhaps my un-swan like neck was the cause of all the trouble. I had to change my direction as I reversed. The steering was very stiff, and, feeling in too awkward a position to manage it, I thought it better to stop and pull forward a little. Imagine my horror when my foot slipped off the foot-brake.

I heard a crash and expected to find a large part of the Reserve Unit in ruins, but luckily I had only smashed a small glass case containing rubber gloves for handling live wires. It taught me a lesson, and it was a long time before I trusted myself to reverse in that drive again.

Every, morning at eight o'clock and in the afternoon at four the alarm bells would ring for test calls. The squads on duty that particular day would immediately rush outside and form up in squads to receive an issue of pistols. This took about three minutes, by which time the Riot Van would be ready to move off. The order would then be given to board the Riot Van and a trial run would be made, special riot drill taking place on the way.

The different squads with their respective duties are divided up in the following manner:

The Stand-by Squad. — This consists of twenty-four Chinese under the supervision of two foreigners. But a squad of twelve Sikhs, also under two foreigners, stand by as well. They are confined to the Reserve Unit for twenty-four hours, and are not allowed to leave under any pretext whatsoever. They have to be ready to answer any emergency call at a moment's notice.

They are all kept very fit and disciplined by marching drill followed by Riot Drill twice a day, when the alarm bell rings, and the Stand-by Squad and the twelve Sikhs immediately form up, draw their pistols from the armoury and board the van, which then moves off. After proceeding a short distance, one long blast on the siren is given by the officer in charge, and the Riot Van immediately stops. On another signal from the siren, the squad dismounts and forms up outside in front of the van, with the foreigners on either side of the Chinese, all with batons drawn. The order is then given, "Stand by to advance," and then, "Advance." After advancing a short distance towards the imaginary mob, the word given to charge. Later, when a whistle is blown as the signal to retire, the Sikhs move forward with their *lathis*. On their retirement the banners are unfurled and shown to the imaginary mob, and the Sikhs are then told to load their rifles and fire.

This is the drill in preparation for riots.

The Special Service Squad.—This squad is also confined in the Reserve Unit, but is allowed out in the evenings after five o'clock. When needed, it is sent to act as armed escort for the transport of large sums of money. For instance, large companies require police protection when paying their employees each month. As this involves many thousands of dollars, it would be a fine haul for the numerous armed robbers of Shanghai. Besides escorting money, the Special Service Squad acts as guards over safes and vaults, attends race meetings and does any special service required.

The Night Guard Squad.—This squad stands by for twenty-four hours and does the same routine as the Stand-by Squad, except that while the latter are allowed to sleep at night, the Night Guard must remain on duty. The two foreigners stay in the guard-room waiting for any riot calls or priority messages that may come through. The Chinese are posted outside the Reserve Units, two of them doing a two hours' spell of duty at a time. When coming off duty at eight o'clock in the morning, this squad is given leave for twenty-four hours.

They are the first line of advance at any call that comes through during their time on duty.

The Reserve Unit also does the work of seeing that the block-houses in the Settlement are always properly equipped and in good condition. These small square brick towers, built on the boundaries of the Settlement facing Chinese Territory, are equipped with machine-guns, water and rations. They are really miniature forts with loopholes in the side walls. In time of emergency they are manned by special Blockhouse Squads, who also form part of the Reserve Unit personnel. Should the situation be so serious that the Police Force cannot cope with it, the Shanghai Volunteer Defence Force or the Regular Troops take control. At such times these blockhouses play a very important part in the defence of the Settlement, and a foreigner has been specially appointed to see that they and the boundary gates are kept in good order. For Shanghai remains always in a state of defence, fearing attack from within or without, and sometimes from both at the same time. I doubt whether there are many large cities in the world with special squads of police kept in constant reserve to deal with possible riots. No one has yet heard of a Riot Squad Van in London, and as the late driver of the Shanghai van I hope they never may.

III

At the beginning of my time with the Reserve Unit there was rather a quiet period, which was lucky for me, as it allowed me to get a good grasp of my duties before anything serious happened. Meanwhile I kept myself fit by joining in the various games and sports that were organized to relieve the monotony of the life. For instance, we played basket-ball, badminton, volley ball, tennis, wee golf and billiards, and in the evening we would retire to our canteen for a quiet drink and a game of cards, darts or ping-pong. I was also a member of the Shanghai Police football and tug-of-war teams, besides doing quite a lot of boxing at the Reserve Unit, although I never became a member of the team there. I had, however, nearly realized my ambition in this sport in India in the Royal Tank Corps when I was one of a team from my company that tried to enter for the All-India Boxing Championship, and was only prevented from doing so by the authorities refusing to pay our expenses. As we could not afford it ourselves, we had to give up the idea, to our great disappointment.

We organized our sports ourselves, for there is little encouragement for sport in the Force, and even what I have mentioned above is now a thing of the past. When I left Shanghai, the Night Guard and Stand-by Squads had no time for it, as they were being ordered out twice a day in the Riot Van on armed search-parties.

But my knowledge of boxing helped me on more than one occasion. I remember one night a friend and I decided to go dancing, or rather he decided to dance and I went to watch, for at that time I couldn't dance myself.

I was sitting drinking a little beer and watching the girls (only watching, no more champagne this time), when my friend came up and said that he had been annoyed by an American stealing his partner half-way through a dance. This rather amused me, but I told him to try gentle persuasion by explaining the rules of dancing to the ignorant Yankee. This seemed to have no effect, for a little later I saw him mixed up in an angry crowd of Americans. I strolled up to see fair play (if I couldn't dance, at least I could box), and suddenly received a nasty blow in the face. I seized my assailant and pushed him into the street, and there we went at it hammer and tongs. I punished him rather severely until he shouted for the gang, and the whole crowd of Americans were soon on the spot, followed by my friend, who pulled me aside into an empty garage, and we made off home for the Reserve Unit.

The next day I had a nice black eye, which I told everyone had been caused by my friend slamming a door in my face, as my superiors would have called me irresponsible if they had known the truth; but I'd rather be so than shrink from seeing fair play, as they so often do for the sake of red-tape.

When I had gone through the various duties and driven the Riot Van daily for some time for test calls, I was considered capable of leading a squad in any emergency, and was allowed to take over the duties of a reserve driver. There were three of us — the Russian, another Britisher and myself — which meant that we could all have a little leave.

The bullet-proof vests and shields were all made in the Reserve Unit by Chinese, under the supervision of a Russian sergeant.

Many of these Russians have been there for five or six years, instead of the usual term of six months of the rest of the staff. In spite of this, their knowledge of police duties remains very scanty, and in the opinion of the rest of the force they are extremely inefficient. But the Heads of the Police like them, considering them a more sober, level-headed and conscientious body of men than the average Englishman, whom they label irresponsible for no reason at all.

I was one of the irresponsibles in the eyes of the authorities in those early days, and most unjustly so, it seemed to me. For instance, I got into trouble at the depot for over-stepping my time at night and being away from my quarters after 1 a.m. But so long as it didn't interfere with my duty, I couldn't see that it mattered a tinker's curse what time I came in, and such restrictions were treating a responsible body of grown men like a lot of schoolboys. And the unfairness of it was that it did not apply to the married men, who were allowed to return to their homes whenever they liked, and I know from experience that they are some of the worse offenders, if trying to enjoy life a little when you are off duty can be called an offence.

But the Russians would never have done such a thing. With no country of their own, their jobs as policemen mean security to them, and they are ready to hold them down by any sort of bluff or mean trick, and to put up with any sort of discipline in a cowed, frightened manner. The result is that they are considered conscientious and hard-working, while the far more efficient English policeman, who has many commendations to his credit and not a single bad point in his actual work, is frowned upon as an irresponsible schoolboy. Such a travesty of the truth creates a good deal of bad feeling in the Force, and is probably at the bottom of my dislike of the Russians. When you have suffered from such injustice, it is difficult to be quite fair.

But to return to my experiences of the work of the Reserve Unit itself. At last I thought I had some chance of excitement when the alarm bell rang one day while I was playing a game of volley ball. I scrambled into my tunic, drew my pistol and, being on Night Guard duty, soon had my squad ready for any scrimmage. We boarded the Riot Van and dashed out with sirens screaming and bells clanging.

A friend of mine, the other reserve driver, was driving, and made a record run to the other end of the Settlement, a marvellous performance. After weeks of inactivity, we were all keyed up to concert fighting pitch, both Chinese and foreigners. Arriving at a certain road, we halted, and were given the order to dismount. We lined up in front of the van, my squad leading. Down the road about fifty yards away I could see a large crowd of Chinese shouting and waving banners. I thought that I was in the real thing at last.

The order was given to advance, and off we went, myself on the extreme right of the squad. All the men were wildly excited, and I knew that they would not let me down. Then came the word to charge, and in perfect order we ran towards the crowd with batons drawn. A young Chinese constable next to me rushed madly at the mob, striking out on all sides with his baton. I had got in a few blows myself when I heard whistles being blown in the rear and shouts of "Retire!" The whistles had been blowing before we attacked the crowd, but had not been heard owing to the cries of the mob and the Chinese police.

We retired and, to our surprise, were reprimanded for our action against the mob. The whole riot was a put-up job, a test call to see how we would co-operate with the military, who now came up in the rear of our van. The crowd had consisted of Chinese police recruits disguised to represent a frenzied mob. Unfortunately, owing to some hitch in the arrangements, we received the order to retire too late, and several of the poor men were severely injured. I realized that when a Chinese policeman starts fighting, nothing can stop him, and it was lucky that the affair did not end in a worse tragedy than a few broken limbs. At least it showed me my men's mettle if there were a real call.

Then we rehearsed it all again, and the military took over when we were supposed to be unable to cope with the crowd. They advanced with fixed bayonets, and in reality would eventually have fired on the rioters.

Rather an amusing incident occurred when the deputy of the officer in charge was giving a demonstration with the tear-gas. It is carried in a canister like a fire extinguisher. In disconnecting it from its holder, this officer released the tap by mistake, and received the full force of the gas in his face. He hurled the canister to the ground and collapsed, with his eyes streaming with tears. Luckily he was not seriously injured, and enjoyed the laugh against himself later.

It formed a little comic relief to our bitter disappointment with the whole affair, for we had fully expected some real excitement at last in our rather monotonous existence.

At about this time it was decided to form a Chinese Police drum and fife band. Considering the wide difference between Chinese and Western music, its discordant character and the fact that most of the policemen were ex-farmers and had little knowledge of their own music, the task seemed well-nigh impossible. But not so to a great friend of mine, Jim Franks. He had been a corporal for many years in the Royal Marines, and had been in charge of a drum and fife band on a warship in the China Fleet. He was now at the Reserve Unit, where his pleasant personality and ready wit, combined with overwhelming energy and zest for life, were much appreciated, especially by me.

Everyone said that he was attempting the impossible in trying to teach the Chinese our music, but Franks would not agree. When he started, I remember he used to come to my quarters with a large board, on which he had drawn lines covered with all kinds of funny-looking figures which he called notes, telling me that he was going to teach them the scale.

After a time he found this method an impossible one, and finally decided to teach them by ear alone. I have seen him take an hour to teach a man two or three bars of one tune on the flute, patiently going over and over the same piece of music until the man had mastered it. I have also seen another effect of this method when he rushed to the canteen after a few hours' practice and swallowed half a dozen glasses of beer straight off to soothe his frayed nerves.

It seemed to me enough to drive anyone crazy, and after listening to the terrible discord for about ten minutes, it was as much as I could stand myself. Bugles were another instrument that had to be learnt, with disastrous results as far as peace in the Reserve Unit was concerned. But at last, after many weeks of steady persistence on the part of Franks, the first tune was learnt — "The Stein Song," which, I think, is an American fox-trot. Franks' round face beamed with pleasure when he marched his band on to the compound and they played that tune. If the time was somewhat ragged, at least it could be recognized, and that was an achievement in itself when you looked at the stolid, inscrutable faces of the bandsmen.

Then came more weeks of practice while he taught them a marching tune, and finally, after months and months of uphill work, he turned out a most excellent drum and fife band. It would play every year on the race course at the annual Police Review, and he was often complimented on its smartness and efficiency by various regimental bandmasters. To realize what a triumph that was, you should have heard their first attempts.

Unfortunately, after a time some difference arose between him and his superiors — quite a minor affair — but he was transferred to a station for duty. By then he had safely formed the band, and the authorities could safely dispense with his services, for which he never received due acknowledgement. Fed up with such casual treatment, he resigned not long afterwards, and is now in England, where, like myself, he finds his service in the Shanghai Municipal Police is not much help in making both ends meet.

But Jim Franks should have his niche in history, for he was the first if not the only man ever to form a Chinese drum and fife band. It now plays at Chinese weddings and funerals, gaining "face" for the rich Chinese who can afford to pay two hundred dollars for its performance, two hundred dollars which Jim would find very useful himself now, only, having been a policeman, he cannot expect payment for such little services as music-teaching, even to Chinese.

At about the same time there was a bad epidemic of poultry-stealing in the Settlement. It reached such a point that drastic steps were taken to put a stop to it. Everyone was warned to keep a good look out for the thieves, but the stealing still went on. Finally one night some chickens were stolen from a poultry yard quite close to the Reserve Unit itself, and it seemed as if the thieves were trying to make a laughing-stock of us, as of course the news of the theft quickly circulated among the Chinese. Even more drastic steps were taken to catch the thieves, and innumerable detectives and uniform police were mobilized from an adjoining station for the purpose. Night after night they patrolled the neighbourhood, and lay in wait for a further raid at half the poultry yards in the district.

After many weary nights, at last they caught the culprit — a mongoose which a policeman had kept as a pet and then lost, one of the few criminals caught in Shanghai not taken to court.

The Police Armoury is situated near the Reserve Unit. All weapons used in the Force are checked over here. No one had any excuse if his pistol failed to act in an emergency, as it was his duty to report any defect as soon as it occurred, so that it could be sent to the Armoury for repairs. It is quite easy to drop a pistol in the course of one's duty and do it serious damage, so even that had to be reported. The Armoury makes a quarterly issue of ammunition to all stations. This ensures every policeman having ammunition in good condition, for it deteriorates after a time, although some can probably be used after many years.

Before going on any armed search-party, we used to get about a dozen Chinese police and conceal pistols and little packets representing narcotics on their persons. They would then be lined up, and every Chinese policeman going on the search-party would individually search them. It was surprising what could be missed.

We used to strap pistols to their ankles and under their armpits and conceal them in their waistbands, between their legs, across their backs and on their heads under their hats — in fact, in every spot on the human body where they could be concealed.

We did the same with the small packets, often putting them in their ears, noses and mouths.

Tests were also made for entering houses harbouring armed robbers or desperate criminals. We would form a party, all armed and wearing bullet-proof vests, and with one man carrying a bullet-proof steel shield. He led the way up a spiral flight of stairs that adjoined our quarters, and four Chinese followed behind. It was not a very good example of the staircase in a typical Chinese house. The whole thing is usually a ramshackle affair with very narrow stairs, often little more than a ladder, with a concealed landing at the top and an exit on to the roof. But we were told what to expect in reality, and got a certain amount of anticipatory thrill while practising this test.

We often used to argue about the value of our steel vests and the measure of safety they afforded, especially after the experience of one of us with regard to them.

While out on search-party one day, this man had run into some armed robbers who had opened fire upon the police, and a regular battle had ensued. When he returned to the Unit, two bullets were found embedded in his steel vest. As it was found on inspection that the shots could only have been fired from a pistol of a very small calibre, and as the officer stated that he had felt something of a shock at their impact, it was decided to make improvements in the vest.

Some time after this, I was with some of the fellows in the Reserve Unit when our officer in charge came along with one of the new bullet-proof vests. He explained some of the improvements, and then told me to put it on, to test its fit, as I thought.

I think someone ventured to question whether it really was an improvement on the old model, whereupon he drew his .45 automatic Colt pistol and fired at me point blank.

"There, isn't that better than the old?" he said. "Did you feel anything?"

I had to reply in the negative, but afterwards I told my friends that I got the shock of my life when he started to fire, as the surprise made me forget that I was wearing a steel vest at all.

Our search system was specially adapted to the conditions of Shanghai. We split up into four parties, and each party had its particular area in which to operate. We thus formed a network over a large area without the various parties interfering with each other. A police search-party in Shanghai does far more than keep a look-out for individuals wanted by the authorities. We stopped all suspicious characters loafing in the innumerable alley-ways and entered all the tea-shops and food-shops frequented by the criminal classes.

The old trick of the female decoy was often employed by armed gangs, and we had to keep a constant look-out for it. Several rickshaws would be seen coming along a road with a Chinese woman in the first one and men in those following. As a woman, she is allowed to pass, but the others are all searched for arms, even the coolies, but nothing will be found. It is, however, an armed gang off to commit a robbery. The woman is carrying the pistols, which she will hand over to the men near the scene of action, receiving them back again when the crime is committed. This has probably all been known to the rickshaw coolies, but they are far too interested in their fares to tell the police about such an unimportant detail to them as an armed robbery.

Steps have now been taken to prevent this trick by means of female searchers attached to each search-party.

But in spite of this strenuous regime that I have been describing, we managed to get some fun out of life. Jim Franks saw to that, for my friend the leader of the Chinese drum and fife band was the practical joker of the Reserve Unit. I can well remember a couple of jokes that we played on one of our fellow-officers.

The quarters of the Unit were arranged in the following manner. The first storey was for the officers during their probationary period, the second for the sergeants, the third for the Russians and the top floor for the officer in charge and his deputy.

Each floor had its own private telephone. One day Franks telephoned through to the sergeants' quarters and told the Chinese boy that he wished to speak to Sergeant Bloomy, as I shall call his victim. On receiving the message in the canteen where he was having his usual drink, the sergeant dashed to the telephone and heard a voice say:

"Is that Mr. Bloomy?"

"Yes."

"Well, I'm Captain Jones," continued Franks. "I have just arrived from England with a parcel from your mother. I knew her years ago, and hearing that I was going to Shanghai, she asked me to give it to you."

"Very kind of you, I'm sure."

"I'm now staying at the Astor House Hotel. Will you come along and fetch it?"

Of course Bloomy agreed, and returning to the canteen, stood drinks all round on the strength of this new-found friend. He was quite broke just then, as it was the end of the month, but he could do this on tick. When it came to thoughts of a possible expensive evening with the Captain, however, he hurriedly borrowed forty dollars — about three pounds — from Franks.

We only heard what happened next day. Apparently he went to the Astor House Hotel Bar, where Franks had told him to look for the Captain, and ordered himself a drink. Then he looked for a man carrying a parcel. As luck would have it, the bar seemed crowded with men carrying parcels of all shapes and sizes that night. Selecting what seemed to him a likely man, Bloomy went up to him, asked him if he were Captain Jones, and on the reply in the negative felt he could do no less than suggest a drink that was never refused. So he went on, until I think news of a lunatic giving free drinks to anyone carrying a parcel must have gone round, from the number of people he said he treated. Anyhow, besides getting very drunk, he spent the forty dollars that he had borrowed without ever meeting Captain Jones. Later on Franks solved the mystery for him.

But Bloomy got his own back later on. We used to keep a poultry farm just outside the Reserve Unit. One day Franks entered his quarters to find half the menagerie running about the room, ducks and geese quacking on the floor, a pig snoring peacefully in his bed, and several rabbits nibbling the pillow-case. An effective *riposte*, as it was several days before a strong farmyard smell left his quarters.

At last I had my first real call, with nothing sham about it this time. We were carrying out some small duties one day when the alarm bells rang. We soon boarded the Riot Van and started on our way, being told that it was an armed robbery call out. My ambition was realized at last — I was a member of a duly organized body of police going into action. The police cleared the streets for our race to the scene of the crime. Arriving at a narrow street, we immediately surrounded a whole block of Chinese houses. The Chinese police were posted back and front, with several foreigners in charge. I formed one of the party detailed to enter the house in which the armed robbery was taking place. We put on our bullet-proof vests. I led the way, carrying a steel shield, with a Scotchman following immediately behind me carrying a Thompson machine-gun. So we entered the house.

We couldn't hear a sound, and the order came to proceed upstairs. It was a very narrow, steep flight with a landing overhead concealed from view. I held the shield well in front and over my head, with the Scotchman ready to fire at the slightest movement above. It was very dark, and no one but the robbers were supposed to be on the premises.

We had climbed about half-way when I thought I saw something moving in the shadows above. There wasn't a sound, but suddenly something white appeared at the top of the stairs. Asking no questions and not waiting for any orders, the Scotchman opened fire with a burst from his machine-gun. A Chinese came tumbling down to the bottom of the stairs. He was already dead, I think he had about twenty-three bullet wounds.

For a start it didn't seem too bad, and I felt quite satisfied with the result of my first battle with Chinese armed robbers. I was a little previous, however. We scoured that house from top to bottom without seeing anyone else, and then went through the whole block of houses, but with the same result.

The robbers had made their escape through a skylight on to the roof, from which it was quite easy for them to run along the other roofs and get clear away, either before our arrival or afterwards by sneaking through our cordon at some weak point.

Why had one man remained behind? Who was the Chinese who lay riddled with bullets at the foot of the stairs? Inquiries were made, and he was found to be the Chinese cook employed in that particular house. Apparently, on the entry of the robbers, he had become frightened, and, instead of leaving with the other inmates who had raised the alarm, he had hidden himself in some upstairs room until he heard the police arrive. Then he had dashed out on to the landing, to be met by us with our machine-gun. It was a case of pure bad luck, for if he had shouted when he came out of the room, our man would not have fired.

So the result was not quite so satisfactory or so distinguished as I had imagined, but it was nevertheless a great experience for me and an example of how the Reserve Unit dealt with these outbreaks of crime.

Another day a large part of the Reserve Unit were paraded and the officer in charge told us that we were to be sent on a special and highly important mission. He divided us up into squads of four Chinese and one foreigner, and told us to wear different-coloured cloths round our arms to distinguish one party from another.

We were then marched to a district quite close to the Reserve Unit and given our final instructions. We were to enter every house in this section, each squad being allotted so many houses to search. Pieces of chalk were handed round so that we could mark the houses as we searched them, to avoid any chance of our going over the same ground twice. In that maze of alley-ways and narrow roads it would have been very easy to do so, without some definite system of classification. We were told to search only for arms and ammunition, and not to bother about anything else. Apparently information had been received that a hoard of arms had recently been hidden in the vicinity, and this was the object of our search. We were not to trouble about anyone trying to escape, as American Marines, whom their authorities had given permission to cooperate with us, had been posted at the end of each alley-way and at every street corner.

So with pistols drawn we started on our way. I had a party of four Chinese with me, all wearing khaki bands on our arms. This helped us to keep in touch with each other. Whenever we entered a room, one or two of the Chinese would keep guard over the inmates whilst the remainder did the searching. We practically turned the rooms inside out, searching the beds, underneath the carpets, behind the pictures on the walls, in the drawers and in every conceivable place where arms might be concealed, not forgetting the persons of the inmates themselves. We discovered large quantities of narcotics, and in one room about thirty tins of raw opium. On informing one of the inspectors in charge of this, he told me to confiscate the lot, but to make no arrests.

The search lasted for hours, but we found very few pistols and very little ammunition. Perhaps false information had been given, as so often happens. It was an interesting experience for me, however, and I had all the thrill of leading my party into house after house, never knowing what we would find within, and fully expecting to be attacked.

I had another similar experience when we were organized into parties to make a thorough search of a beggar colony which was suspected of harbouring armed robbers. I have never taken part in a more filthy job. The arrangements were roughly the same as before. The houses inhabited by the beggars were just huts made of mud and straw in an indescribable condition of dirt and filth. I soon left the actual searching to the Chinese, and stood with pistol drawn at the entrance to these hovels. Their insides were more than I could stand. They were alive with vermin, and housed beggars absolutely eaten away with disease. Again we had no luck—not a robber nor even a pistol was to be found. I was glad when the job was over, however, and we could return to our quarters and have a bath. But a lucky thing did happen a few days later. A fire broke out in this beggar colony, and razed it to the ground. Whether it was a pure accident, or whether some policeman, sick at searching such a foul hole, made sure of never doing so again, I can't say.

We had rather a peculiar mission one day. Several of us were detailed to proceed at once to the Foreign Section of the gaol in Shanghai. When a number of tear-gas bombs were issued to us, we wondered what strange duty we were in for this time.

Arriving at the gaol, we were told that a Russian prisoner had somehow barricaded himself in his cell and refused to come out. The door had jammed, and he absolutely defied everyone to effect an entry and haul him out. It was a difficult situation, and the authorities didn't know what to do. They certainly couldn't shoot him; on the other hand, they could hardly leave him there to starve. He was therefore warned that if he didn't remove the obstruction at the door, a tear-gas bomb would be thrown into his cell. He replied that he didn't care if a dozen were thrown.

So we closed the outside wooden doors of the cell and threw a tear-gas bomb through the peephole. After a time we opened the doors and looked through the hole. Although half blinded by the gas, he still refused to come out, and another bomb was flung in. This time it had the desired effect. Although in a very sorry plight, he managed to clear away the barricades that he had erected, and we half carried him to hospital. I'm sorry to say the poor fellow died there some days later owing to the effects of the gas. Whether to call his attitude that caused his death obstinate stupidity or courage, I don't know. It seemed rather silly to us, and the waste of a human life all for nothing.

The Communistic element that existed in Shanghai, especially among the student classes, meant many calls on the services of the Reserve Unit.

We were cleaning up their demonstrations one day and successfully dispersing them by means of the Riot Van and its sirens, when we encountered a bunch of students who were shouting, waving banners and attracting quite a large crowd. They were standing on a small stone bridge that ran over a narrow waterway.

We approached them in the Riot Van, sounding our sirens and the big bell, but they merely laughed at it and us, and completely ignored the order to disperse. So we dismounted, formed up and charged them with our batons. They showed fight, and must have been sorry for themselves afterwards, for some of them were bowled over into the creek, a drop of about ten feet from the roadway, which must have cooled their ardour. The frenzy of these crowds has to be seen to be believed. It is no use talking to them, action is the only thing, and that as quickly as possible. They understand nothing but brute force.

Some kind of strife always seems to be going on in the International Settlement. If we were not dealing with riots in the streets, we were being called out to settle mill strikes or disorders of employees of the large companies, wages generally being the subject of the dispute.

The mill-workers were a class apart. In some mills only women and girls are employed, the latter from the age of twelve and the former up to sixty and over. They all work in these mills from about six in the morning till seven at night for a bare living wage. The result is that strikes are very common, and the police are often called in.

A mill strike was once in progress in the district in which one of my friends was stationed. Out on patrol one day he saw a large crowd of female mill-workers demonstrating in the street.

He went up to disperse them, thinking that, being women, they would not give him much trouble and would disperse at a word from him. He should have known better, for the female mill-worker is just as big a ruffian as the male. They seized my friend, dragged him across some spare ground and dumped him into a cesspool—one of the open pits dug in the ground that are the only sanitary arrangements in some parts of Shanghai. He was lucky to escape with his life.

A very serious strike took place once among the Korean bus inspectors. They complained that they were not receiving as much pay as the Russian and foreign inspectors, and went on strike to enforce their demands. We were called out one day to proceed to the omnibus depot, and on arrival found a vast demonstration going on outside the gates. The strikers had commandeered the offices of the bus company, and were trying to obtain what they wanted by direct action. The situation was beginning to look rather ugly, and they were ordered by the police to clear out and to state their terms and complaints in an orderly manner. This only seemed to enrage them the more, and we were told to remove them by force. When the mob saw the treatment meted out to their representatives, they too began to take matters into their own hands. They rushed towards the offices, to be met by a charge from us. The crowd were fighting mad, and it took us several charges and all our skill to subdue them.

When the main fighting was over, we discovered that several of the Koreans were lying badly injured on the ground. We removed them to hospital and remained on duty in the vicinity for several days, but except for a few half-hearted demonstrations, nothing much happened, and finally the men came to terms with the bus company.

This was not the end of the matter, however, for the Japanese started an intensive inquiry into the treatment of the Korean inspectors by the police.

Although the Japanese control and govern Korea, they despise the Koreans, and I think they would have received much harsher treatment from the Japanese themselves if this incident had happened in Japan. But the fact is that if any Japanese national or dependent of Japan comes into conflict with the Police Force, the Japanese Consular officials always make inquiries, and invariably prove that their subject was in the right. Then they demand an apology, which, strange to say, they nearly always receive. The power and influence of the Japanese in Shanghai are very strong, and they usually get what they want.

IV

Opium-smoking has been the curse of China for ages. Nowhere has it been worse than in Shanghai; and, although various measures have recently been taken to check its ravages, it still remains one of the darkest blots on the city's social life, and in fact in the life of the whole country, for the habit is widespread. A very short time ago a national campaign was launched to try to suppress the drug traffic and opium-smoking throughout China. Some progress has definitely been made, but it is too soon to say whether it will really succeed. If it does, it will make an enormous difference to the moral and physical standards of the Chinese as a race, and perhaps bring about that awakening of which the peoples in the West so often speak with mingled hope and fear. From my personal experience, nothing hinders the regeneration of the country more and nothing is a more fruitful source of crime. Besides improving the virility of the race, its suppression would transform the criminal life of the city, and thus have a considerable effect on the work of the police. But its total suppression is far too much to expect, at least for many years to come. The habit is much more deeply engrained in the Chinese people than tobacco-smoking in the West. Progress is bound to be slow, but even in the comparatively short time that I worked in Shanghai I noticed several improvements.

Since returning to England I have been much surprised to read the report of some former Commission on opium-smoking. It states—supporting its arguments with charts and diagrams—that opium has no injurious effect on the Chinese as a race, and that it is of little more importance than tobacco-smoking in other countries. It even goes so far as to suggest that most of the Chinese opium-smokers indulge in the habit quite moderately, and that there is no more harm in it than in the cigarettes of the Western world. The report concludes with the theory that the strenuous life of the majority of the Chinese, the absence of any form of healthy relaxation and the lack of home comforts are the natural cause of indulgence in drugs in China, and consequently their excuse, as the sedative effects of opium-smoking and the restful position in which it must be practised appeal strongly to the philosophical temperament of the Chinese.

This sounds all right in theory, and there is a small percentage of truth in some of these statements. For instance, I have personally been acquainted with Chinese lawyers and business men who smoke an occasional pipe of opium to soothe their nerves and ease their minds, as we sometimes smoke a cigarette, pipe or cigar, and it probably does them no more harm. But in reality such opium-smoking forms a very small part of that done in Shanghai, and it all works out very differently in practice. My personal experience led me to conclusions quite unlike those of this Commission.

If I could take these learned gentlemen to Shanghai, not as a Commission but as policemen, to go out on nightly raids of the opium dens, I don't think that they would be quite so certain about the harmless effect of opium-smoking. As a purely social custom, it can cause as much, if not more misery than betting, on which they doubtless frown. Whether he can afford it or not, the Chinese addict must have his pipe, and will borrow, pawn the clothes that he is wearing, or even steal to obtain it. On arrest, they are brought to the police station, and usually spend one night there before being tried in Court. I have been on duty in the charge-room and have heard and seen these Chinese in the cells groaning and writhing in agony, until I have had them sent to hospital. The treatment they receive there is quite simple, but if they didn't have it they would be seriously ill and perhaps die; it consists of a couple of pills containing a quantity of opium. Deprived of such treatment, the opium addict would eventually die in his cell, as not infrequently happens.

In my opinion, opium is literally a poison destroying the minds, morals and physique of the Chinese. I think they know this themselves, for ninety per cent. of the suicides in Shanghai kill themselves with opium. A little family trouble, a slight touch of melancholia, a moment's depression, and the sufferer buys twenty cents' worth of opium and, as they say, returns to his forefathers. The Commission states that the average Chinese cannot afford to buy opium. This is not quite true. The poorer classes cannot often buy pure opium, but the stuff they do buy is far more injurious and much more deadly in effect. They buy and smoke opium ash and dross, and even drink small quantities of liquid opium.

Some years ago the so-called control of opium in Shanghai was nothing but a racket of the worst possible kind. First of all the drug was smuggled into the city. The Customs officials, both Chinese and foreigners, winked at the matter then, and made small fortunes for themselves by conveniently closing their eyes to the little consignments of opium always passing through their hands.

I remember one of the Customs officials telling me one day that in the old days his monthly earnings were four times that of his regular wages. He rather bemoaned his fate, and would certainly not have agreed that progress was now being made.

For things are very different now. Not long ago a foreigner — a Swedish subject, I think — who had been a Customs inspector for over twenty years, was sentenced to a six months' gaol sentence for attempting to obtain money from a Chinese business man by promising to let some goods through the Customs free of charge. For this he had suggested that he should receive $5000, but the Chinese reported the matter to the police, and the man was arrested.

After being smuggled into Shanghai, the drug is distributed to various traffickers, whose agents sell it to the opium dens.

Some years ago, if you were a policeman patrolling the streets and mixing with the crowds of pedestrians, you would suddenly feel something placed in your hand.

It was impossible to say who had put it there, and when you opened it — for it was usually an envelope — you would find that it contained ten dollars.

Then, again, you would be going off duty, and you would find a letter addressed to you with your name and police number on it. Opening it, you would probably find twenty dollars. Later on you would discover that not only you, but the whole Police Force were receiving something, graded in amount according to the rank of the recipient. One of the most appreciated attentions of all was when you returned to your quarters and the Chinese boy said:

"Master, some Chinese bling twelve bottles beer."

It was one gigantic racket. This was the way that the "conductors" of opium dens obtained protection from the police. But it is all a thing of the past now. The authorities have tightened up the discipline of the Police Force, and a big opium racket certainly does not exist now, although some racketeering on a small scale is still carried on by the Chinese police.

There are innumerable wharves along the Shanghai waterfront, and at one time they were much used for the unloading of opium. I remember one case in particular. At about three o'clock one morning a Sikh policeman was patrolling the roads near some of these wharves. He suddenly heard the sound of a motorcar engine running on a certain wharf. Becoming suspicious, he waited on the roadway, as the dockside was badly lit, and he dared not investigate the wharf itself. So he stood just clear of the dock gates and waited.

A motor-lorry appeared at last, and dashed through the gates on to the roadway. He called out to the driver to stop, but it proceeded on its way, disregarding his shouts and signals. He gave it one more chance, but then, seeing the driver accelerate in a desperate attempt to escape, he put the .303 carbine that he was carrying to his shoulder and fired at the lorry without further hesitation.

It immediately swerved, and, after mounting the pavement, collided with a wall and came to a full stop. On examining the shattered vehicle, the Sikh found that the driver was dead. He had shot him through the back of the head, his bullet having gone through a small glass window in the rear.

Further examination revealed that the lorry was loaded with opium, running into thousands of dollars' worth. A thorough search of the wharves and docks failed to produce any signs of the other smugglers. Rumour said that when the lorry had been loaded, a Chinese Superintendent of the Police had been there to draw his "squeeze" or hush money. I don't know whether it was true or not, but it was freely stated then that such a man was the head of one of the opium trafficking organizations. There were certainly some very strange personalities in the Chinese branch in those days.

Chinese hotels in Shanghai are under police supervision and are periodically inspected. This is an obvious necessity as they harbour (and some owners know it) many opium addicts, and often criminals of the most desperate kind.

It is a regular occurrence for a Chinese of quite a respectable class to go to one of these places with a small bag or attaché case, engage a room for the night and, taking his opium parapher-nalia out of his bag, smoke there for hours on end. If the case is brought to court, the proprietor usually pleads ignorance that opium was being smoked on his premises. These hotels are also a retreat for gamblers and the better class of prostitute.

Raids made on hotels of this kind at various times have disclosed not only gamblers and opium-smokers, but Chinese members of the Police Force itself, just having a *tête-à-tête* with a girl friend on strictly conventional lines, and it has kept them there until the early hours of the morning.

On the whole, however, conditions in Shanghai with re-gard to the use of and the traffic in narcotics have very slightly changed for the better, although large quantities of opium still flow into the Settlement through various channels. A lot is brought in from the country agents taking it direct into Chinese Territory, where the authorities are more easily bribed. Thence it is smuggled without much difficulty across the boundary into the Settlement.

Trains running into Shanghai from the districts outside often bring with them drug-traffickers. If they are dealing with agents in the International Settlement, they are soon traced by means of informers, but the situation is really much more complicated than this.

As with so many problems in Shanghai, the biggest difficulty in the matter of controlling the drug traffic arises from the complicated nature of the governing bodies of the city themselves. Inquiries often cool off when it is known that on arrest of the offender, it would be discovered that the drugs had been obtained in Chinese Territory or the French Concession. This applies particularly to minor offences. There is more co-operation when it is thought that trafficking on a large scale is being carried out.

Until quite a short time ago the punishments inflicted on opium-smokers, traffickers and the "conductors" of opium dens were not heavy enough to have any appreciable effect. A person taken to Court for a first offence of opium-smoking would only receive as a penalty a fine of about ten to twenty dollars, and for the next offence of the same kind would get quite a short gaol sentence. Larger fines and longer terms of imprisonment were certainly given for subsequent offences, graded according to their more serious nature; but this was really quite a failure as an attempt to diminish narcotic crimes. So the Nanking Government decided to wage a desperate war on the use of all drugs. The big Youth Movements that were then coming into existence did much valuable propaganda work by stating that the health and strength of the Chinese nation were being sapped by the taking of drugs, and that the youth of the country would decay unless something decisive were done in the matter.

So, driven by fear of the demoralization and deterioration of the race, the Chinese authorities at last made a serious attempt to tackle the problem, and very heavy punishments were ordained for these narcotic crimes.

A person charged with a first offence of smoking opium is made to pay a fine of about fifty dollars, and is also given a term in gaol; but before serving his sentence he is sent to an anti-opium hospital. Here he receives the best possible treatment for the drug mania, and enjoys certain privileges in hospital as an ordinary citizen. He remains there until it is considered that a cure has been effected, and then he is sent to gaol to serve his sentence. This finishes off his cure, and on release he is thought to be absolutely free from the opium habit.

If he relapses and is arrested again for the same crime, he is given a heavier fine and a longer term of imprisonment. He is also sent again to the anti-opium hospital for the same treatment, but he is deprived of the privileges that he had before.

If he relapses again, and is arrested for the third time, he is given the death sentence without any option whatsoever. As someone once remarked, as a cure for drugs this is absolutely certain, although rather drastic as a treatment.

Whether these new laws mark a turning-point in the suppression of the drug traffic it is too soon to say. The Chinese go to great extremes to obtain their drugs, and what I saw in Shanghai does not make me very sanguine that even these very severe punishments will have much effect, at least for some time to come. The Chinese is a fatalist by nature, and I think he believes that if he wants to smoke a pipe of opium, it is his fate to do so, even if it involves his own death.

These laws not only affect Shanghai, but the whole of China, and perhaps more progress is being made in other districts than in that cosmopolitan melting-pot. But whatever the truth, at least a better attempt is being made to deal with the scourge than in the past, and there is still time for the campaign to produce results that would astonish the world; for I am convinced that if the smell of opium ceased to pervade the land, a new China, morally and physically stronger than she has been for centuries, would arise.

The smell of opium! Once smelt, it is a scent never to be forgotten. No one who has ever experienced that sweet, aromatic,

pungent smell can ever mistake it. Even now, many months after leaving China, if by any strange chance I could pass a house
in an English street in which someone was smoking a pipe of
opium, I know quite well that I should be aware of it by the
smell without the smallest shadow of doubt. That is what would
happen in Shanghai when on patrol. I would be out on duty
walking along a street, and would notice by the smell that opium smoking was in progress. It would probably be someone
smoking a "family pipe," as we used to call it, perhaps some
rich old Chinese enjoying his daily pipe to cure some of his old-
age ailments. He would probably die if deprived of it, and this
kind of smoking is winked at by the police. It is only when opium becomes a commercial enterprise and large profits are made
by sapping the vitality of the younger generations that I for one
rejoice in arresting the culprits.

Drug-taking on the streets is quite a common sight, especially
amongst the coolie class. First of all a person buys a small con-
signment of morphine or heroin, which is made up into small
paper packets containing minute quantities of the drug. Then he
employs various coolies to sell them on the streets at twenty cents
a packet. Rickshaw and wheelbarrow coolies and other low-class
working-people buy these drugs, some even going without food
to do so, retire to a secluded spot, take out a cigarette, sprinkle
a little of the drug on the end and then smoke it, inhaling the
heroin or morphine with the tobacco smoke.

I have often walked down somewhat unfrequented alley-
ways and seen dozens of coolies sprawled out on pieces of
matting having their little smoke. I never arrested them, but
confiscated the remainder of the drug and tried to find out
from whom they had obtained it. If I managed to trace it back
to the sellers themselves, I generally found that the drug-traffickers resided either in Chapei or in the French Concession.
As any attempt to set the law in motion against them in these
circumstances was an extremely complicated business, involving representations being made by one set of authorities to

another, it was usually abandoned at the outset. Sometimes, however, sufficient information was received from the sellers to make a roundup worth while.

As usual, the rickshaw coolie is a cloak for crime, and the narcotic gangs find him a useful go-between. At one time the transport of considerable quantities of drugs was known to be going on under the very eyes of the police, but the most careful search of hundreds of rickshaw coolies failed to reveal how it was being done. The investigation had been going on for some time without any result when somehow or other a certain rickshaw came into the hands of the police. On examination, a sliding panel was found at the back, and in the hollow recess behind it a large quantity of opium was discovered. This was how the drug was being carried about Shanghai, and for many weeks it had successfully evaded police search. Photographs of this rickshaw were then sent to all stations showing the different positions of the various secret panels, and this method of transporting drugs came to a sudden end.

But the smoking of opium is the most frequent crime as far as drugs go in Shanghai. It is absolutely rife in the city. Hundreds of opium dens have been raided and thousands of Chinese have been arrested, but still it goes on almost as badly as before.

The popular conception of an opium den, founded probably on the romantic imaginations of the writers of detective fiction, has little connection with reality. These writers seem to imagine that opium is always and only smoked in rooms hidden by silken tapestries and containing several bunks, on which the smokers recline at ease with the comfortable thought that a secret exit is there to give them a means of escape should the police interfere. I worked in Shanghai as a policeman for six years, but I never saw a place quite like that. Now for reality.

The usual opium den is an ordinary room in quite an ordinary Chinese dwelling-house. It can be termed a den only in so far as it is always dirty and the house is a filthy wooden hovel. Here a party of eight to a dozen people collect. They receive their pipes and smoking paraphernalia from the tenant of the house, who is called a conductor, and generally some form of watch is kept outside to give warning of a police raid.

Opium-smoking requires certain peculiar instruments—at least, the Chinese always conform to a sort of ritual in their smoking, and it necessitates a regular paraphernalia.

First of all there is the pipe. Usually it has a long hollow wooden stem with a very large mouthpiece at one end and a metal cup at the other, fastened to it by means of a metal band. The more expensive pipes have bands of embossed silver, and these are often confiscated by the police in opium raids and kept by them as souvenirs.

The opium is kept in a metal container, and other instruments include a pair of tweezers for handling the opium and some pieces of metal called picks which are used for plucking the opium from the container. Red pills and raw opium are what is usually smoked.

A pill about the size of a pea is held between the tweezers over the flame of a small lamp. It is then placed over the hole in the bottom of the cup, and the smoke is then inhaled. About three or four inhalations are supposed to exhaust the pill's life. Several of these pills are smoked, until the smoker falls off into a deep sleep. As he becomes addicted to the habit, more and more pills are required to induce sleep.

The raw opium is mixed in the container until it becomes a sticky substance. A quantity is then wound round the pick and placed in the cup, where it is worked into a small ball. It is then held over the lamp and smoked in the usual way. The remaining ash and the residue of prepared opium, which is called dross, are also smoked.

The police usually gather information about these opium "dens" from informers, employed unofficially by the Chinese detectives. These informers frequent tea-shops and food-shops and mingle with all sorts of criminals. Some of them go to the opium dens themselves, but gladly give the show away to the detectives for a few dollars. Anyhow, having collected some information, the informer telephones to the detective employing him at his station, and a meeting is arranged between them, generally in a tea-shop, which has led to it being called a tea-shop conference.

The informer hands over the addresses of some of these opium dens to the detective, who forwards them to the senior Foreign detective at the station, who immediately applies for a search warrant from the court. In the meantime a careful watch has been kept on the premises by detectives to ascertain the regular hours of the opium-smokers. This ensures a full quota being there when the raid takes place and a large number of arrests. The search warrant is sent to the station in a sealed envelope, which is then handed over to the senior detective. This precaution is taken to prevent any information leaking out to anyone at the station concerning the whereabouts of the intended raid and the whole affair is kept as secret as possible.

This may seem rather strange, as it suggests that the police cannot trust each other. As a matter of fact, that is partially the truth, and the reason for so much secrecy. Cases have been known when rumours and more definite information have gone round a station concerning a prospective opium raid, with the result that when the detectives entered the den in question, the birds had flown. But the situation must not be judged as if the personnel of a Shanghai police station were the same as in England. The conditions are quite different, and proper precautions have to be taken to meet them. For instance, the informer himself would probably net twenty to thirty dollars from the owner of one of these houses if he double-crossed the police and "tipped him the wink" when his premises were likely to be raided. And the Chinese employed at a station can easily and quite accidentally drop information of considerable importance to outside individuals. If they saw the search warrant in the case of an opium raid, they might unintentionally talk about it in the presence of someone who would immediately sell the news to the "conductor" involved.

I have worked with some good Chinese in a station, but also with some of the most crafty and cunning people I have ever met.

I remember one day, whilst on charge-room duty, a small Chinese child was brought into the station, having been found straying in the streets. I went through the usual procedure — that is to say, I circulated a message giving a description of the child to all stations, in case any inquiries were made. Then I gave the child some food and kept it at the station. A little later a Chinese coolie employed by the Police Force stated that he knew where the child lived. I should have sent for the parents to take it away and obtained particulars direct from them for reference, but I decided to send the coolie with the child, telling him to get the name and address of the parents. I saw the Chinese clerk whisper to the coolie, but I thought nothing of it. The latter returned later with the required particulars, and I thought that the matter was finished as far as I was concerned.

But on the following day a Chinese superintendent appeared and made discreet inquiries about the affair. In the end it transpired that the clerk had told the coolie to demand some recompense from the parents for the return of their child. This had been paid, and probably nothing more would have happened if the child's father had not been a friend of the Chinese superintendent.

Suspicion naturally fell on me, as I had acted in an unorthodox way in the first place. So I tackled the Chinese clerk, who confessed to what he had done. I saw the superintendent, explained what had happened, and the whole affair was amicably settled, the money being refunded to the child's father.

This was quite a small affair, but it shows what cunning and unscrupulous Chinese there are working alongside us in the Force.

To return to the opium raids. They cause a lot of friction between the uniform and detective branches of the Force. The Chinese detectives are allotted certain sections in their districts, and they are supposed to discover and report any opium-smoking or gambling going on in them. They do this to some extent, for they can be efficient at their job if they are so inclined. But they cannot live up to their reputations as detectives, and gain "face" by means of fine clothes, without some form of addition to their pay. So some of these dens are not reported, and hush money or "squeeze" is taken—not personally, but through the informers, who receive it from the "conductors" of these houses.

This may go on for some time without any of the parties being found out, until a uniform man in the section, unaware of the situation, reports one of these "squeeze" houses. This means that the detective loses "face" because crime is being enacted under his nose, presumably unbeknown to him (for of course he cannot mention his hush money). So he has to regain it by making more arrests, and he loses more money thereby. Ill-feeling between the detectives and the uniform men has become so bad that it has led to a curious and almost unprecedented result—the Chinese branches of the Force are nearly doing their full duty against crime.

An opium-raiding party will consist of about six detectives, with one uniform man in attendance. They proceed in the station motor-car to within a short distance of the opium den. They alight and cover the house back and front. Then some of them enter the premises with pistols drawn for use in case of emergency, and rush with all speed to the room where the smoking is taking place.

It will probably be a typical Chinese room, small, ill-lit, scantily furnished with a bed and a few family pictures on the walls. The opium-smokers will be found on the bed, on the floor, on chairs or anywhere that seems to them a comfortable resting-place. A Chinese woman will probably be in attendance, besides the conductor of the opium den himself.

If they have not been warned of the approach of the police, they will resign themselves to their fate, some of them trying to clear themselves by saying that they have come to see a friend or to play Mah Jong, the universal recreation of the Chinese.

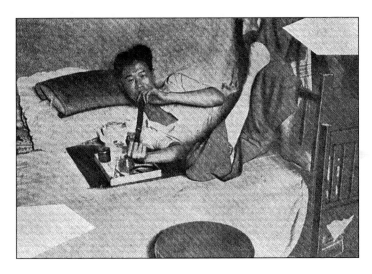

Top: A Chinese Coolie Smoking Opium
Bottom: The Paraphernalia Used for Opium-Smoking, with the
Inevitable Teapot

If they are warned, then it is surprising what they will do, so great is their fear of the police. Irrespective of the height from the ground, they will jump from the windows, and often do themselves such serious injury that they cannot escape, and the police pick them up from there.

I remember one curious case of the Chinaman's little regard for pain that happened when I was charge-room sergeant. An opium raid had taken place one night, and the raiding-party had just brought the opium-smokers to the station. One of them, a middle-aged Chinese, seemed to be limping a little, so I asked the officer in charge of the raid if anything were amiss. He told me that this man had jumped to the ground from the second storey of a house when the police had raided the place.

While the others were being finger-printed, I sat this fellow down on a stool and asked him if he were in pain or felt hurt. He replied:

"Veh iau Ching. Ih nyih nyih Toong." (It's not important, I'm only a little sore.)

I wasn't satisfied, and I sent him to hospital for treatment. Later on I received the doctor's certificate, which ran: "Fractured pelvis. Very serious." He remained in hospital for over six months.

The prisoners at the station, especially after a big raid, will be classified in the following manner. As their names are taken, the Chinese clerk numbers them by dipping his pen (which, like all Chinese pens, is like a small paint-brush) into some ink and writing or painting their numbers on the sides of their faces.

After particulars have been taken, they are fingerprinted and thoroughly searched. Then, if it has been a raid by the uniform branch, they are interviewed by the detectives to see if any further information can be obtained from them.

The Chinese are natural gamblers, and gambling is as rife in Shanghai as opium-smoking. It is difficult to say which causes the more misery and crime, for the Chinese can never resist the temptation to have a gamble, even if it means that he has to pawn his own clothes to do so, as he so readily does for his pipe of opium. I cannot think of a case in which gambling was the direct cause of a murder, but it probably has been so more than once.

A few years ago there were many dog-racing courses in Shanghai, two of the main ones being in the International Settlement. The latter were eventually closed, as they were considered to be enticing the Chinese to gamble too much. I doubt whether this has had the desired effect. I think the result has rather been that the Chinese, unable to gamble publicly at the dogs, have gone more and more to the private gambling dens. Moreover, the one remaining dog-racing course in the French Concession attracts a crowd many times larger than those that used to attend the two courses in the Settlement.

The favourite indoor recreation of the Chinese is the well-known game of Mah Jong. Played like dominoes, the clink of the bricks on the board can be heard in most streets at any time of the day or night. It is played in tea-shops, food-shops, hotels and dwelling-houses, four persons playing together for any stakes that they can afford or not afford, as the case may be. They become so expert at the game that they can tell by touch what is inscribed on the bricks.

The Chinese seems to me a good gambler, if by that one means a man who wins or loses with perfect equanimity and without showing his feelings. The fatalism of the race probably plays a part in this, and prevents them from giving way to the excitement of Western peoples.

Lotteries are one of the most popular forms of gambling in Shanghai. They are forbidden by the police, and rather heavy sentences are imposed on offenders. The most famous is organized on a big commercial basis. For this, you buy a ticket that may cost you from five cents to five dollars. When the draw takes place, your ticket may bring you hundreds of dollars in return.

It is rather surprising how many of these lotteries manage to remain secret, considering that publicity is the very essence of their existence. But in spite of the police using informers in an attempt to suppress them in the same way as the opium dens, they are always springing up on all sides. They certainly should be wiped out, for they are a swindle from start to finish, the only person having any chance of gaining anything being the man who runs one.

I came across many curious methods of gambling among the Chinese while on duty in various parts of Shanghai. I have seen them laying odds on the number of seeds in a water-melon, a race between a couple of land crabs, and playing many peculiar games with cards and dice. But the strangest of all was that which I discovered while on duty in the charge-room.

A party of police had just returned from a gambling raid. They had arrested about a dozen Chinese, and confiscated some weird and wonderful gambling apparatus. I noticed a beautifully carpentered box with one side covered with a fine mesh of bamboo canes and two small doors let into it. Then there were several deep earthenware pots complete with lids, a small set of Chinese scales and some straws specially cut at one end so that the tips resembled paint-brushes. On inspection the earthen pots were found to contain a pair of crickets—those things that you hear making loud chirruping noises in the fields in summer-time.

I asked in amazement what all this paraphernalia was for and what crime should be entered on the arrested persons' charge-sheets. The Chinese inspector told me that he was going to charge them with "gambling with crickets," and on my gasp of astonishment agreed to give me a demonstration.

First of all he took a male cricket out of one of the pots. They are kept in pairs, one male and one female, as grouped thus they will not fight. Then he took another male out of one of the other pots, carefully matching him in size with the first one. This is where the scales came in, and as he weighed the two crickets as if the absurd little things were two boxers going into the ring, he told me that matching them evenly was most important. When the two crickets were finally selected as nearly as possible of the same size and weight, he placed them in the arena — the carved box that I described above. The straws are now brought into play while the gamblers place their bets on their favourite. The crickets are tickled with the straws until they become so infuriated that they attack one another, and fight on until one retires in disgrace or is left dead or dying in the centre of the arena by the conqueror. The Chinese inspector told me that an old rickshaw coolie will sometimes have a stroke of luck in his search for a good cricket, and light upon a champion that makes his fortune.

One of the oldest Chinese customs is "squeeze." It is hard to define in precise terms what it really is. If I call it hush money or a bribe, it must be remembered that in many cases it is a fully recognized custom among the Chinese.

A common form of "squeeze" occurs in the rackets run by the loafer class in Shanghai. These people do no work, but form into gangs of hooligans who are always kicking up trouble in the city, and even demand money from shopkeepers and traders under threat of violence if it is not paid. In a way this is more a form of extortion than actual squeeze.

A Chinese will open a new shop, and instead of doing a little trade as he expected, finds that he is doing nothing. He discovers in the end that a gang of loafers are standing outside the shop obstructing all would-be purchasers from entering. They refuse to move until they receive their squeeze. If he calls the police, the loafers have naturally decamped before their arrival, to return as soon as the shop is left unguarded. The authorities do everything in their power to stamp out this racket, but they are faced with almost insuperable difficulties, as the loafers always disappear before the police arrive, and it is impossible to put a police guard over half the shops in the city. So in the end the shopkeeper usually pays them their squeeze, hoping at last to be left in peace. But then the gang will probably demand more squeeze to protect the premises from the attention of other gangs. Finally rival gangs will engage in a regular warfare for superiority — all at the expense of the poor shopkeeper.

Another form of racket is quite common among the Chinese police themselves. A foreign policeman in charge of a certain section will find that there are innumerable obstructions, consisting chiefly of bales of goods placed on the pavements outside many shops in his district. He will complain about the matter to the Chinese policeman responsible for that particular area, and will receive the assurance that the obstructions will be cleared away immediately. What has happened previously is this: the Chinese policeman has warned the shopkeepers, but the latter have been very polite, begged for the favour of a little grace and on some squeeze being handed over this has been granted.

The same sort of thing happens with regard to traffic accidents. For instance, an accident occurs in the street between a motor-car driven by a rich Chinese and a rickshaw pulled by a coolie. Although it is probably only a very trivial matter, it is the policeman's duty to take full particulars and to report the matter to the station. In most cases the rickshaw coolie will be in the wrong, but the driver of the motorcar, not wishing to lose time and "face" at the traffic court, will suggest to the policeman that the matter should be settled on the spot by his paying for whatever damage has been done to the rickshaw. This will be agreed upon, but not before the policeman has received his recognized squeeze. He gets the same kind attention from the opium dens and gambling-houses in his section.

A foreigner shopping in Shanghai will pay more for his goods from a Chinese shop than the Chinese themselves. For instance, if I buy some soap I may pay a dollar for it, but if I send my Chinese servant on the errand, he will return with the same quantity of soap, and at the same time give me back twenty cents. He will also have received, however, ten cents from the shopkeeper as squeeze. He will bargain for this rebate or squeeze on the strength of his master's patronage.

I have been involved myself in two incidents connected with squeeze. They took place in very abnormal circumstances, and many of my companions were guilty also (if, considering everything, we were guilty of the heinous crime of accepting bribes from the public — one of the worst crimes in the police calendar in England; but far worse are committed in Shanghai). I thus have no hesitation in confessing to my two solitary and rather unsuccessful attempts to take a small share of the profits made at the expense of the Chinese public. When I think of the whole racket, I feel rather proud of my restraint, but I some-times wonder whether I was the biggest fool or the wisest man in the Force. On these two occasions there was no risk, and it was easy to get away with it because of the Chinaman's usual fear of the police.

It was just after the Japanese and Chinese War in 1932, and I was on duty at a station on the borders of Chapei.

During the war, the Chinese had evacuated Chapei, and at this time the people had not yet begun to return. It was absolute-ly deserted, and there were not even any police in the district.

I was in charge of four Chinese policemen detailed to patrol a certain area of Chapei, a job that I shall never forget. The whole place stank abominably. For two months the refuse had been al-lowed to rot in the streets, and the authorities of the International Settlement were having to clear it away to protect the health of the people.

We were walking down a street in which there were several semi-foreign houses, when the Chinese sergeant told me that he suspected that something fishy was going on in one of the houses a little farther on. As a matter of fact, he knew perfectly well what was happening, but he wanted to tempt me to enter the place. So, leaving the Chinese constables at the corner of the street, I went along with the sergeant.

We passed many empty houses, and then stopped outside one that looked no different from the rest. I opened the gate and walked up a small drive to the front door. My appearance had an almost miraculous effect. Long before I could knock on the door or proceed to investigate, dozens of Chinese swarmed out of the house, jumping through the windows and leaping over the fence and running for dear life. It gave me quite a shock to see that apparently deserted house suddenly teeming with such activity.

I certainly had my suspicions aroused, but on entering I received another and even more startling surprise. The whole bottom floor had been converted into one large room, that was now filled with gaming tables. Thousands of dollars were strewn about the tables, and the gamblers had even dropped them on the floor in their hurry to escape.

Not a soul was there, and I found myself in rather an awkward position. Normally I should never have entered the premises. I ought to have reported the matter to the station, and then a search warrant would have been obtained and a raid made. But this did not quite apply to Chapei, especially when abandoned by its own inhabitants. At the best of times, we did not much care what the Chinese did there.

I was still hesitating, wondering what I had better do and looking eagerly at so much wealth, when two Chinese in foreign dress came into the room. They excused themselves most politely, and asked to be forgiven for running this gambling-house. I at once assumed a stern and official, not to say officious attitude, and told them that I would have to arrest them for conducting a house for the purposes of gambling. They became very frightened, and one of them placed fifty dollars in my hand. I refused it with a show of indignation, and again said that I would have to take them to the station. Whereupon they gave me a hundred and fifty dollars and the Chinese sergeant twenty-five, telling us to call every day at a certain time for the same amount. As the house and district did not really come under our jurisdiction, I decided to accept it, and began calculating how much I should net if I continued on this patrol job until Chapei returned to normal conditions.

Next day I set off to receive my further instalment of money for nothing, accompanied by the Chinese sergeant. He told me on the way that he had seen a foreign sub-inspector near the gambling-house that morning. This brought me to a halt. I had no wish to hamper my promising career in the Force by being accused of accepting bribes while on duty, so I sheered off and decided to have nothing further to do with the matter.

I need not have been so circumspect, however. A few weeks later I found out that I was not the only person who had been receiving gifts from that source.

Another time I was on charge-room duty. A Chinese had been arrested on suspicion of being the head of a large gang of narcotic traffickers and manufacturers. I think myself that he was innocent, although he had probably inherited his father's profits from dealing in drugs.

The Chapei police were demanding in no measured terms that this man be handed over to them, but we could not let him go until a full investigation had been made. I am afraid that his life would have come to a speedy end if the Chapei police had got hold of him then.

As he was a rich man, he could afford to have good food and warm clothes brought to him in his cell at the station. He was allowed to receive such things, and a certain number of visitors at the discretion of the detective in charge of the case.

I happened to be on duty one evening when one of the prisoner's friends came to see him. Knowing that he had been accorded the privilege of receiving visitors, I gave the required permission for the man to be conducted to his cell. It was with some surprise that I found an envelope containing thirty dollars on my desk. I pocketed the money and asked no questions, but I knew what it was for. To contradict the librettist, there are times when a policeman's lot *is* a happy one.

There are only about three Chinese Clubs in the International Settlement that are exempted from police supervision or interference. One of them was in a district in which I was once working. I was going on charge-room duty one day when the officer whom I was relieving told me that this particular club had invited several members of the station, including myself, to a dinner on the following night. I told him that I was too busy and refused.

The next day I heard a telephone message from one of the heads of the Police Force to a detective who had also received the invitation (Headquarters are not the only people who listen in) to the effect that nobody was to attend this dinner-party. He mentioned everyone who had been invited by name, except me, my refusal apparently excluding me. He then said that he was considering having the whole station personnel transferred elsewhere, obviously thinking that there was some dirty work going on at this club between the Chinese and the police, and that this dinner was a subtle means of corrupting the Force.

V

I SHOULD THINK that crime was worse in Shanghai than in any other city in the world both in amount and in degree. The cosmopolitan character of this metropolis breeds its own special crimes and criminal methods, which means that the police have to invent completely original means to deal with them.

Most of the crime committed is done by the Chinese, but a large amount must also be attributed to the Russians. The latter are expert pick-pockets and they are always to be found on the race-courses and dog-tracks, besides practising their skill on the passengers in the trams and buses. Whatever may be said against the Russians in the Police Force, the big decrease in the crime committed by their countrymen must be ascribed to the skill of their detectives. They are particularly clever at shadowing Russian women shoplifters, and have considerably reduced their ravages of recent years.

Since the Russian Revolution, Shanghai has sheltered thousands of refugees from that country. Unable to find work in the city, they have taken to crime and prostitution. One sees them living under worse conditions than the poorest Chinese coolie. Losing all sense of self-respect, they join the beggars in the streets, and even live on the earnings of immoral women. Others cease to care whether they live or die, and when they have begged twenty cents from someone, they spend them on a concoction far worse than methylated spirits or even petrol. Having swallowed this awful stuff, they lie dead drunk in the streets until arrested by the police. When sentenced to a few days in gaol, they are only too glad to get food and a bed free.

There is one Russian famous for his liking for gaol. He is called the "King of Beggars." I think the last time I saw him in court he was receiving his fifty-fourth sentence for vagrancy. Life holds nothing for such people outside prison.

Those retaining a little decency and self-respect obtain a variety of jobs that bring them just enough to live on, no more. Some become bodyguards to rich Chinese or watchmen for the large companies. Many join the Chinese Army if they cannot find other employment, and the remainder become criminals to save themselves from starving. Some of them may call for pity, but the majority can only be despised for resorting to such degrading forms of wage-earning, pimping for harlots being one of the least unmentionable.

The menace of the armed criminal is a comparatively recent thing in Shanghai. It has only developed to its present alarming proportions during the last twelve years. In that short space of time the armed robbers have literally set up a reign of terror in the city, and transformed the usual conflict between police and criminals into a bitter civil war in which he who shoots first has the best chance of surviving. Before then the police in the streets were unarmed, and it was not the usual thing for a man to slip his pistol into his holster before going on duty, as we all do now. The shooting of a foreign police officer was the indirect cause of every officer in the Force now carrying a pistol.

A Chinese shop had been robbed by a gang of armed robbers, and the alarm had been raised. The foreign officer saw one of them trying to escape by running down an alley-way. He gave chase, but was handicapped by having no pistol. As he overtook the robber, the latter turned and fired at him point blank and he received a shot in the stomach. In spite of this he still carried on in pursuit of his assailant, and getting within striking distance, picked up a large shovel and smashed it down over the robber's head, collapsing as he did so. The robber was killed and the officer received a first-class Police Medal for pluck and gallantry under fire.

This type of criminal increased to such an extent that they became an absolute menace to the public and the social order, while forming an almost insoluble problem for the police. As there seemed a danger of the armed robbers getting the upper hand and literally terrorizing the city, the Police Force was radically reorganized and the C.I.D., or Detective Branch, was considerably strengthened to cope with the situation.

The innate fatalism of the Chinese means that these robbers will stop at nothing, and armed robbery and kidnapping have become the two major crimes in Shanghai.

The Municipal Police Force therefore has a very large Detective Branch, comprising British, Russian, Japanese and Chinese. The latter do the donkey work, so to speak, while the others sift the evidence provided by them and so build up their case. Thus the Chinese detectives obtain through their informers the first inside knowledge of criminal haunts, the criminals themselves and the crimes they are plotting to commit, and submit all their information to the Foreign detectives to be analysed and examined. The Russian and Japanese detectives generally work on cases affecting their nationals.

The detectives themselves pay the informers whom they employ. Good cases are sometimes distinguished by pecuniary rewards besides seniority, but in spite of their low wages Chinese detectives are never short of money, and manage to hire the services of as many informers as they require.

Many criminals who have fled from Shanghai want to return, and often try to sneak in by train. News of the attempt is frequently passed on to the detectives by their informers, and then a regular party is organized to suit the occasion. Several rickshaws are brought into the station from the street, and the coolies paid off to compensate them for whatever time they may lose. A full-dress masquerade is then staged. The Chinese detectives impersonate both coolies and passengers, all carrying concealed pistols. Arriving at the railway station, the "passengers" alight and mingle with the general crowd. At last the suspect arrives, and takes a good look round, for he fully expects watchers to be waiting for him. Satisfied that no one has spotted him, he finally jumps into a rickshaw, unaware that he has been carefully manoeuvred into one of those - pulled by a detective, and in a few minutes he finds himself in a police station where he undergoes a cross-examination which he will never forget, whether he be innocent or guilty.

When information is received that certain premises are harbouring armed robbers or kidnappers or desperate gangs, the detectives make their raids wearing steel vests and carrying bullet-proof shields. There is every reason for these precautions. Although no crime may be taking place at the moment except that of the possession of firearms, the raid is none the less dangerous. For these gangsters are always such desperate men, besides being dangerous fatalists, that the police must take them by surprise if a pistol duel is to be avoided. And it must always be remembered that, having everything to lose by capture, an armed robber shoots to kill.

A typical Sydney Street affair occurred in Shanghai some years ago. A gang of robbers were besieged in a certain house by the police, but in spite of the cordon drawn round them and the hopelessness of their position they refused to surrender. Periodically a fusillade of pistol shots broke from the windows in the direction of the police. The Riot Van was called out, and for some time a steady machine-gun fire was directed on the room in which the robbers were known to be. When later on there was a lull in the robbers' fire, a ladder was propped against the window and a policeman went up with a couple of tear-gas bombs. As he neared the top, he was met by more shots, but managed to fling one of the bombs inside. As the firing still went on, however, it was decided to rush the room from the inside. The person doing all the damage was then found propped against the window, mortally wounded. He was the only survivor, but he didn't last long.

The whole place was absolutely riddled with bullets, and the man himself was full of lead. How he had managed to survive so long and to continue firing most of the time was a mystery—at least, it would have been if he had not been a Chinese armed robber, for such men always fight desperately to the bitter end.

It would be almost impossible to get such criminals to "squeal" against their gangs in England, if such a situation arose there; but this is not the case in China. The Chinese are said to be the only people who understand their own race, and they have their own methods of dealing with recalcitrant criminals. When an armed robber or kidnapper is arrested and the Chinese detectives want to obtain information from him concerning the rest of his gang and their whereabouts, they sometimes employ rough-and-ready but usually effective third-degree methods of their own. They have probably convicted an innocent man more than once, but they have doubtless been the only possible means of convicting some of the guilty ones on many occasions.

It is not for me to judge the rights and the wrongs of the matter, nor perhaps for anyone who has not made a profound study of the Chinese, their ways and customs and their present state of social development. China is not Europe, their standards are different from ours, especially in regard to the infliction and endurance of pain. It often seemed to me that I was back in the Middle Ages in this respect. I was amazed by some of the stories of these third-degree methods that I heard, and by some special cases that came to my notice. I know for certain that such methods of extracting required information are from time to time employed by the Chinese; but they are doubtless unknown to the authorities and responsible officers. It is a pity that these officials do not know what we in the lower ranks had certain knowledge of. If they did, it would doubtless soon cease.

Let me take a typical instance of the sort of thing that goes on. A prisoner is brought into the charge-room, full particulars concerning him are taken down and then he is sent to the detective office for further inquiries and investigations. There he is asked to reveal certain information that would lead to the arrest of the remainder of his gang. He probably replies with a fictitious address, and then leads the detectives all over Shanghai in an attempt to find it.

When he has bluffed them in this way several times, they become angry and fed up. Back to the station they go, partially strip him and smack his feet with a life-preserver until he is ready to talk. Even then he probably takes them on another false errand. This often means that, on returning to the station, they proceed to more drastic measures. This time he is laid on his back on a long wooden form with his head dangling unsupported over the edge. His arms and legs are bound down, and he is told that this is his last chance. A Chinese detective sits astride the criminal and pummels him, while a light gag is tied across his mouth. Then another detective brings a large kettle of tepid water and pours it slowly down his nostrils until it is practically empty. He is then released to see if this torture has had the desired effect.

It says something for the Chinaman's courage and stoicism in face of pain that men have been known to take the detectives on a wild-goose chase after this. Furious then, they bring him back again, give him another and stronger dose of the water torture, finishing up with some electric shocks from a battery. This usually makes him speak, and he confesses everything.

That is the sort of thing they do. It can only be hoped that time will lead to the suppression of these cruel third-degree methods of obtaining information.

I have said that the Chinese policeman on ordinary duty is so lazy that he always has to be watched to prevent him from shirking his work. But when an emergency arises and courage is needed, then it is quite a different matter. Perhaps he does not always use as much strategy as the occasion demands, but then he never holds back, and woe betide any armed robber whom he meets in even battle.

I was once at a station in a district where armed robberies were a regular occurrence. One evening the alarm was given, and in a few minutes about a dozen of us in our bullet-proof vests were speeding to the scene.

Arriving at the entrance to a very dark alley-way (there was only one light, about forty yards away), we were directed by onlookers in pursuit of the robbers. A sub-inspector and I cautiously led the way along this narrow lane. We suddenly saw the figure of a man lying beneath the solitary light. We both loaded, our pistols, an example that was followed by those behind us. I think now that if firing had started we should have stood in more danger of being shot by our companions behind than by an enemy in front. As it was, the figure remained quite still, so we advanced, and found a Chinese robber badly wounded with a bullet in the chest. He was already unconscious.

What had really happened was that the robbers had been seen by an Indian watchman in the first place. He had fired on them with his rifle and missed. A Chinese policeman had then arrived on the scene, and, seeing them escaping, had given chase. He had shot one of them and, leaving him wounded on the ground, had continued in pursuit of the rest. Later he returned and reported that he had lost touch of the robbers on the boundary of the French Concession, into which they had fled.

The plain-clothes search-parties on the streets are much more useful and efficacious than those in uniform, as they escape detection as police by the criminal classes. They usually wear bullet-proof vests concealed under raincoats, and carry their pistols in their pockets until an actual search is being made. Such a search-party is formed of two foreigners and four Chinese policemen. A very sad misunderstanding connected with these search-parties occurred one evening between two different stations.

The detectives had learned that an armed robbery had been planned to take place that evening at a certain time at a certain place in an adjacent district. Now, information gained by detectives entitles them to proceed to any district in the Settlement. So a short time before the robbery was supposed to take place, they left their own district and crossed into the suspected area. They found the appointed spot to be a very poorly lighted street, and just as they were marching down it, they noticed a party coming towards them. They immediately drew their pistols, and when they saw that the approaching party were carrying arms, they opened fire, for they were taking no chances. A fierce duel ensued, and it was only when someone recognized an acquaintance in the opposite party that the firing ceased, but by then several men on both sides had been severely wounded. Then it was discovered that the suspected armed robbers were the members of a plain-clothes search-party operating in their own district. Each side had thought the other the desperate gang which they were in fact both chasing.

The desperate measures that these armed robbers will employ if driven hard are well illustrated by the following incident, that happened at a station to which I was once attached.

During an armed robbery staged by a very large semi-political gang of Chinese, one of the robbers was severely wounded and had to be left behind when the rest of the gang made off. He was picked up by the police and taken to hospital. A Chinese detective was stationed by his bedside to try to obtain some information from him about his companions should he regain consciousness. I must mention that the hospital was situated on a main road and was heavily guarded by the police.

The next morning two quite respectably dressed Chinese obtained admittance on the pretext of visiting a sick friend. They entered the ward where the robber was lying unconscious, one of them waiting outside to watch the main entrance and another standing by the door. The first man looked slowly round the ward, saw the man lying in the bed, which happened to be the first on the left on entering, and without any hurry or flurry shot his wounded comrade dead to seal his lips for ever, so that he could not disclose the whereabouts of the rest of the gang. This done, he shot the Chinese detective dead also, before he had a chance to draw his pistol. Then he and his companion ran down the steps leading to the courtyard of the hospital. Here they saw a Chinese policeman belonging to the French Concession bringing an injured man into hospital. To avoid all chance of subsequent recognition, they shot both the policeman and the patient. Their motto certainly was "Dead men tell no tales," because when the policeman began to crawl away seriously wounded, one member of the gang fearlessly returned and callously finished him off.

Then they rushed out through the hospital gates and, mingling with the crowd of pedestrians, were soon lost to sight, having perpetrated one of the most sensational crimes ever committed in Shanghai. It took place in one of the busiest centres of the city under the very eyes of the police, and reads more like a melodramatic incident in a detective story than grim reality. The whole thing had been most carefully planned in advance, but I should hardly have believed it possible if I had not been at the time at the station near the hospital.

The next day the detectives there received information that put them hot on the trail of this desperate gang of criminals. It says something for the skill of the Detective Branch that within a couple of days several members of the gang had been located and arrested. On this occasion there had been for once real co-operation between them and the police in the French Concession and Chinese Territory.

A perfect arsenal was discovered at the gang's headquarters. I believe that the police found twenty-three pistols, a large quantity of ammunition and several bombs and knives. More hard work by the Detective Branch during the ensuing weeks succeeded in rounding up the remaining members of one of the most desperate gangs that has ever operated in Shanghai. Many women were also arrested, as it was found that they had been concealing weapons in their homes.

The Chapei Police were very interested in this gang, and whilst on remand at the station the prisoners were taken several times into Chinese Territory to be questioned by the police there. If they had anything to divulge, it must certainly have been obtained, for there are no restrictions to third-degree methods in Chapei, and, as I have said, it takes a Chinese to understand a Chinese.

Whilst the gang were detained at the station, they were all handcuffed to a large table in the detective office, and when removed to Chapei they were likewise handcuffed, with the addition of leg-irons.

I was charge-room sergeant at this station at the time, and although normally we did not carry pistols inside the station, I did then, concealing one in my pocket. Further precautions were also taken. The station gates were closed and bolted, and an Indian guard was placed over them inside and out. If this gang were desperate enough to shoot their way in and out of a hospital, they might well attempt to do the same thing at a police station. We were not giving them the chance if we could help it.

Armed robberies were a daily occurrence then. They were generally committed by about three or four Chinese, only two or three of them being armed. They would enter any kind of shop or money exchange, intimidate the inmates and abscond with money, jewellery or anything of value on which they could lay hands. Frequently the shop people would not report the matter to the police until many hours after it had occurred, which added to the difficulties of apprehending the robbers. This was due to their fear of the gang, who always threatened to return and kill them if a report was made within a certain time.

But even in Shanghai crime has its lighter side, as the following incident will show. It is also a typical example of the Chinese attitude towards crime, a sort of cunning brilliancy of mind that treats it much in the same way as some business men in the West treat rather a sharp deal. It further represents the desperate measures which they are prepared to take to attain the desired end.

I received a message one afternoon from the central control room via the teleprinter, which reported that a motor-car had been stolen from outside some offices in the central district, the commercial part of Shanghai. I immediately gave orders for the message to circulated through the district by means of the street telephones. About an hour later a Chinese constable reported that he had found the wanted car abandoned on the boundary between Chapei and the Settlement. He also mentioned that a Chinese shop-assistant wanted to make a statement concerning the theft. I had him brought to the station, and interviewed him myself. He said that his master was the owner of a shop that stocked attaché cases and trunks of all descriptions. Just after lunch a car had driven up and stopped outside the shop, a young Chinese had entered and said that he wanted to buy a trunk for his master, saying that he was his chauffeur. He asked if he might take two or three trunks "on appro," so that his master could make the final choice himself. The shopkeeper, delighted to make a sale, agreed to these terms, but, with the cunning of the Chinese, sent his assistant along with the chauffeur to see that it was all above-board.

The chauffeur blustered a little, saying that his master was such a well-known man it was casting a reflection on him to mistrust his servant; but he finally consented to this arrangement. When he and the assistant arrived at the boundary, he said that his master did business in the Settlement, but resided in Chapei, and had not troubled to take out a licence for his car there as he used it chiefly for business purposes. As they could not therefore drive on into Chapei now, the chauffeur suggested that he should take the trunks to his master, and leave the shop-assistant to look after car.

"There are so many car thieves about just now," he added, "one has to be careful."

The shop-assistant felt quite satisfied, as the car was worth much more than the trunks. So the chauffeur went off, but he did not return. The assistant waited for an hour and then reported the matter to a patrol policeman, when it was discovered that the car was the stolen one whose description had just been circulated by me. The bogus chauffeur—for such, of course, he was—had invented this daring and very ingenious plan of stealing a car for a short time in order to steal forever a couple of travelling-trunks. And he got away with it.

Kidnapping is another crime that seems peculiarly attractive to the Chinese. Gangs of armed men are again the principal performers. They hire a taxi that is probably on its way back to the garage, and tell the chauffeur, under threat of immediate death if he disobeys, to drive them to a certain place. There they will forcibly kidnap their victim and drive off, generally to one of the boundaries.

If the driver is lucky, he is allowed to go unmolested, but usually he is shot and left dead beside the abandoned car, so that no tales may be told.

Communication is then established with the victim's relations, and negotiations proceed according to plan. Ransom is demanded, and they threaten death to the victim if it is not paid, and also to the other members of the family if the matter is reported to the police. The relatives often hand over the money, as they are afraid to take any chances, well knowing the callousness of these gangs and their readiness to resort to desperate measures.

If they have the courage to tell the police, then weary weeks of watching, waiting and tracking ensue. The relatives' houses are carefully guarded by the police. Informers are sent out to gather any scraps of information available, but false trails are often laid by the gangs and a lot of hard work frequently ends in failure. Detectives disguised as rickshaw coolies follow any likely clue, and traps are laid in an attempt to entice the gangsters into the open. Finally perhaps a meeting is arranged between a relative and a member of the gang. When it takes place, some spurious money is handed over by the relative, and immediately an old rickshaw coolie strolling along the street with apparent unconcern is transformed into a detective complete with pistol. The gangster caught with the dud money on him easily surrenders to a little third degree, and it is not long before the kidnapped person is free and the remainder of the gang arrested.

The wealthy Chinese who have sought refuge in Shanghai from the bandits that infest their native towns take various precautions against these armed gangs. They will live in a fairly busy district near a main thoroughfare. Large iron gates protect the main entrance to their houses, and they have special Chinese, Indian or Russian watchmen, who are armed and come under the supervision of the police. Another watchman patrols the grounds. And when these rich men leave their houses either on business or pleasure, you will notice that they sit in the rear of their cars, with a Russian or Indian armed to the teeth sitting beside the chauffeur in front. Their bodyguards follow them about everywhere until they are safely back in their houses behind locked gates.

I have mentioned before that there were some rather shady characters among the Chinese branch of the Municipal Police Force. One in particular was a Chinese detective sergeant who had been for more than twenty years in the Force. What he had accumulated in hard cash from his own criminal exploits was never disclosed, but it must have run into many thousands of dollars. Finally he left the Force and was soon afterwards arrested as a member of a gang of armed robbers.

The case dragged on for months in court, and his full history was slowly brought to light. It was proved that for many years, whilst serving in the force as a trusted officer, he had also been the head of three large gangs who dealt respectively in opium, armed robbery and kidnapping.

This again reads more like the fantastic exploit of some hero of detective fiction instead of the actual achievement of a police officer in a centre of modern business and industry. When I think of such extraordinary things happening in the great modern city that is Shanghai, I always recall with some amusement what was said to me in London before I joined:

"In general, the duties of the force consist of routine work of a modern business centre, modified as necessary to suit local requirements."

This Chinese detective certainly made his own interpretation as to what modifications were necessary. The inside information obtained from his work as a detective helped him considerably in his criminal activities. He was too clever, however, to let his gangs simply rob and kidnap without encountering any opposition. That would have aroused suspicion. But once their deeds were accomplished, it was quite easy for him to lay false trails that enabled them to escape. They committed murder several times during these robberies and kidnappings, but thanks to their friend and master in the Force they were never brought to justice.

But the Chinese detective sergeant finally was, and he received the following judgment. He was given a long term of imprisonment for his activities with the opium gang, and was sentenced to death on the three counts of armed robbery, kidnapping and murder. He appealed, and, after spending thousands of dollars in his own defence, managed to secure acquittal on one of the death counts. When I last heard of the case, he was still battling for his life against heavy odds. His money was running low, and without it I fear he is doomed.

I often wonder how many Jekyll and Hyde policemen there are in the Force in Shanghai, and how many of the men with whom I personally worked are leading this double existence. I'm pretty sure I must have knocked up against some such adventurers without knowing it.

The vindictiveness of these gangs when some of their comrades have been arrested and sentenced often assumes menacing proportions and has terrible results. Some years ago a young Britisher in the Detective Branch was filled with ambition, and set out to make a name for himself. He worked very hard and conscientiously, and succeeded in rounding up several badly wanted gangs of criminals. He received promotion, and success followed success, until he found himself the youngest detective inspector in the force. The work had tired him, his nerves were strained and he took a holiday. At least, this was the story that was surmised.

But his nerves had been frayed, not so much by his work as by the letters which he had been receiving for some time from various gangs, threatening him with death in the most horrible form in revenge for his arrest of their comrades. Knowing the Chinese as I know them now, I have no hesitation in saying that such a letter is enough to upset the nerves of the strongest man, for the gangsters will let nothing stop them if they are determined on revenge.

Although time passed after the receipt of this letter without anything unpleasant happening, I don't think the poor fellow ever quite got over it. It was not so much that he could pin down any actual reason for his fears; he lived in fear of the unknown, and that is something much worse.

The daring and recklessness of the gangs also appear in an incident that occurred not thirty yards from a police station.

A British sergeant had played an important part in the arrest of a certain gang. It had happened some time before, and he had probably forgotten all about it. He had just left the station, and had arrived at a crowded point in the street near a Chinese hotel and dance-hall. As he passed the latter, a shot rang out, and the officer fell dead. The murderer escaped in the crowd, and was never heard of again. Subsequent investigation suggested that a member of the gang which the sergeant had been instrumental in arresting had taken his revenge.

When one thinks of the heavy punishments inflicted for such crimes, the Chinese seem a more enigmatic race than ever. Even their fatalism fails to explain such criminal daring. For an ordinary armed robbery with no shots fired there is a sentence of anything between seven and fifteen years in gaol. (Incidentally, many of these robberies are committed with dummy pistols. Cleverly carved out of wood, and then painted, they are such a good imitation of a pistol that they deceive most people at a short distance.)

For armed robbery in which shots are fired, and for kidnapping, the death penalty is the rule. And of course all murderers receive the death sentence. But the Chinese, and especially those of the lower classes, have so little regard for life that even such severe punishments do not seem to reduce the amount of crime in the city to any appreciable extent.

This contempt for human life governs many of their actions. You must always take it into account with the coolies. Perhaps it explains the strange behaviour of the one involved in the following incident.

A rich Chinese found out that his wife had a lover. Not wishing to take the matter to court, probably on account of the loss of "face" that such action would involve, he sought some other means of revenge on the man who had supplanted him in his wife's affections. He formed a plan, and took immediate steps to put it into execution.

He found a Chinese of the coolie type and explained to him how his family's honour had suffered from this lover of his wife. He said that he had finally decided to kill the man. The coolie agreed that it was a good idea; anyway, he knew that the lover had done wrong. Then the rich Chinese suggested that the coolie should kill the lover for him.

After a little debate and argument over terms, it was settled at last that the coolie should kill the lover for ten dollars (about thirteen shillings), the money to be paid over when the murder had been well and truly committed.

The coolie watched the lover for several nights, and then killed him with a large hammer in a secluded alley-way one evening. But he was only an amateur murderer, after all, and he was soon arrested. The rich Chinese was soon brought to court also, and they were both sentenced to death.

But it only shows what the Chinese coolie will do for a little money. It would probably have taken him three weeks to earn ten dollars by ordinary work, and he considered it quite an achievement to obtain them in a few minutes, although it meant taking a man's life. He had no sorrow for his victim, and it seemed to him quite worth while. But these poor unintelligent coolies, who are little more than dogs themselves, will kill a man as readily as others will slaughter cattle.

The authorities themselves, however, show as little regard for human life as do the coolies. And none less than the Chinese military authorities.

One day I was acting as escort for some money that the Power Company was sending to one of its substations on the boundary between the Settlement and Chapei.

A Britisher in charge there asked me if I could do anything about the dead body of a Chinese soldier that had been lying on some waste ground near the station for some days. As he luridly put it, "Besides hardly being a decoration to the landscape, I don't think it's improving our health. The wind's blowing that way and — well, you can see, or rather smell, for yourself."

I asked him how the soldier had come to be in such an outlandish spot. He replied that four days before he had seen a train stop at this point, where the track runs near the sub-station, and several Chinese soldiers alight. One of them had his hands tied behind his back. The others had stood him up in a convenient position, shot him and returned to the train, which then proceeded on its way minus one soldier. A few discreet inquiries among the Chinese in the neighbourhood made it clear that an execution of this kind was a regular occurrence there.

The explanation of the whole matter was that many Chinese desert from their regiments in the country and flee into Shanghai. When caught the military authorities don't trouble to escort them back to their regiments, but stop the train on the outskirts of the city, and, finding a convenient spot, execute them. This is what had doubtless happened to the fellow who had offended that English official's sense of — propriety.

VI

SENSATIONAL CASES OF armed robbery occur so frequently in Shanghai that it is difficult to pick out the most interesting, but perhaps the following forms a good example.

It occurred in February 1929 in the Y'Poo District. The first watch were just coming off duty in the station there, guns were being handed in at the armoury, and reports were being submitted to the desk sergeant. Foreigners, tired and hungry after a weary four hours' patrol in Shanghai's most scattered and largest district, the Yangtsepoo—or the Y'Poo, as we called it for short—were leaving the charge-room for their evening meal, when suddenly the burglar alarm went off. This was an ingenious American invention, an extremely delicate and highly sensitive piece of mechanism known as the "Ever-Open-Eye Burglar Alarm." It operated in code simultaneously with an alarm bell, a red light and a tape machine, the latter punching a series of holes in a moving tape, Morse fashion. A code-board giving the addresses of the buildings in which the alarm was installed hung alongside. They were usually the homes of very wealthy Chinese merchants, large factories or banks. The alarm was set in motion by a concealed button placed in some convenient position in the building.

"Drat the thing!" remarked the desk sergeant, as the tape began to unwind itself into a hopeless jumble after a few seconds' coding. "Another false alarm, I suppose."

However, the first coding proved to be the address of a very wealthy and important Japanese cotton-mill owner, situated some fifteen minutes' ride from the station. Within three minutes a posse of police, fully armed and equipped with bullet-proof vests and shields, were roaring along in a high-powered car to the scene of the alarm. The house was situated in a lonely spot some fifty yards off the roadway, surrounded by a high bamboo fence with one small entrance and a crescent-shaped drive leading up to the front door.

Dashing through this entrance, the police were immediately greeted by the sight of a thug emerging from the house with a shot-gun under his arm.

"My God, look out!" exclaimed one of the officers, whilst another called on the thug to stop, the necessary warning before opening fire.

The robber took no heed of the warning, but dropped the shot-gun and took to his heels, making for the exit on the opposite side of the drive to that by which the police had entered. Luck favoured him, for the inky darkness made accurate shooting impossible. A number of shots were fired at him, but he made good his escape across country into Chinese Territory outside our jurisdiction.

Meanwhile movements had been observed in one of the front bedrooms of the house. Rushing round to the rear, one of the officers arrived in time to see another of the gang in the act of opening a window in an attempt to get away there. The officer opened fire, at the same time taking cover behind a coal-house some yards away from the main building. The thug was seen to withdraw, shot in the leg in two places, as it was afterwards discovered.

As the police were uncertain how many of the gang were still in the house, a call was made to the station for further assistance, while they formed a cordon round the building to prevent the remaining thugs from escaping.

Suddenly a figure leaped out of an upstairs window, shouting, "Don't shoot," in English. This proved to be one of the male Japanese inmates of the house. From him it was learnt that the remainder of the family, including several women and children, were huddled together in a downstairs room, in which they had been locked by the gang soon after they had forced an entry.

The Riot Squad now arrived, having been called out to deal with the situation. An entry squad was immediately formed, consisting of five foreigners, one armed with a Thompson sub-machine-gun, the others with automatics and bullet-proof shields. The first thing they did on entering the house was to release the terrified family and take them out of the danger zone.

Then began the systematic searching of the darkened rooms. Each one was entered with the tension of expectation known only to those who have faced such moments. The basement rooms being drawn blank, the party moved up the stairs. When almost at the top of the first flight, a figure emerged out of the darkness in front of the advancing body of police. They opened fire, for it was seen to be one of the gang. The machine-gun quickly found its mark, and the thug soon toppled to the bottom of the stairs with several bullets in his vitals.

The rooms on the first floor were then searched, but without success. The officer first on the scene suggested, however, that there must be some other members of the gang somewhere, so a further, and more thorough search was made. At last the thug who had tried to escape by way of the bedroom window at the rear of the house was found buried beneath a pile of empty boxes in one of the attics. It was discovered later that he had been wounded by his companion, and had then dragged himself to this hiding-place. He was given no chance to use his gun, for as soon as he was spotted four shots were fired, and they all found their mark. The bulk of the loot from the robbery was found on his person, consisting of jewellery amounting in value to some ten thousand dollars.

Another case of even greater interest occurred in April 1933. It happened something like this.

"Raid?" exclaimed one of the first watch coming off duty, as he spotted the usual arrangements being made in the charge-room.

"Yes," replied the sergeant on duty. "Big one too, by the look of it. Chief's going. Matter of dope, I believe. Going yourself?"

"You bet! Where's the joint?"

"No idea yet. Chief's got the warrant."

A few minutes later the order was received to fall in. Three car-loads of uniform police, consisting of ten Chinese and five foreigners, were told to follow the Chief's car. Until it drew up at the entrance to an alley-way on the famous Nanking Road in the very heart of the city, not more than three minutes' ride from the Station, there was no indication as to where the raid was to take place.

Then things began to move quickly. The Chief issued his orders. In a few seconds every officer knew what was expected of him. The house, a large old building of the usual Chinese type lying some fifty yards inside the alley-way, was surrounded and entered. The basement revealed all that could be desired from the police point of view. The inmates scurried furtively away in an attempt to avoid arrest, trying at the same time to put out the lights. Then sacks upon sacks of opium pills were found, together with the entire plant for their manufacture. The whole gang were soon arrested, as their account-books and records of their distributing centres were also discovered.

It proved to be the largest opium-pill manufacturing plant ever found in the Settlement. Some idea of the tremendous traffic in the drug may be gained from the fact that ten huge sacks of these pills were seized. The pills were sold at ten cents each, reaching a phenomenal price before being sold to their final purchaser. This raid also put a stop to the activities of a gang of international dope traffickers. All the opium pills that were seized then were handed over to the Chinese Maritime Customs, and subsequently destroyed.

Another case of armed robbery of some interest once took place in the Sinza District. The station there received a telephone message one day that armed robbers were raiding a house in the Chengtu Road. Three foreigners in the charge-room were immediately detailed to deal with the matter.

The Indian patrol motor-cycle being at hand, they lost no time in reaching the spot, picking up, en route, the Chinese police constable who had reported the robbery. A heavy front door was found to be locked, and attempts were made to burst it open. Two Chinese constables rushed to the rear to prevent escape that way. After several attempts the door was burst open, and as the police rushed into the house, they saw a robber in the act of opening the back door, with a heavy calibre revolver in his hand. But before he could use it, the police opened fire, and killed him instantly. Then a second robber was seen at the top of the rickety stairs, just about to use his automatic; but again the police guns roared a fraction of a second first, and he toppled down the stairs shot through the head and stomach.

Later the terrified inmates, who had been huddled and locked into a small upstairs closet, were released. It was found that the two robbers had been in the house for almost an hour before the alarm was raised by a neighbour. They were two members of a gang of notorious Zaushing bandits who had been working in the Settlement for some time.

The most remarkable feature of both the robbery and the subsequent police raid was that they occurred in broad daylight at about ten o'clock in the morning.

One of the most sensational armed robberies that has ever taken place in Shanghai was the attack on the Post Office in September 1935. The robbers carried off $91,000, killed a coolie and a guard, wounded another man, and made off in a stolen car. And all this right in the centre of a populous business district.

In a manner suggestive of the latest gangster film, a band of armed Chinese walked into the loading yard of the Post Office in broad daylight, mowed down three employees with fire from their automatics, and seized bags containing $91,000 in banknotes and coins. They escaped in a stolen hire-car driven by one of their confederates.

It was the first time in its history that the central Post Office had ever been looted by armed robbers. The speed and precision with which the crime was carried out suggested that the robbers were thoroughly familiar with the procedure followed in transferring money to the bank.

Shortly before 9.30 a.m. the money was being taken from the Post Office treasury in the building into the loading yard to be placed in a safe contained in the armoured van used for collections and transfers to the Postal Savings Bank. The yard was full of people, including Chinese police with rifles. The bandits were thought to have been there for some time, and to have mixed with the crowd until their opportunity had come. The money was being carried by a coolie accompanied by two postal guards armed with pistols. Suddenly five men drew large automatic pistols and opened fire on the coolie and his escort. He slumped to the ground with an agonized cry, and released his grip on the money-bags. With two bullets in his back and two in the abdomen, he was soon dead. The two guards were also shot, but one of them managed to fire three shots at the robbers as they picked up the money, dashed across the yard and scrambled into their waiting hire-car outside. Before the chase could be taken up by the police, they had driven off at high speed.

The hire-car, whose number was noted by the bystanders, had been engaged by one of the bandits in the International Settlement early in the morning. The chauffeur had then been ordered to drive to an outlying district, where the rest of the gang were waiting. There they seized the driver, bound him with rope, and left him helpless in a deserted spot off the road. Then they drove the car back into Shanghai and kept it with a man at the wheel near where the robbery was committed.

After the crime they again drove out to where they had assaulted the driver, and abandoned the car in the same spot. For some time all trace of them was lost, but finally the gang were rounded up and sentenced to very heavy terms of imprisonment.

Before bringing to an end my account of some of the more thrilling and exciting armed robberies and kidnappings that came my way, I will give some typical examples of the sort of thing a resident in Shanghai sees almost every day when he opens his morning paper. He may very well find such headlines as these:

ARMED ROBBERS SHOT DEAD BY POLICE IN WAR ON GUNMEN WHO SLEW CONSTABLE
Battle with Underworld during Looting of Private House: Detectives Risk their Lives in Big Round-Up

Six Chinese armed robbers were shot dead yesterday by British police sergeants, one of them disposing of three single-handed. . . . The inspector in charge of the station received information that armed robbers had penetrated into a house in the district. . . . On arrival, the sergeant broke open the door and encountered one of the robbers on the stairs armed with a pistol, attempting to escape. He immediately fired and shot the robber dead.

Another robber appeared on the staircase, and the second sergeant shot him dead, the corpse rolling down the stairs to his feet.

There were two more robbers upstairs. One of them stuck his pistol through the half-open door. At great personal risk, the same sergeant managed to kill him, and finally accounted for the last robber. . . .

One of the men was identified as a Chinese who shot a policeman last week. . . . All the dead robbers were dressed as wealthy Chinese.

Or perhaps he will find an account of some armed kidnapping such as:

KIDNAPPED FORTUNE-TELLER HELD FOR RANSOM, RESCUED BY POLICE FROM FOREIGN HOME
Captors Held for Trial, Aged Victim Tells of Abduction, Imprisonment in Servants' Room

Startling discovery of a kidnappers' den. . . . Two foreign dwelling-houses raided. . . . Five inmates alleged to be members of a big gang of professional kidnappers. . . .

The victim, well known in Chinese circles. . . . Most of the rich Chinese ladies, superstitiously inclined, have had their fortunes told by this weird-looking, half-blind old man. . . .

Found at the back of the house with two guards armed with loaded revolvers. . . . The police fired several shots and disarmed the kidnappers. The victim was released. Arrests were made.

On leaving his house, he had been caught by a gang of men and driven in a motor-car to a house, where he was detained. . . . Asked to surrender a large sum of money, he refused, and the gangsters threatened to cut off his ears. He felt the blade of a knife sticking against his face.

He decided to commit suicide one night because he could not bear the physical pain inflicted on him. . . . He heard several shots fired, and thought the kidnappers would come to kill him. He hid underneath heavy blankets and said Buddhist prayers, when a detective came and told him he was safe.

Such are the kind of events that are reported daily in the newspapers in Shanghai, proving that I have in no way exaggerated the prevalence of this type of crime in the city.

But besides the problem of crime itself and how to deal with such an incessant variety of major crimes, committed with all the ingenuity of the Eastern mind, there is the problem of where to put all the criminals — at least, those whom the police succeed in catching. Even in China it takes a little time to sentence a man to death and execute him; and then, of course, there are all the people whom you simply can't bump off in this convenient way, and yet can't leave at liberty to steal and pilfer. They all have to be kept behind locked doors somewhere.

I think the International Settlement has the largest accommodating prison in the world. On an average throughout the year between five and six thousand Chinese are always incarcerated there. It is situated on the outskirts of the city facing a main road. Having been very recently built, everything is most up to date and spick and span. It covers a large area, and is almost a self-contained town in itself. The long-sentence prisoners are put to work in various large shops doing carpentry, printing, boot-making and things of that kind. All the boots of the Chinese branch of the Police Force are made here, as well as all the furniture used in the offices and quarters of the whole police. The stationery to be found on the desks of the Municipal Councillors, besides that of the other officials, is all prison made.

As may well be imagined from the kind of prisoners confined there, conditions within the gaol are extremely hard, and the regulations particularly strict. Prisoners serving very long sentences are confined to their cells in irons, and I should not like to imagine how many perish under this treatment before their sentences expire. The short-term prisoners can often be seen in groups of about six working in the grounds. They are all chained together, and the washing, scrubbing and general up-keep of the place are done by them.

This enormous number of criminals, including many of the desperate armed robbers and murderers that I have previously described, necessitates a particularly large staff of prison warders. The superintendent of the gaol is a Britisher, who comes directly under the control of the Acting Commissioner of Police. It is the latter who is called the Governor of the gaol, but it is only a formal title, for the actual work of governing the prison is done by the superintendent, and the whole responsibility for it falls on him.

He has a foreign staff of British and Russians under him, and after them come the Chinese and Indian warders. The latter are on duty guarding the cells and the innumerable gates leading from the cells to the main gates of the prison. They are also in charge of the working-parties, exercise-parties and the general routine of the gaol.

A curious if not comic situation arises from this arrangement of the nationalities, but one fully to be expected in Shanghai, with its conflicting interests and peoples. One set of prison officials has to keep a very strict watch over the other — that is to say, the foreigners have to see that the Chinese and Russian warders do not themselves commit the same crimes as some of the prisoners whom they are supposed to be guarding. In fact, their chief work is to see that the warders under them don't shirk their duty, and it is a whole-time job. A prison warder has many opportunities of obtaining "squeeze," and a large amount of smuggling, chiefly of correspondence from the prisoners' friends and relations outside, goes on. But there are times when the spectacle of prison warders being watched as if they were criminals seems rather to belong to the world of comic opera than to grim reality.

The gaol is said to be pretty well fool-proof, and as far as I know no one has ever succeeded in bringing off an escape. There are dozens of iron grilles, all double-locked, between the main entrance and the cells, and a very high wall surrounds the whole prison, with watch-towers in it at various points. Day and night they are filled with relays of guards supplied by the Russian branch of the Shanghai Defence Force.

The very large prison hospital is always pretty well full of patients. Tuberculosis is very prevalent among the prisoners, and I should imagine that the disease is the natural result of some of the prison conditions.

The death cells are completely isolated from the rest. It can be safely said that there are never less than a dozen Chinese incarcerated in them awaiting their fate. Like so many things in China, it takes a long time even to be duly sentenced to death; and delay and procrastination, in this case perhaps much appreciated, according to the temperament of the prisoner, are the general rule. After being sentenced to death at court, the prisoners have to wait for final confirmation from the Government at Nanking, and it always takes a long time. Some of them wait months, and then probably they lodge an appeal. As a way of prolonging one's life, it is an ideal arrangement, but the uncertainty and suspense must be agonizing.

The Foreign Gaol adjoins the Chinese Section. It accommodates every nationality apart from the Chinese — both the unrecognized foreigners and those having extra-territorial rights. The majority of these prisoners are Russians, mostly pickpockets, shoplifters and vagrants. Americans sentenced to long terms of imprisonment are sent to the McNeil's Island Penitentiary.

British subjects serve their sentences either in Shanghai or Hong-Kong.

The armed robbers, kidnappers and murderers whose exploits I have previously described wait in this grim iron-and-steel cage for the final outcome of their sentences. Throughout their trial a gang charged with such crimes are imprisoned here, and are transferred each day to court under heavy guard, which is usually supplied by the Reserve Unit.

When I was serving in the Unit, I often acted as a member of this guard. When it is needed, a message is sent to the Reserve Unit asking for its services. If the gang are notoriously desperate men, and there is a possibility that an attempt may be made to rescue them on their way from the gaol to court, a small police raiding van is used, and the usual guard is increased by the addition of a motor-cycle guard, consisting of three foreigners armed with a Thomson machine gun.

The armed police escort wait for the gaol van as it passes through the prison gates with its load of gangsters. On arrival at court, more armed police are on guard inside and outside the building. This precaution is made necessary by the fact that the relatives, and probably even some members of the gang to which the prisoners belong, attend these trials. There is always a large crowd of Chinese in the body of the court, and it is impossible to exclude them.

The trial begins, and follows the usual routine. The prosecution is conducted by the Chinese Police Advocate. The judge does quite a lot of cross-examination himself. But as there is no jury under Chinese law, perhaps it is as well that he should try to find out the truth himself, for the final decision rests with him alone.

One of the most peculiar and amusing features of a trial in a Chinese court is the presence of interpreters. Some of them are Chinese. Their work is not, as might be supposed, between the foreigners and their own countrymen, but between the various dialects in China itself. They are employed to prevent any misunderstanding between the judge, prisoners and witnesses, but the dialects are so complicated that I doubt whether they always succeed. And there are so many of them, it is like a meeting of the League of Nations with none of the representatives completely understanding the language of the others, and the interpreters being in no better position.

In most cases the judge himself understands, but it is beneath his dignity to speak anything but the Mandarin dialect. It is difficult to describe exactly what this is, but if I say that it is the language of politeness and officialdom, some conception of its nature will be gained.

The trial goes on. The gang plead their innocence, and say that the confession of guilt which they made in prison was forcibly extracted from them by the cruel and wicked police using brutal third-degree measures. They are sentenced to death. They receive this quite calmly, and immediately apply for leave to make an appeal against it. They are returned to the death cells, and there await the result of their application. If permission is granted, the armed police conduct them back to court in the same way.

When their appeal is tried, they sometimes have their sentences commuted to life imprisonment. They are allowed to appeal against this if they are dissatisfied and think that they have a chance of a further reduction. But if they are actually so foolhardy as to appeal for a second time, they probably receive the death sentence again. And this time it is final, and no further appeal is allowed.

In some cases a term of imprisonment is given besides sentence of death. This they will serve, and then, when it is completed, and not before, they will be executed.

Having received their final sentence in court, they seem to resign themselves to their fate, but not before they have seized some opportunity of telling the detectives what they think of them. Often unable to understand what they were saying, I realized by the tones of their voices that their language was hardly polite—"something awful" would be a better description of it.

Even when you don't understand the sense of the words, Chinese seems a delightful language in which to swear.

They are then left, perhaps for months, in the death cells in solitary confinement with no exercise, before the final confirmation comes from Nanking. When this at last arrives, preparations are made for their final attendance at court. This is simply a formality.

I have personally attended dozens of these executions as a member of the armed escort. I will select a typical example, when we escorted a gang of six men to their death.

We arrived at the gaol at about half-past one. Three of us formed this motor-cycle escort, and we accompanied the gaol van to court. The doomed men were then brought before the judge, who went through a whole lot of routine that ended in his reading the Nanking Government's sanction of their execution. Then he laid aside his pompous manner and, according to a clause in Chinese law, allowed them to make their last request.

As so often happens at such moments, the Chinese love of food influenced them even at this solemn occasion. They requested food and wine. Meanwhile the gaol van had been taken inside the court grounds, and the sentenced men were bundled into it. This gave them an opportunity of another verbal attack on the detectives. I noticed that they did this with complete *sangfroid*, and without the slightest excitement or hysteria. As invective, this made it all the more telling.

The food and drink were given to them in the van. It consisted of a meal of Chinese food of the better variety, accompanied by a bottle of wine, which I imagine was of less good quality. Anyhow, the only man who touched it was sick on the way to the execution ground, but they all thoroughly enjoyed their food. When they had finished their meal, we started on our way. As we passed through the court grounds, their friends and relatives cried out and waved their hands in farewell.

We now proceeded to a Chinese gaol named the Taichaoping Prison. This is situated in Nantao, or Chinese Territory. We had several miles to go and our way passed through the French Concession. Special permission had been granted us by the French and Chinese authorities in these areas to allow us to pass through carrying arms, which we were usually never allowed to do. At the border of the French Concession we were met by a French policeman, who jumped on to the gaol van and escorted us through his territory to the Chinese border. Here he left us, and we proceeded with all haste to the prison.

We had left Shanghai behind, and were now in the countryside. The condemned men had probably been farmers themselves before turning to crime for a living, and it may well have been a painful reminder to them of a happier past. Behind us a couple of hired taxis were in view. Some policemen were bringing several Shanghai business friends along with them to witness the executions. Perhaps they were some of the people who write to the newspapers complaining of the brutality of the police in their dealings with the poor Chinese, who they consider are naturally a peace-loving, inoffensive race. If so, their feelings had become bitter against the callous Chinese then, and they were only too eager to see them executed. It seems to me a perverted sort of taste. I was there because I was doing my duty, but I cannot quite understand how people, and especially women, who form the majority of these seekers after morbid excitement, can find pleasure in witnessing the following scene.

When we arrived at the gates of Taichaoping Prison, they were opened by the Chinese warders. Grim, cunning, treacherous-looking fellows, with nothing humane about them, they seemed to me like vultures waiting for their prey, and the last people with whom I should like to be left alone in the interior of China.

On passing through the gates we were surprised to find an atmosphere entirely different from the grim work that was shortly to be carried out there. The drive was well kept, and bordered with flower-beds either side, the trees were in full bloom and the birds singing, and it seemed more like the drive of a stately park in England than the road leading straight to a prison execution ground.

I could not help thinking of the feelings of the condemned men. I imagined them struck by this sudden revelation of Nature in all her glories, and smitten by pangs of regret from the knowledge that if they had lived a better life, they would still have been able to live to enjoy such beauties. Even the most callous murderer, the most brutal armed robber and kidnapper, may be sensitive to the charms of Nature, especially in China, where he has probably led a quiet, sober life tilling the fields and watching the sunsets, and the changing seasons before coming to Shanghai and having his simple mind turned to the glittering rewards of crime. I can only say that, coarse and brutish as some of these murderers are, the possibility of their having such thoughts as they enter that prison of death does not seem at all strange.

Winding along that drive we at last halted, and, looking round, I noticed that we had drawn up alongside a well-kept plot of ground with a beautiful stretch of green turf that was nevertheless marred in some places by splotches of red, a sudden reminder of where we were. There were several Chinese warders standing round, armed to the teeth with long-barrelled German Mauser pistols. They certainly looked as if they meant business. The grass plot was surrounded by a green hedge, with a high and very solid brick wall at one end. As the plot was not very large, it was decided to bring only three of the condemned men out there at a time, for safety's sake.

Three of them were therefore brought from the van, all handcuffed together. They were greeted by a Chinese priest, not of any of the Chinese religions or beliefs, but a Roman Catholic. He tried to convert them to his faith, and spoke to them for about five minutes. Only one of them decided to adopt a fresh religion, remarking as he did so that his last one had not been much use to him. The priest blessed him, and placed a Roman Catholic medallion round his neck.

They were then taken to a table at which a Chinese judge presided. He went through the routine of reading out their sentence again, and asking them if they wished their valuables, if any, property and clothing to be handed over to any relatives. This settled, their handcuffs were taken off and returned to us.

The Chinese police, or warders as they like to term themselves, then took charge. The condemned men, by the way, were now smoking cigarettes that some of us had given them, and as far as I could make out they were thoroughly enjoying them. They were then each handcuffed with their hands behind their back. Their hats were left on their heads, as the Chinese have a superstition that it is better to die fully dressed, so as to be ready for the life after death.

They were then walked to the centre of this plot of ground. By this time they were quite hilarious, passing jokes with the spectators and threatening the detectives who had arrested them with all kinds of unpleasant punishments. They said that they would return to earth in so many years, haunt them and put curses on them, the Chinese being great believers in reincarnation.

The Chinese police made them kneel down and stood behind them with pistols drawn pointing towards their heads. As if everyone felt the approach of death, an intense silence fell on the scene, broken only by one sound, that may seem almost unbelievable to those who have not seen a Chinese execution.

The Chinese warders and police live inside the prison grounds with their families. At that awe-inspiring moment young children from the age of three to twelve were running about and playing in the yards behind the doomed men. Some of them were even watching with the intense curiosity of children.

A Chinese official standing well to the rear of the execution ground blew a whistle, and immediately three shots rang out.

I saw two of the criminals fall to the ground, but imagine my horror and surprise when one of them remained kneeling and started to swear at his executioner for missing him. What had happened was this. At the critical moment when the whistle

Top: At the Execution Ground — A Condemned Man being
Questioned by the Judge before his Execution
Centre left: A Chinese Walking to his Execution with the Usual
Cheerful Fatalism
Centre right: Execution by Slow Strangulation of a Murderer
Bottom: After an Execution — Settlement Police are Awaiting
Confirmation of Death

blew, the condemned man had unconsciously closed his eyes and bent his head, with the result that the bullet had passed harmlessly over the top.

But the Chinese policeman rectified the mistake without any apparent flurry or excitement. Grasping him by the hair, he turned him to the front again and shot him through the head.

If any of them make the slightest movement after this, another shot is fired into them whilst lying on the ground. I myself saw one man, only a little fellow (they say that the smaller they are, the tougher they are to kill), receive five shots before he was pronounced dead: one in the back of his head, two in his ears and two in his chest. Whilst this is being done, they might be animals, considering the way the police treat them, kicking them over to find a place for the next shot.

The dead men were then propped up against a boulder, and official photographs were taken to ensure that the right men had been shot.

In this case three others had to be shot. With any civilized people, the natural human instinct would have been to remove the bodies of the first three from sight, but not so with the Chinese. The last three were brought out and the same procedure gone through. They must have heard the first three shots, and now they had to kneel down with that gory sight in front of them. It was enough to cow the bravest of men. But it had no effect on them, and they went to their death as stoically and as unconcernedly as the others.

Just after they were shot, I got another shock. Some Chinese women and children rushed to the scene and dipped copper coins in the blood of the victims, while one girl brought a dozen Chinese cakes, which she soaked in the blood. All this was supposed to keep evil spirits away from their households.

The coffins were half hidden behind the hedge, but the bodies were not removed right away, but left to lie there over-night, with a small piece of wood laid across each with the deceased's name written on it.

On the following day they were removed, placed in the coffins and buried, unless claimed by the relatives.

When these men were pronounced dead, we were able to leave, glad to get away from such a scene until such time as duty called us again to act as escort to the death van.

Execution by shooting is reserved for such crimes as armed robbery and kidnapping; but for murder itself the form of execution is death by slow strangulation. I have witnessed two such executions, and I hope I shall see no more.

The same procedure takes place at the gaol, court and Taichaoping Prison as before. The only difference is the final execution.

A post about six feet in height and four inches square is driven into the ground. Two large holes are drilled in it close together, so that when a person kneels down the holes are nearly flush with his neck.

I have seen both a male and a female Chinese executed in this way, the procedure being the same in both cases. The man was placed in a kneeling position in front of the post, his arms being handcuffed at the back of it. A leather band was then fitted over his head, with an extension that fitted tightly under his chin. He was then blindfolded, and a specially made rope was passed round his neck and the two ends were slipped through the holes in the post. They were then made fast to a special stick, and when this was turned it tightened the rope round the man's neck like a tourniquet being tightened round a limb. About two turns were given first, and then it was left for a short time. The murderer began to find some difficulty in breathing. The rope was slackened about half a turn, and then, after a pause, given one full turn, which meant that it was now half a turn more than at first. This slackening and tightening went on for fifteen minutes. Then all movement ceased in the body, and it was sealed to the post until the following morning, when it was removed for burial.

The Chinese prefer this form of execution, because they like the body to be whole at the time of death, fearing that evil spirits can enter it through bullet-wounds.

VII

TOWARDS THE END of 1931 everyone in Shanghai realized that the dangerous situation which had long existed between the Japanese and the Chinese was rapidly approaching a crisis. We had all been aware that the intense hatred between them might at any moment cause trouble, and now some kind of a clash seemed inevitable.

Then the Japanese sent an ultimatum to the Chinese Mayor of Shanghai stating that unless certain articles were signed by a certain time an attack would be made on Chapei. On this the Chinese population of Shanghai panicked, and thousands of them left Chapei, which was practically evacuated, and sought refuge in the International Settlement.

At this particular time—January 1932—I was stationed at the Reserve Unit, and was on night charge-room duty. I was not thinking of the Japanese—or the Chinese, for that matter—as I fully expected to hear that a settlement had been reached at any moment. At about midnight I suddenly heard a distant sound that seemed to me like machine-gun fire. When this had gone on quite regularly for some minutes, I decided to go outside and investigate. I thought my suspicions must be wrong when a Chinese policeman remarked that someone was having quite a celebration, judging by the sound of the firework display. For the moment I believed him, but when this regular rat-a-tat was reinforced by the boom of heavy gun-fire, I realized that I had been right after all.

Telling the Chinese policeman to keep a sharp look-out and immediately report anything unusual to me, I returned to the charge-room, and shortly afterwards received a telephone message from the central control room (we had not yet got the teleprinter) to the effect that the Japanese had attacked Chapei. It appeared that they were entering Chinese Territory in armoured cars, and were meeting their first opposition from the Chinese police, and that a sort of guerilla warfare was going on in the streets and houses.

Everyone, including the Japanese, fully expected the whole affair to be over in a few days. It was generally thought in Shanghai that the Japs would simply walk into Chapei, and demand their terms, which would be meekly accepted by the cowed Chinese. We all imagined that conditions would be normal again in a comparatively short time. The very reverse happened, however.

The Japanese found that the Chinese soldiers—the famous 19th Route Army under the equally famous Colonel Tsai—had dug themselves in round Chapei, and were going to take some moving, although the result was a foregone conclusion, considering the predominance in heavy armaments of the Japanese. They had all the equipment and training to be expected of a first-class military nation, while the Chinese were so badly equipped that many of the soldiers were wearing cloth caps and no shoes, and their only armaments were rifles with a bandolier of ammunition. What few guns they had were old and obsolete, and any determined resistance on their part even for a few days seemed quite beyond the bounds of possibility.

But hold out they did for weeks, to the amazement and admiration of many foreigners in Shanghai. They were defeated in the end, but no one had expected such a long-drawn-out resistance in the face of such overwhelming odds.

Meanwhile the International Settlement was in a most dangerous and precarious position. Chapei formed one of its boundaries, the French Concession and the river forming the other two. All the gates on the French and Chinese borders were closed, and the Shanghai Defence Force were mobilized and posted in all the blockhouses facing Chinese territory. Chapei was slowly being evacuated, with considerable loss of life.

The various nationalities had sent for detachments of their military and naval forces to protect their interests. Different areas were allotted to the British, American and Italian soldiers and sailors, who remained on duty day and night. The British sent for reinforcements from Hong Kong, and the Americans from the Philippine Islands. The harbour was crowded with the warships of the various Powers, all standing by in case of emergency, and the situation looked very ugly. The very existence of the International Settlement, with its Council, on which so many nations were represented, seemed to be at stake.

I had the feeling that at any moment we might be quitting Shanghai, at least for a time. Such feelings became all the stronger when, like every other Britisher, I received one day a special notice from the British Consulate. It consisted of a blue card stating that in the event of a definite evacuation order I was to proceed at once to the Metropole Hotel near the Bund, with as little clothing and as much food as possible.

Things were indeed looking serious, our ships were all prepared to take us off, the battle was being fiercely fought out in Chapei and the surrounding districts, Japanese planes were dropping incendiary bombs on the important buildings, and the whole area was slowly being razed to the ground. Even the Commercial Press, where irreplaceable manuscripts and books centuries old were kept, was burned down and completely destroyed. It was said that here alone damage was done to the extent of over a million dollars. The Chinese were making a most heroic stand, however, in spite of their poor resources.

I was stationed in a part of the Settlement quite near the river and also close to the Hongkew District, in which the Japanese colony lived. It was now fast becoming a centre of Japanese activity. Large reinforcements of marines and infantry were being rushed from Japan to Shanghai, and it was here that they were first stationed when they arrived. A big school was speedily renovated and turned into a hospital. Although the newspapers always stated that there were very few Japanese casualties, I often saw lorries loaded with wounded on their way to this hospital, which happened to be quite close to the Reserve unit. About a quarter of a mile away the Japanese had an aeroplane depot. Here they would take off for their flight to Chapei, only about half a mile away, do their ten minutes' bombing and return safely with little fear of being hit by the Chinese, whose only protection against these raids was the rifle.

The British Admiral of the China Fleet told the Japanese authorities that if their 'planes flew over the Settlement, he would be forced to give orders for them to be fired upon. This warning had the desired effect, and we were not bothered by Japanese 'planes flying overhead. But we nevertheless felt as if we were practically at war ourselves.

Japanese gunboats and cruisers were very busy at a place called the Woosung Forts, quite near Shanghai. It was held by the Chinese, who had fortified it with some very ancient canon. It was surprising what a long time it survived a daily shelling by these Japanese warships. The British and American navies stood by watching developments. It was a strange mix-up. A Japanese cruiser lay in the docks quite close to a British warship. She was the object of much Chinese fire, and shells were frequently dropping near her, until one day a shell dropped on the quay-side near a British ship. It exploded (an unusual happening, for most of them were dud) and killed two British sailors working on the quay at the time.

Whilst all this was going on, I was confined to the Reserve Unit, which we had converted into a miniature fort. The Chinese police had filled dozens and dozens of sacks with sand and placed them in suitable positions under our supervision. We arranged them so that at a moment's notice we could have closed the large wooden gates and with the aid of these sandbags have withstood an organized siege. We were normally all armed, and had unlimited stores of ammunition. This, together with our machine-guns, we kept in one special room.

Tucked away there in a corner of Shanghai, we were right in the midst of the Japanese activities, and only a few hundred yards from the battlefields of Chapei themselves, nothing but the Japanese colony separating them from our troops. We consisted of a body of about forty men, two women and one child, expecting any day to be attacked or to find ourselves in the very centre of a battle between the opposing forces. We were in direct communication with our Police Headquarters, and got most of the news regarding the situation, but we had the feeling that at any moment we might be cut off, especially if anything serious or startling happened at our end.

A foreign policeman was posted day and night on the flat roof of the Unit. He had a wonderful view of Chapei from there, and could get some idea of what was happening. Our main anxiety was that either the Japanese or the Chinese might take it into their heads to commandeer the Reserve Unit as the best post of vantage in the neighbourhood. As I have said, it was a well-fortified stronghold and would have made an excellent defensive position for either party.

The foreigner on the roof was given a pair of binoculars, and he periodically scoured the surrounding country to see if anything unusual was happening. A telephone had been installed on the roof and connected with the charge-room. So he could report to us there any suspicious movements of troops or aeroplanes in the vicinity, and then everyone would stand by until more satisfactory news arrived.

If an actual attack were reported, we had received our orders. First of all, the women and the one child were, if possible, to be conveyed to the safety of our warships. We were to collect on the roof, taking there all our fighting equipment, including several lengths of rope. The Reserve Unit was to be defended until orders were given to retire. As a last resource it was considered that this could be done by our making fast these ropes, clambering down to the ground, and making our way as best we could to our ships in the harbour.

The police station to which I went when this war was over was the scene of great activity and danger. It was situated quite near Chapei—so close to it, in fact, that some parts of the pavements belonged to us and some to the Chinese, so the conditions and difficulties may well be imagined. One of the duties of the personnel of this station was to rescue all the British subjects residing in Chapei. It was quite a common sight to see a police officer loaded with the personal effects of someone whom he had rescued, struggling along under fire in the danger zone. Later on all the men at this station were highly commended by the Commissioner for loyalty to duty under very trying conditions.

They remained there even when their rescue work was over, although the Chinese police had been transferred elsewhere; but it was considered that it would give a good impression for English police to remain at a station so close to the scene of hostilities. But when a couple of stray shells had exploded in the grounds of the station and done quite a lot of damage, fortunately without causing any casualties, the authorities realized that it would be madness for them to remain, and they too were temporarily posted for duty in an adjoining district.

Most of us at the Reserve Unit were confined to the building. But my friend Franks, the bandmaster, was in charge of the blockhouses at that time, and he went out on daily tours of inspection to see that they were all in proper order. I accompanied him one day, and shall never forget the experience. The war had now been in progress for about three weeks. I had not left the Reserve Unit since the beginning, and I was amazed at the changes that I found everywhere.

In that short space of time the International Settlement had been converted into a typical war zone. Leaving the Reserve Unit in a police motor-car, we went down a road that runs near, and parallel with, the river. I noticed that Japanese marines in full fighting kit were posted on both sides of the street at intervals of about ten yards. They were also posted outside the entrances to some of the docks, and they rigorously searched anyone entering or leaving. As we neared the Japanese colony, I saw heaps of sandbags piled at all the street corners. We decided that we had better walk here, which gave me the opportunity of having a good look round.

Several Japanese marines armed with rifles and ready for action were stationed behind each of these piles of sandbags. Machine-guns were posted at intervals along the roads, and although the Settlement police were still on duty, patrolling the streets as usual, the Japanese were in complete control of that district, and there was no disputing the fact.

I received rather a shock whilst cautiously making my way with my friend through this part of the Settlement. Japanese marines were entering all the Chinese shops and searching them and their inmates for arms and ammunition. They were doing so without the slightest interference from anyone. They smashed the doors and windows, and even set fire to some of the shops, without encountering any opposition. Part of this work was being done by Japanese civilian volunteers called "Ronins." They committed many atrocities and brutalities, taking the opportunity to vent their national hatred of the Chinese on the unfortunate inhabitants. I saw them running absolutely amok, stopping all the Chinese in the streets and ill-treating them, in many cases leaving them more dead than alive.

From time to time I heard shots being fired. This seemed rather strange to me, and I felt rather inquisitive, for, after all, we were in the International Settlement, and I knew that the war zone had not officially been extended to include our territory.

I soon discovered what was happening. Coming out on to the main road from an alley-way, I saw a Japanese marine fire his rifle at the roof of a Chinese shop. There was no apparent result, and I thought he was only bluffing, trying to frighten the people and show them what they would get if they made any trouble. But in the short time that I was there I saw several Chinese deliberately shot by the Japanese in this manner. I will not pretend to judge these shootings, but I should say that most of them were in cold blood. If a Chinese were seen inside a building and the Japs thought he looked suspicious, they shot at him, and obviously shot to kill. On the other hand, they could hardly be blamed for taking no chances, as it was a well-known fact that Chinese snipers were seen taking pot shots at Japanese marines from the roofs.

Having seen enough of the situation in the Japanese colony, we returned to our motor, and proceeded on our tour of inspection of the blockhouses. Arriving at the outskirts of the district, we were held up by a big crowd that had congregated outside a large chemist's shop.

A lorry belonging to the Japanese landing-party was there, with several marines in attendance. Just as we came up, the whole Chinese staff of this drug store were driven out by the Japanese at the point of the bayonet and bundled into the lorry. It then drove off, and we learned that they were being taken to the Naval Headquarters for interrogation as suspected snipers. They have never been seen or heard of again.

A short time ago further inquiries were made about them, as one man was quite an influential Chinese, but without result. From the moment when they were bundled into that lorry they have utterly disappeared. They must obviously have been shot by the Japanese on the charge of firing on them from the top of the building.

Quite close to the police station which I mentioned as being shelled was a large piece of ground known as the Japanese garden. Before the trouble began it was used as a playground and garden for the Japanese community, but during the war a rather unpleasant smell of burning bodies could often be noticed coming from it. I have an idea that this may have been connected with the disappearance of the staff of that chemist's shop.

My friend now suggested that as we had to pass the court building (which although in Chapei was rather out of the war zone), it was a good opportunity to view the ruins of the city, and probably get a few thrills.

We clambered up a long stone staircase on to the flat roof, and it was certainly worth the trouble. It was a marvellous sight.

Top: CRUDE TRENCHES DUG BY THE CHINESE DURING THE
SINO-JAPANESE WAR
Centre and Bottom: THE DEAD BODY OF A YOUNG CHINESE SOLIDER
LEFT ON THE BATTLEFIELD

Chapei was simply one mass of ruins. Buildings were being blown sky high in front of our eyes. First we could hear the dull roar of the gun-fire, and then see house after house collapsing and falling in ruins.

A Japanese aeroplane swooped up from the aerodrome that I have mentioned before. It flew at a great height right across Chapei, then, suddenly diving very low, it dropped several bombs, and safely made off back to its base. A few rifle-shots could be heard — the rather half-hearted attempt of the Chinese soldiers to bring the raider down.

Standing there on that court building, we watched the devastation of Chapei. For the moment I felt the thrill of the neutral who can enjoy the spectacle of wholesale destruction with the comfortable thought that he is immune from attack from both sides. But this did not last long. Soon rifle bullets began to whistle unpleasantly near, and we decided to skip before it became too warm. As it was, we had not only got a glimpse of the war, we had been in it and that seemed thrill enough for the moment.

But visiting the blockhouses gave us more excitement. They were manned by the Shanghai Volunteer Corps, who were also posted along the boundaries of the Settlement. Typical scenes in France during the Great War could be seen. Battlements of sandbags were everywhere. All the soldiers were wearing the familiar steel helmet and gas mask. Hastily improvised dug-outs could be seen bearing names suggestive of the trenches on the Western Front. "Windy Corner" was a prominent one, and it was certainly most appropriate, with the countless stray shots knocking about.

Heavy firing was going on not fifty yards away, and our machine-guns were trained on Chapei. If any attempt had been made to enter the International Settlement by force, the attackers would have met with a warm reception. It seemed wonderful the way the fighting was confined to that particular area of Chapei.

One night a party of Chinese had attempted to cross one of the bridges that span the creeks separating Chapei from the International Settlement. Some American infantry posted there had threatened to fire on them, and they took the hint and retired. I think there was a little promiscuous shooting by the various defence forces in the Settlement; but, considering the state of tension in which we all were, there was remarkably little. At least it served to show that any invaders would get it in the neck.

My friend got quite a shock when he visited one of these blockhouses. Unbeknown to us it had been manned by Japanese. When Franks entered and started to ascend the ladder leading to the top, he was suddenly confronted by a couple of bayonets held by two sturdy little Japanese marines. I remember him shouting "Juin-sa," which means policeman, and then he dived down the ladder and we left, satisfied that someone was manning the blockhouse, anyhow.

I was struck on many occasions by the goodness of the Salvation Army at this time. In Shanghai during the Sino-Japanese War they worked tirelessly. All through the night they visited the different troops in the Settlement, supplying them with hot tea, coffee and cakes. The police and the defence forces all appreciated their attentions, and if it often seems funny the way that particular organization gets a good and bad name in all parts of the world, it certainly earned a good one then.

I took every opportunity that came my way of sneaking out of confinement in the Reserve Unit and getting some idea of what was happening. One day I had just finished a spell of duty at one of the stations which were now all manned by us. I was about twenty yards away from the station when I saw a Chinese pedestrian turn and call a Japanese marine "Ts loo," meaning pig. He then walked on, but not very far, because the Jap, shouting something in his own language, crept up behind him and ran him through with his bayonet, killing him instantly. Callous as this may seem, it is nothing to what would have happened if the positions had been reversed.

It must also have annoyed the Japanese the way some of the Chinese obtained protection in the International Settlement, and in the circumstances they can hardly be blamed if they killed on the slightest provocation.

One of the many tragi-comedies of the time occurred when a party of us were detailed for night duty on special patrol. We were to guard the Post Office, which was in the district of the Japanese colony. I have often wondered what our little party could have done in face of any real attack. We had nothing but our usual pistols, while the Japanese had machine-guns trained on the Post Office only a short distance away. They had extinguished all the street lights, and the place was pitch dark when we arrived.

One of our fellow-officers took a little rest, and leaned against an electric-light standard, watching with intense interest the occasional shots fired by the Japanese at some Chinese out after curfew. Suddenly he was seen to start running furiously, until he turned the corner of the Post Office building. When at last he reached us by running right round, he said that the Japanese had apparently mistaken him for a Chinese whilst leaning against the standard, and had fired a short burst from a machine-gun in his direction. He had heard the whistle of the bullets and their plonk as they struck the lamp standard, and that was enough for him; he had scampered for dear life. We could not persuade him to return to that beat again, and in fact no one else volunteered for it either.

We used to take our men from the Reserve Unit to the stations along all the main roads at night. On the way we would be stopped dozens of times by the Japanese sentries posted at close intervals along the roads. They would stand in front of the car while another pushed his bayonet inside. The best policy was to stick your head out, show your uniform cap and shout, "Juin-sa"—the Japanese for policeman.

The Chinese in the streets near the Japanese colony were scared stiff, and would only approach it under dire necessity. I soon began to realize that the Japs knew how to master the Chinese, and to make them feel that they are the under-dogs. While

a Chinese will take practically no notice of an ordinary policeman, and sometimes even swear and curse at him, it is a different
story when a Japanese naval patrol comes along the street.

All round Shanghai hundreds of Chinese were rushing into
the city to escape the onslaught of the Japanese. Colonel Tsai and
his gallant 19th Route Army were receiving no help or reinforcements, and they were beginning to weaken. The dead bodies of
Chinese soldiers killed in action were piled high at all the boundaries, and it now seemed a matter of days before the war would
be over.

From the Reserve Unit we could see Japanese troops every
day on their way to the firing-lines. And then the lorries returned
to the hospital with their wounded. But the Chinese were obviously suffering the heavier losses.

Remarkable feats of heroism were performed by the Japs,
and one in particular comes into my mind. They were advancing
when they encountered a barbed-wire entanglement that completely blocked their way. It had to be cleared. So two Japanese
loaded themselves with high explosives, threw themselves into
the midst of this entanglement, and blew it and themselves to
smithereens. There may have been no other way of destroying it,
but at the time it seemed a curious waste of the lives of two good
soldiers. But the ways and minds of the Oriental are impossible
to follow, and perhaps these men felt a great honour was being
bestowed on them by being allowed to immolate themselves in
this way. A very nice monument has now been erected to them
in Shanghai, and it is probably all the recompense they needed.

One day at the Reserve Unit some of us were detailed to
escort a large batch of Chinese refugees as they were brought
in. They had been arrested by the Japanese authorities and been
released only after a rigorous questioning. I have seldom seen a
more pitiful and tragic sight than they represented. We housed
them in a large gymnasium at the Reserve Unit, and several Chinese nurses and doctors attended to them. They needed all the
attention that they could get, for many of them had been ill-treated

by the Japanese and had numerous bayonet wounds. By the look of them, they considered themselves martyrs owing to the punishment that they had received. They were given excellent treatment, and, when cured, were allowed to leave and join their relatives. Even their stolid faces expressed astonishment and relief; they had obviously resigned themselves to a crueller fate.

Towards the end of this Sino-Japanese War two of us in turn were allowed four hours' leave in the evening. It was sorely needed. At one time I had not been out of the Unit for over a month, and there were others who had been confined to that block of buildings much longer than that. It was beginning to tell on our nerves, and we wondered how much longer we could last without someone going crazy. So it was with a light heart that a friend and I left the Unit one evening at about five o'clock. Although off duty, we had been told to wear our uniforms and to return before curfew.

We managed to hire a couple of rickshaws—a lucky break for us, as they were rarely seen in those days, especially in that part frequented by so many Japanese marines. We visited the sergeants' mess of the Royal Army Ordnance Corps, where we had several good friends. Strong guards were posted outside, but we soon forgot about the war when once through the gates. We passed a glorious four hours, talking about our various experiences, but they had had a dull time compared with ours. Then we drank beer and played billiards until we discovered, to our surprise, that it was well past curfew hour. Leaving in a hurry, we found that we had a good two or three miles to walk. Luckily for us, we stopped a motor-cycle and sidecar going in our direction, and found that it belonged to a man returning to the Unit after performing special duty. He took us home, but we were stopped many times by the Japanese marines on the way.

After that we decided to find some other means of transit for our next leave, and I bribed an old Chinese police sergeant with a few cigarettes to lend us some bicycles. I have seldom enjoyed a leave so much as those few short hours, but suddenly the pleasure came to an end.

My friend and I, who were in the same Riot Squad together, were paying our usual visit to the sergeants' mess. We had just settled down to our beer and a good game of billiards when we heard a sudden shout of "Guard turn out."

We all rushed to the windows, and there saw hundreds and hundreds of Chinese rushing towards the centre of the city, shouting in what seemed a most happy mood. But the whole affair was obviously considered serious, as the military were all standing by, so we made a hurried exit and returned to the Reserve Unit.

On our way we were alarmed by a tremendous noise, the loudest that we had heard in that by no means quiet war. It seemed as if all the machine-guns and artillery massed in and round Shanghai were being let off at once. Starting so suddenly, it certainly appeared as if a successful attack was being launched on Shanghai by the Chinese. If we had any doubt in our minds then as to who were the aggressors, the behaviour of the Chinese community dispelled it (quite mistakenly in reality). They all seemed to go stark, staring mad. We were pushed off our cycles and forced to make as much headway as we could on foot until we got clear of the mobs. We were glad to arrive back at the Reserve Unit, in time for whatever trouble was brewing.

But that was only the beginning of a night of real excitement. We were just explaining the situation to some fellow police when the alarm bells rang throughout the Unit.

As we turned out as quickly as we could, we learned that dense crowds of Chinese were massing in the centre of the city. They were said to be fighting, and absolutely crazy with joy. I wondered why, for I knew very well that the Japanese were the victors in the struggle.

Apparently the rumour had gone round that the Chinese had captured a number of Japanese generals and other officers, and this was considered sufficient occasion for wild rejoicing, although the Japanese had won the war. I think that all the fire-works in the place had previously been bought up by the Chinese in the hope of celebrating their own victory. Deprived of this, they were not going to lose a chance of a firework dis-play, and when a few of the enemy's generals were captured, they seized upon it as an excuse for lighting every firework in their possession.

I have never heard such a noise — a continuous volley as if every rifle in the place were being fired. It was absolutely deafen-ing. No wonder that we had imagined an invasion!

Arriving in the centre of the town, we found that thousands and thousands of Chinese were crammed on the main thorough-fare in the International Settlement. Every available policeman had been mobilized to cope with this struggling mass of stark-mad, joy-sodden humanity, and that it was exclusively Chinese humanity only made it worse. The police were working hard to keep the mob on the move, and their discipline and coolness in the face of that frenzied crowd were a joy to see. Batons were in full swing, and some progress was being made.

We were given the order to form up. The only thing that wor-ried me was whether the Chinese police would stand this strain on their sense of duty. It was a hard test of their loyalty to the Force, for they were asked to charge their own countrymen at a moment when national passion had been roused to fever point by the war. But when the order came to advance, they stood the test all right, and although some of them may have attacked somewhat half-heartedly, the majority gave us all the support we needed.

It was quite impossible to keep together as an organized body. It soon became a matter of every man for himself. I know I struck out right and left with my baton. I was pushed and pummelled all over the place, and received some nasty blows, that I returned with interest. I was lucky to escape so lightly, for several of the police were injured, but fortunately not seriously. On the other hand, we accounted for a number of Chinese. Fine as it may be to celebrate victory, such jubilations have to be kept within bounds, or anything might happen. Finally we managed to disperse the largest gathering that had ever massed in Shanghai.

Two days later, the hostilities being over, two or three of us decided to visit the battlefields. We set off in uniform, an advisable precaution, for without it we should never have been allowed through the Japanese pickets. The battlefields were a remarkable and awe-inspiring sight. We came across trenches crammed with the dead bodies of Chinese soldiers, boys of sixteen and upwards, all very poorly clothed and equipped. Mules and horses were lying dead and rotting in the fields. Mustard gas and petrol had caused the agonizing death of many Chinese. And whole families lay huddled together just as they had been mown down by the Japanese machine-gun fire. It was strange to see the shattered coffins of Chinese who had been dead for years, which had been left above ground according to the prevailing burial custom. They were blown to pieces. This desecration of the dead brought home to us the horrors of war more than anything else, for we were in a land where ancestor-worship is very strong. But on every side we felt the sorrow and the despair of war. The stench was unbearable, and after taking some photographs in the hope that they might educate younger generations in their struggle for peace, we returned home, never to forget these horrible scenes.

It took Shanghai a long time to settle down to normal conditions after this war, if indeed it ever has. For the friction between the Chinese and the Japanese remains as bad, if not worse than before. I don't think they will ever be friends now. My experience in the Police Force, working alongside them both and dealing with their respective countrymen, confirms me in this opinion. Although the average Japanese policeman treats the Chinese with his innate courtesy and politeness, and they laugh and joke with one another in public, what they say behind each other's backs is a very different matter. I have been with the Chinese when a Jap has passed by, and their remarks are both untranslatable and unprintable. They know that the Japs are now top-dogs, and they hate them all the more for that.

The Sino-Japanese War has certainly increased the power and prestige of the Japanese in Shanghai to an extraordinary extent. They now do many things that other nationals dare not do, and they usually get away with it. I'm afraid that our behaviour during the war in some way lowered our prestige in the eyes of the Japs. They seem to think that they did all the dirty work of teaching the Chinks a necessary lesson, and that the English did nothing but look on when they were not getting in the way. We on our side have become rather bitter against them, especially in the Police Force, as the result of recent events, or perhaps it would be more accurate to say that we are annoyed with the authorities for favouring the Japs at the expense of other nations.

For instance, since the trouble, fights and scrimmages between the Chinese and Japanese have become much more common, and in some parts of the city are almost a regular occurrence. As police, we try to be fair to both sides and to remain strictly impartial. It is sometimes a difficult job. The Japs always assume that they are in the right even when patently in the wrong, and it is often very hard to keep one's temper, especially when they begin to tell us what to do and to order us about. When in great difficulty, we can inform the Japanese Consulate Police, but this is seldom much help, as they always side with their own countrymen. So we generally have to sit in the background and watch the wrong party win the case, well knowing that if we were free to conduct it in our own way the result would be precisely the reverse.

I recall one case in particular that embittered our minds against the authorities and made us realize the limitations of our powers as policemen.

A foreign sergeant (an Englishman) was on patrol one evening in the Hongkew District, in which the Japanese colony was situated. He saw two Japanese sailors ill-treating a Chinese woman. She happened to be a prostitute who had been soliciting on the streets. In the ordinary course of events, they ought to have reported her to a policeman, if she was causing trouble, and then make an official complaint at a police station. They certainly would not have struck her in the circumstances unless she had been Chinese.

The foreigner strode up and strongly reprimanded them for striking the woman. He had every right to do this, but they flew into a rage and cursed and swore at him, while a large crowd of Japanese supporters gathered round. They all backed their countrymen up, and things began to look rather ugly, so the Englishman drew his pistol for self- protection. At that moment a Japanese naval landing-party patrol came on the scene, and without any questions being asked whatsoever, they whisked the policeman off to their headquarters. Our officials were informed of the incident, and finally a deputation, including the Japanese Commissioner and the Commissioner of Police himself, went there to investigate and to ask for his release. After much talking and parleying, the foreigner was finally released at about three o'clock in the morning.

The Japanese authorities demanded that police action should be taken against him, and he lost three months' seniority. It seemed to us a sentence satisfactory to the Japanese, and to them alone. Be that as it may, it certainly meant that we lost a lot of prestige in their eyes.

Another case of the same kind comes into my mind. A foreign detective sergeant and a party of Chinese detectives were making a raid on a house in which some armed robbers were suspected of hiding. Somehow or other they made a mistake and searched the wrong house. The Chinese detectives went up into the bedroom and pulled a man out of bed, treating him fairly roughly, according to what was stated afterwards. He turned out to be a Japanese. It certainly is rather difficult sometimes to differentiate between them and the Chinese, but on this occasion the detectives probably took advantage of their mistake, and, under pretence of thinking him one of the robbers, manhandled him before they released him.

The Japanese authorities demanded a strong inquiry into the whole affair. The foreigner would have fared badly if he had not been able to prove that he had remained outside the house, and left the detectives, who were from another station, to conduct their own raid. As it was, he was given the benefit of the doubt and exonerated, to the fury of the Japanese.

But final proof that the Japanese are now the most favoured nation in Shanghai came when I was on charge-room duty at my last station one day. The Commissioner was visiting us, and he suggested that we should be a little more polite to the Japanese in the course of our work than we had been recently.

I fear that if the Commissioner had heard our comments on his advice, he would have thought that we needed further lessons in politeness.

Until now we English have been the predominant influence in the International Settlement in Shanghai, and I am prepared to boast that the Municipal Police Force has been an important element in maintaining our prestige. But if the police are to use sweet words to every Japanese they meet and wink at their illegal actions, then it is time that any self-respecting Britisher left Shanghai.

VIII

A HOLIDAY-MAKER sight-seeing in Shanghai may leave with pleasant memories of having spent a glorious time. He will boast of the magnificent things that he has seen: the fine streets and the wonderful lights at night, his experiences of the famous night life of the city, and tell his friends all about the fine spree that he has had in the "Paris of the East."

Ignoring the Chinese community, it seems to him a modern business, commercial and shipping centre, with its public utility companies and efficient Police Force, a noticeable absence of red tape and a reputable press—a city, in fact, where half the nations in the world mix and mingle with apparent ease and good fellowship.

It is not perhaps strange for a casual visitor to Shanghai to receive such an impression, but it is rather curious that a large percentage of the foreign population residing in the city should have the same. Their knowledge is extraordinarily limited. They go about their daily business, enjoy their social life, attend their clubs, dinners and dances, and take what seem to them exciting jaunts on Saturday nights visiting low-class cabarets and houses of ill repute, proudly boasting of their inside knowledge of Shanghai's underworld. But most of them have never seen an opium pipe, and unless they read their morning papers they would be quite unaware that armed robberies and kidnappings were such a frequent occurrence. If they glance sometimes at the smart officer on point duty or patrolling the streets, they think perhaps that he leads an ornamental rather than an active and dangerous existence. If they are the morbid seekers after vice and excitement that I have mentioned above, maybe they envy him his opportunity of entering the darker parts of the city perhaps unknown to them. They would probably be surprised to learn that in this respect a policeman's lot is not a happy one, at least in Shanghai.

I could take these sightseers on a tour of the city at night that would astonish them, and I hope afford them little pleasure. I know for certain that what a policeman sees around him during an ordinary term of duty in parts of Shanghai gives him none. There is no need for us to hunt for vice, our trouble is that we cannot escape from the sight of it.

The oldest profession in the world is practised on a terribly large scale in this meeting-place of all types and conditions of people from every corner of the globe. Although the police do all they can to suppress it, prostitution seems to many the easiest solution to the problem of earning a living, and it is still rife all over Shanghai.

Some years ago they had a system of licensed brothels, which were regularly visited by recognized medical men. Not being with the police in those days, I cannot say whether it was abused or neglected, but anyhow the authorities abandoned the scheme. I cannot help thinking that this was a mistake. It must have done something to diminish disease that is now so prevalent in the city. But it is doubtful whether it could be adopted again now with any chance of success, for prostitution has increased to such an extent that it is no longer a question of unlicensed brothels, but rather of a deliberate commercial enterprise, if it may be called so. Hundreds and hundreds of Chinese girls, each accompanied by their *amah* or nurse, line the streets in the heart of the city, all soliciting for prostitution. There is much keen competition, among them. While the girls try to attract the passers-by, the *amahs* keep a good look-out for the police. The girls employ their charms, if they have any left, quite indiscriminately on Chinese and foreigner. Their first attempts are always verbal. They often reminded me of rickshaw coolies touting for hire. A prospective customer would be followed along the street by one of these girls, with the *amah* trotting along behind. If unsuccessful by this means, they would grasp the person's arm and entreat him to accompany them to their rooms.

In a few years their lives are wrecked by this mode of living, and girls who are really quite young look like middle-aged women, so blighted are they by disease. Parents often sell their children when no more than twelve years of age to the conductor of one of the brothels. Many cases connected with this shameful traffic come to the knowledge of the police, and prosecutions ensue. A father would often sell his daughter for about fifty dollars, receiving a first instalment of perhaps twenty from the purchaser. Later on he has to ask again and again for the balance, always being met with a refusal, on the grounds that the girl has been a poor bargain and is not earning enough money.

Most of these girls deserve to be pitied, because they often put up a gallant struggle against such a life, but they are usually defeated in the end. It is a recognized old Chinese custom, I believe. A go-between or middleman will nearly always find a buyer for them, drawing a prearranged amount of money for his services. It is such a usual occurrence among the poorer classes that it is treated as an ordinary business transaction.

The police take stern measures against all this prostitution. Special plain-clothes squads, composed of several Chinese policemen with a couple of foreigners in charge, are detailed nightly to round up these girls and their *amahs*. They go off in a police raiding van at all times of the night between 9 p.m. and 2 a.m. leaving the van in a quiet spot near where the round-up is to take place.

The Chinese policemen will be specially dressed in their Sunday best for the parts that they are to play in the performance. They mingle with the jostling crowds of Chinese, and stroll unconcernedly along the roads infested by these girls of ill repute, who can easily be recognized without questioning them; but the police wait until the girls approach and solicit one of them in plain clothes for prostitution. Then they arrest them. The police van is soon loaded with girls and their *amahs*, who are driven straight off to the station and deposited there. The van then returns to the field of action, and the whole routine starts again from the beginning. This will go on until the station concerned is packed out.

The result is often rather a comic situation in the charge-room swarming with these girls. Most of them are old offenders, and they treat the matter very lightly, loudly and shrilly protesting their innocence in an attempt to gain a little "face" in front of the others. Some of them will try to look demure and virtuous, but such an attempt is usually a dismal failure, owing to their appearance. Others, accustomed to be arrested, pour out an apparently inexhaustible stream of profanity against the police for being so cruel as to stop them from earning their living. Others, again, seem to consider the whole affair simply as a piece of bad luck, and blame themselves for their own poor strategy and stupidity in allowing the police to arrest them. The latter type pass away the time laughing with and sometimes at the police. It is often most embarrassing for some poor Chinese policeman when he is picked out as the object of their attentions. Their jokes are apt to have a bitter sting in the tail.

"Ai-ya, Di-kuh nyung z lau bang-yeu," will say one of them, pointing at some Chinese policeman, and even sometimes at a foreigner. This means, "This man is my friend," and I have often seen a young Englishman blush—of course with anger, for I am not suggesting for one moment that there is any truth in the remark; but it is enough to upset a man and make him swear, to have such a thing said to him in front of his companions. For the girl goes on:

"Bang-yeu noong nyung-tuh ngoo. Ngoo-kuh hwo-li noong kyau-tuh va," which means, "Friend, you recognize me? You know where I live?" (or literally, "You understand my home?")

When they have gone through the usual formalities at the station and have been searched and their names and addresses taken, they are bundled off to court. There they are detained in the cells until brought before the judge at about ten o'clock in the morning. Unfortunately, when they are taken from the cells to the court they seem to forget their previous attempts to preserve some "face," and they let loose a torrent of oaths and indulge in the most unpleasant gestures reminiscent of their trade.

They are lined up in the dock in batches of a dozen at a time. On a Monday morning after the week-end there may be several hundred of them to be dealt with, which might be thought to mean a busy day for the judge. But not a bit of it. A Chinese policeman will bear witness that "he, together with a number of other policemen, arrested them soliciting for prostitution." The judge will then make some cross remarks and pass the recognized sentence of a ten-dollar fine on girl and *amah* in rotation. The court is soon cleared, and the merry throng go home to get painted up for the following night. Whatever may be the advantages and disadvantages of this system, it certainly means that the girls go on filling the coffers of the court.

Besides the street prostitutes, there are those in the common brothels, or "dives," as we term them. If these places are not doing sufficient trade, definite methods of advertisement are adopted. They are, of course, little more than hovels in some alley-way somewhat renovated and decorated up. Look-outs or "pimps" will stand at the corner to entice passersby to visit their "most beautiful Chinese girls." Usually Chinese men, these "pimps" were the people that we really took a delight in arresting. Mean, despicable creatures who lived on the earnings of these poor wretches. Whenever I laid hands on them myself, I always gave them something to remember me by. They thoroughly deserved all the thrashings they got from the police. They even paid their fines in court out of the girls' earnings, and I was always pleased to see them receive a stiff gaol sentence. They haunt the bars frequented by seamen and sailors, and tempt them when they come out, perhaps a bit drunk, with their inane cackling of:

"Pletty girls, master. I take you, rickshaw."

The rickshaw coolies themselves play a big part in the encouragement of prostitution. People often write to the newspapers in Shanghai complaining that they have seen the police ill-treating the coolies. I wonder if they realize what is often actually happening. Surely the unlawful exercise of authority and the use of a little force may be excused when a coolie is being prevented from taking a drunken man to a brothel.

The coolies are the worst type of "pimps." They act as look-outs for probably half a dozen brothels, and collect "squeeze" from them all. If they get a drunken foreigner in their rickshaw, they will either take him to one of these dives, where he is robbed while unconscious, or to some dark alley-way, where he is likewise robbed and man-handled by a gang of coolies, who often do him serious injury.

I remember one night a friend and I had been into the French Concession to spend an evening at the dog-racing track. We were returning home in rickshaws, and suddenly, without any warning, they turned off the main road and darted down an alley-way, thinking that we wished to visit one of these dives. We told the coolies to turn back, but they took no notice, and went on with their patter about "beautiful girls," so we both became rather angry. We were in mufti, but we jumped out and gave them what they deserved. They on their side began to get excited, afraid of losing their squeeze from the brothel besides their fares, which we had refused to pay them. They thus decided to get what they could out of us by force. Attracted by their shouts, more coolies came up and started to attack us. They were in a very ugly mood, and I'm sure we should have been badly beaten by them if we had not made a sudden rush and fought our way out on to the road again. Even then they chased us down the main road until we sighted a French policeman, who treated the whole matter as quite a normal occurrence when we explained it to him. I must say that the coolies seem to me more out of hand in the French Concession than in the Foreign Settlement.

Raids by the police are often made in an attempt to suppress these brothels, but a regular campaign would have to be launched to make any appreciable difference in their number.

There are also special brothels for the Japanese in Shanghai, but most of them are run on quite different lines from the Chinese. They are licensed and kept in strict control by the Japanese authorities, definitely excluding all other nationalities.

But the Japanese colony is crowded with cafés where one can eat the famous "sukiyaki" or drink beer and dance, all in true Japanese fashion, with the most attractive young girls politely executing one's orders. Some of them are certainly centres of prostitution, while others are a pleasure to visit.

Then at night, if you are leaving the dock-side, you will notice many Russian girls and women standing at the entrance to their houses and inviting all and sundry to enter. There are many low-class cafés and cabarets here, visited by the seamen of all nationalities, for they are simply haunts for the Russian prostitutes.

Farther on you come to the Bund, facing the river with all its shipping and commercial buildings. Here you find the Russian street-walkers, who occupy the same beat for months and even years. In spite of repeated arrests, they still carry on in the same place. Farther on, behind the water-front, there are several large houses which may be called "very high-class establishments," under medical supervision and unofficially immune from police interference. Then all over Shanghai there are innumerable cafés and cabarets that, from the smartest and most modern to the lowest and most dingy, are nothing but a cloak for prostitution.

This is only a little of the knowledge that comes to a policeman in Shanghai during the course of his work. He gains it gradually from experience while delving into the life of the city in the course of duty. After a time he becomes accustomed to the atmosphere of the underworld there, learning its language and the habits of its people. It is all part of his work, and he would be no use unless he acquired this knowledge. In a few years there is little that goes on in this respect that is not known to the average policeman.

There is another side of Shanghai that could do with a little cleaning up besides its morals. The Chinese are naturally a very dirty race, unlike the Japanese, who rival many Western nations in their cleanliness. For instance, in spite of the fine work and magnificent plant of the Shanghai Waterworks, it is still essential to have the water filtered and then boiled to ensure a healthy drink, for it comes from the Whangpoo River, with all its filth, mud, manure and even dead bodies floating about in it. But I have often seen Chinese women with a little wicker basket filled with rice, swishing it to and fro in the water by the banks of this river until they think it is — clean! How they survive is a mystery to me.

Of course the foreign quarters of the city have the latest and most modern sanitary arrangements, but that is only a small part. The vast districts inhabited by the poorer classes have absolutely no sanitation in our sense of the word. In spite of the filth everywhere, they seem to thrive on such conditions. At night what are known as night-soil coolies go on their rounds pushing a contrivance like a large metal-bound box on two wheels. They go to each house in their respective sectors and collect the refuse that has accumulated during the day. This will go on from 3 a.m. till about 8 a.m., after which time they are forbidden to appear on the streets. The Chinese quarters of Shanghai in the small hours of the morning have to be "smelled" to be believed. I wonder what a London policeman would say if he could suddenly be transplanted from his beat in some respectable residential district at home to one of these streets. I fear that at the first sight and smell of one of these ghastly barrows even his strong sense of duty might collapse, and he would run a mile in the opposite direction.

Having finished his sector, the coolie takes his barrow to one of the many creeks that run through the Foreign Settlement and empties the contents into one of the open barges there for the purpose. When full, the barges drift down the creeks until they reach the country outside the city, where the manure is sold to the farmers. They literally smother their land with it, and the result is a marvellous stock of vegetation. But apart from anything else, the system has its disadvantages for the policeman patrolling the neighbourhood of these creeks at night.

Such primitive not to say barbaric conditions form a strange contrast to some of the intimate family life of the Chinese with whom I came in contact. There one was conscious of an age-old civilization, a formal and highly developed code of manners and rules of etiquette quite beyond the comprehension of a foreigner. At one time I became very friendly with a young Chinese whose father was an important official in the Nantao Police. I learned much of the peculiar habits and customs of the Chinese from being entertained by him, especially when he invited me to dinner at his parents' home.

I remember the first time I went there. On arrival I went through the usual routine of introduction, making the short polite bow and trying in my best Chinese to convey my salutations to them in the proper way. I was rather crestfallen when my friend's mother replied in perfect English. But, much to my pleasure, it did not affect the dinner itself, which was truly Chinese. I drank the usual cup of tea with them, and then we sat down to table. As his father was not at home, his mother acted as host and hostess, a custom that I believe is quite usual. In China the women rule the domestic side, while the men remain in the background demanding respect.

A bowl of tea that was kept constantly full was placed in front of me, with another bowl of rice. A Chinese spoon, a plate and a pair of chop-sticks were all the dinner service that I had. But I didn't mind, as I had acquired the art of using the chop-sticks, a compliment always appreciated by the Chinese. Nuts, raisins, melon seeds and different cereals adorned the table. They were eaten before, during and after the meal. The Chinese might be called true family or communal eaters. The first course was served in a large dish or tureen, and placed in the centre of the table. Then everyone joined in a tremendous scamper to finish the contents, an absolute race to see who could eat most in the shortest time, it seemed to me.

It made me think of the meal at the end of *Alice in Wonderland*. I found that just as I was beginning to enjoy any particular dish that I really liked, it was whisked away and another course brought along in its place. There were dishes of ham, pork, duck, chicken, fish, bamboo shoots, shark's fin, bird-nest soup (I don't know of what it consisted, but there were no birds or eggs in it), and other Chinese dishes whose nature filled me with suspicion, but which I thoroughly enjoyed. There seemed to be no prearranged order, and the dishes were just brought in and taken out anyhow. The food was certainly not a diet for anyone liable to indigestion. Various Chinese wines were drunk during the meal, and I was thankful when at last it was over. For Western table manners hardly allowed me to imitate the members of the family who casually got up, walked about, had a long chat in one corner of the room and then sat down again. I couldn't very well do this, although I wished that I had been able to, as they seemed to take offence if I refused anything, so I had to keep on eating all the time.

We then smoked (not the family pipe of opium, I'm glad to say) and played Mah Jong for a while. My pleasant evening was nearly spoilt by someone turning on some Chinese music for a while. After that dinner I felt I could not bear that weird sound of scraping glass and squalling kittens, so I dug my friend in the ribs, and he took pity on me and switched off. If my lack of musical appreciation upset them, they were far too polite to show it.

Sometime later on, the same friend took me to a Chinese wedding-party one evening. We had nothing to do at the time, and he suggested that we should go to the wedding reception of a friend of his. I hesitated for a moment, as I hardly liked to butt in without a proper invitation, but on hearing that he had received none himself and being told that it was all right, I agreed.

The reception was held in a large Shanghai hotel in a semi-Western manner — that is to say, the bride and bridegroom wore European dress, although the actual marriage ceremony had taken place in Chinese. At the entrance we were met by the official receiver of the guests, whom my friend knew well. After the usual polite greetings and salutations, he offered us cigars and conducted us to a long table, at which we sat down in the midst of a crowd of Chinese. I was the only foreigner, besides being a complete stranger to everyone present except my friend. Innumerable Chinese of all descriptions were standing round, even coolies and *amahs* residing in the vicinity who had come in quite uninvited to witness the ceremony of the wedding reception. This is, I believe, an old Chinese custom.

I noticed a party of Chinese in one group who remained standing in one spot. I found out later that they were there to make jokes and to keep the guests in a good humour. I was introduced to the bridegroom and had a few words with him, but I never saw the bride, as apparently some Chinese custom kept her absent. I then had the same sort of meal as I have already described.

Being the only foreigner, I was soon the object of general interest, especially as my friend had explained that I was a policeman. I think they wanted to test the drinking powers of the police, for they kept filling my glass with a most horrible sour wine. Fortunately for me, one of the spittoons to be found in every Chinese house was just behind me, and I managed to pour most of it away into it. Spitting is another filthy habit of the Chinese, both male and female. Even without the almost inevitable spittoon, it makes no difference; the floor is good enough for them.

As the meal went on, I noticed that I was the centre of all eyes, and then I noticed that the official jesters were directing their jokes at me. From what I could understand, they were saying all sorts of nasty things about my job as a policeman, such as: he strikes coolies, he arrests prostitutes — in fact, anything that might have made me lose my temper if I had not been careful.

As it was, I thought it very funny, and laughed heartily. In some way, this seemed to make me everyone's friend. I found out later that I had been subjected to the same sort of personal attack as the bride herself had endured a short time before. The idea seems to be to test the humour and temper of the person at whom these pointed and often nasty remarks are directed. I was glad that I had passed this examination no less well than the bride. At least I did not let down my friend.

Sometime after this, he asked me to go with him to a Chinese theatre. At first I tried to refuse, as I thought it would not be very amusing for me, since the plays were always spoken in the Mandarin dialect, which I did not understand. But seeing that I should offend him if I refused, I agreed to go.

The sight that met my eyes when we entered the theatre nearly took my breath away. I had never seen anything like it before. At one end of the big hall I could see the artists on the stage, which was simply a platform with a few painted cloths in the background for scenery; but what astonished me was that nobody seemed to be taking any notice of them whatsoever. The large audience were talking, joking and shouting about their private affairs or anything rather than the play and the actors. But even more curious was the fact that the latter did not seem to mind this in the least, and just went on acting, apparently for their own amusement. They certainly got no encouragement from the audience.

We sat down on a high-backed wooden form. In front of us was a wooden rest for the cups of tea that were brought to us periodically by Chinese attendants. I soon noticed a curious noise, a sort of sucking noise with a continuous crackle in it. I found that it was made by all these Chinese sipping their tea and eating melon seeds. These dried melon seeds seem to take the place of the chocolates that are eaten in Western theatres during the performance, and they make as much noise as the rustling paper wrappers. They put them in their mouths, expertly crack them, extract the kernel and spit the shell out on to the floor, which is apparently quite in order.

The play reminded me of watching a pantomime in England. I think the impression must have come from the gaudy dresses, which are, in fact, the ancient dresses worn by the Chinese— centuries ago. There was a childishness about the acting that seemed to me quite to suit the Chinese mind. But there was no applause from the audience, who treated the whole thing very much like a tea-shop conference; but the end of a dramatic or important speech was emphasized by the clashing of cymbals and the beating of drums. This also happens when any scene is finished. Then no curtain is lowered, and whatever, changes are made in the scene, such as changing the crudely painted cloths in the background and sweeping any debris off the stage, are done in full view of the audience by some attendants.

If I had seen the play soon after my arrival in Shanghai, it might have seemed stranger to me than it did. As it was, with the knowledge that I had then acquired of the Chinese, their habits and their mentality, their style of acting struck me as quite a natural form of expression for them. The Chinese act so much in ordinary life, indulge in so many gestures and have such a keen sense of the drama in their everyday affairs, that the further exaggeration of their style of acting passes almost unnoticed by one accustomed to the former. I had often heard of the peculiarities of the Chinese theatre, but when I visited it I felt that its strangeness had been somewhat misrepresented by Europeans, who probably had little knowledge of the Chinese. This formal style of declamatory acting may well have seemed strange to them, but when you have spent hours in a Chinese Court of Justice, as I have, there seems little difference between the long, pompous speeches to be heard in both places, given the ancient period of these classic plays.

But the casual visitor to Shanghai and its native theatre doubtless receives quite a different impression. It took me a long time to gain whatever knowledge of the Chinese I now have. Of course it was my job to study them, and part of our training was devoted to acquiring some general knowledge of Chinese ways and customs. It was when we came to practical things in the course of our duty, that the real problem started. Like the police anywhere, we had to learn how to size a man up pretty quickly. Without that intuitive knowledge of a person's character, social position and work—a sort of rough-and-ready psychological analysis, it may be called—no policeman is worth his salt, in my opinion. After a time it becomes automatic, and you don't really know why you tick so and so off as a person of no importance and treat another with a certain amount of politeness and deference. But if a policeman doesn't acquire this sort of tact, he can't deal with all the strange situations which he has to handle on the spur of the moment; he will make no end of mistakes and get himself into an awful mess. In fact, if he is congenitally a tactless person, he'd better give up trying to be a policeman and breed rabbits. They multiply of themselves, while our work requires constant attention and diplomacy—at least in Shanghai. As I say, we had to make up our minds about a man in a moment. In your own country, your whole life, experience and education help you, but abroad at first you have to start from zero in this respect. I doubt whether this business of classifying people is an easy one for the police at any time, but when the man you are trying to size up is a Chinese—one of those flat, yellowish, expressionless faces all round you in the streets—it makes it a hundred times more difficult.

It took me some time to differentiate one face from another. But that was only the beginning. All the subtle differences of class and type remained. I could see the broad distinction between a wealthy Chinese and a coolie—the dress alone is enough to tell you that—but for many months I thought I should never succeed in recognizing the various types of the lower classes with which we had chiefly to deal.

I remember being particularly aware of my ignorance in the matter when I went out on my first search-party. The foreigner in charge kept on saying to the Chinese policemen, "Search that man; he looks a proper loafer," or "Don't bother about that man;

he looks quite respectable." All these different types seemed just the same to me then.

I am quite at a loss now to say how I repaired my ignorance. As time went on I suppose I learned from experience how to recognize these different classes and to spot them instinctively without knowing why. But, like any policeman in the Force, if I were in a crowded street I would unconsciously pick out a coolie, an ordinary working man, an opium addict, a student, what we called a loafer, and a typical criminal. But if you ask me what was the distinguishing feature in each case by which I labelled them, for the life of me I can't tell you. It was simply a matter of learning from experience how to sum a man up from his general appearance, until it became an automatic reaction. I would not go so far as to say that I was right in every case, but on an average I should say that I was not far wrong.

But here are a few things that might give the men away to me. In some cases it might be the dress or the features, but both can be extremely deceptive, especially the clothes. Many criminals dress very smartly and well, while many quite respectable Chinese dress below their station in life owing to poor circumstances. I think I learned more from the many small details in a man's appearance that in sum suggest his class and profession. From this broad class distinction it then becomes easier to define the type.

For instance, take the coolies first; they are in the majority and stand well out from the rest. They have the coarse features to be expected in a type of people who are mechanical in their actions, habits and such thoughts as they may have. They conform to the customs of their ancestors, and do just what they did centuries ago. Quite unable to control their emotions — again such as they may have — if they want to laugh, they laugh; if they want to cry, they cry; if they want to kill, they kill. Their general behaviour might be compared to that of the caveman in prehistoric times. The typical coolie wears an old pair of blue trousers tied round the waist with a piece of string, a pair of rope sandals and nothing else. Sometimes, if he has been lucky, he may have got hold of some old jacket. You get to know the coolie more by his appearance than by anything else.

But it is by instinct alone that you recognize the loafer. He has about as little intelligence as the coolie, except that he becomes a little more cunning. His hand-to-mouth existence teaches him that. He might be compared to the hooligan known in other countries, but he is much more ruthless. The loafers usually work in gangs, and sell their services to anyone who wants any dirty work to be done and is afraid to do it himself. They blockade the shops that are being "squeezed" by some racketeering gang, act as decoys for blackmailers, and generally act as jackals for the lions in the crime racket.

The opium addicts, however, are a type definitely known by experience and contact. Even if they have not been reduced to physical wrecks by the habit when carried to extreme, they have a wasted look and their faces assume a dull, parchment-like colour, especially when the effects of a bout of opium-smoking are beginning to wear off. Then their eyes always give them away. They have the kind of bloodshot look peculiar to opium-smokers.

Experience again teaches you to recognize the typical students. They stand out quite clearly from the coolies and the loafers, not, of course, by carrying books, or because they are seen entering a college, which they sometimes do, but by something alert and aggressive in their appearance which the police recognize at once. We have good reason to spot them on sight, for they are the cause of a tremendous lot of trouble in Shanghai, with their Communist meetings and their agitations against the Japanese. When you have charged a mob of these students in a riot squad, you feel that you will never forget them. But perhaps instinct plays a small part in their immediate recognition besides experience.

As for the typical criminal, he defies description. He is to be found in all classes, and you only learn to recognize him after long and bitter experience. He differs chiefly from the criminal in other countries by being more reckless, desperate and ruthless. Where a burglar in England would knock a man down if hard pressed, the Shanghai armed robber shoots, and shoots to kill. I can only say that he has got this savagery in his face. I have often walked along a street and looked with considerable uneasiness at the faces round me. Some of them were undeniably criminal to my eyes, but unfortunately I had no right to arrest them on such suspicion. If I had, I might well have prevented some armed robberies and kidnappings, and perhaps a murder or two; for, like most policemen in the force, I would bet my bottom dollar against being mistaken in spotting the typical criminal. When you have sat day after day in the charge-room at a police station and watched the prisoners being brought in, you acquire a sort of intuition in spotting what they are which never, or hardly ever, lets you down. This is something of an achievement, I can assure you, considering the mystery that the Chinese remain to us in so many ways.

For instance, their apparent immunity from the sensation of pain is astounding. I have had clear proof that it exists, or rather I am left in doubt whether they have any feelings at all, or whether they are able to conceal what they have in face of physical suffering. I was charge-room sergeant at a certain station one day when a case was brought in of a man and his wife who had been involved in a petty dispute over their domestic affairs.

The normal procedure would have been to take particulars and to let them go after giving them a little lecture not to allow it to happen again. (If this sounds a bit childish, I can only say that this is the way that we have to treat the Chinese.) I was making a few entries in a note-book when I noticed that the man seemed rather unwell, so I asked him if he felt ill. He shook his head and said that he was all right, whereupon I went on making inquiries. Then I noticed that he was beginning to perspire freely, and, realizing that something was seriously wrong, I called for the ambulance and sent him to hospital at once. He died next day.

What had happened was this. After quarrelling with his wife, he had become very depressed and despondent. This always happens after domestic troubles among the Chinese, and perhaps comes from their having such a strong sense of family life. But this man was a very bad case. All on account of this little squabble, he had succeeded in swallowing a strong dose of raw opium unbeknown to anyone. I have been told that the drug in this condition would have the effect of a corrosive acid on the inside, and literally burn the man up. But he showed nothing in his face of the pain that he must have been suffering, and even refused to admit to me that he was feeling unwell.

Then, again a Chinese walked calmly into the station one day and said that he had been fighting with a friend and needed police protection. I took particulars as usual, and while doing so noticed that he was holding his stomach.

"Doo bien toong va," I asked him, meaning "Does your stomach pain you?"

He said that he was in no pain, but this time I was not satisfied, and I decided to investigate. He certainly needed police protection all right. On examination by a doctor, it was found that he had been stabbed in the stomach with a very long thin knife that had given him a deep wound without causing much blood to flow. He also died a few days afterwards.

On the other hand, you have to be on your guard against the malingerers who are always turning up at a station with a small bruise or a slightly cut or scratched finger, bemoaning their fate and asking to be sent to hospital. They are usually trying to obtain "squeeze" from someone who gave them the bruise or cut. Or they have lost "face" in some way, and think that they will recover it by persuading the police to reprimand or fine the other person. They frequently pretend that they have been assaulted, and say that they want to take action against their assailant. I have often broken all the rules of "face" and kicked the whole case out of the station, after having had all the trouble of taking a few particulars.

But the most curious example of "face" that I ever came across was connected with a traffic incident. I was a charge-room sergeant at the time, and one day a Chinese policeman on point duty came to the station accompanied by a Chinese in a very angry mood. As far as I could make out, he wanted the policeman executed on the spot, but for precisely what crime I was quite unable to discover. Chipping in when he paused to take breath, I told him to keep quiet for a bit while I received a report from the constable.

He proceeded to tell me the following story. The Chinese had walked across a road which he had closed both to traffic and pedestrians. When he had reprimanded him for his conduct, he had been verbally abused by him, thus causing him to lose "face." The man had then shown him his card stating that he was a lawyer, but he had taken no notice of it, and had brought him to the station for disregarding his signals and using abusive language. As spoken, this report seemed all in order.

The lawyer then told his story. He admitted that he had disregarded the signals, but said that he had done so quite unconsciously. He went on to say that the constable had not simply reprimanded him — in fact, he had done nothing of the sort, but had struck him. This meant that he had lost "face." He had therefore shown him his card, thinking doubtless that it would make some impression on the constable, as a lawyer ranks high in the estimation of the Chinese. It failed to have the desired effect, however, for the constable struck him again. This was more than he could bear, being struck twice by a policeman, and after showing him his card too; so he had come to the station to report the constable and demand that disciplinary action should be taken against him. From his outraged manner, it seemed that nothing but the death sentence would satisfy him.

Even when I had explained the policeman's report to the lawyer, he still maintained his attitude, and emphatically demanded summary punishment for the other at once. I told him to come to the station next morning and see the inspector. I did not want to deal with the case if I could help it. I knew that the lawyer was only making trouble in an attempt to regain his lost "face." He protested that he was a busy man, and could not attend a police station at that time. As he still demanded some action to be taken against the constable, I invented a little plan to smooth things over, although, in my opinion, they were both equally in the wrong.

Taking the lawyer aside, I told him that I would severely reprimand the constable for his conduct in front of the Chinese personnel of the charge-room, which would automatically mean that the lawyer would regain his lost "face."

Then I took the constable aside and told him what I was going to do, explaining that if the matter were reported to the inspector, he would probably be punished. At first he resented this, and complained that he would rather be punished than thus lose "face" in front of the other members of the charge-room. But I told him that I would inform everyone of the situation, and that we would all treat the affair as a joke to get rid of the lawyer. On this he agreed, and we duly carried out my plan, and the whole matter was amicably settled.

I publicly ticked off the constable. The lawyer went away quite happy, thinking that not only had he regained his "face," but that the constable had lost his. While the constable concealed a grin of pride, for he knew that everyone in the charge-room knew that he was really gaining "face," while the lawyer was losing his. By this little stratagem I pleased everyone, but I inwardly cursed at so much trouble being caused by so much folly. Afterwards, of course, I saw the comic side of it.

"Squeeze" is another thing that is always causing trouble. An armed search-party was once out in charge of a foreigner, an Englishman. The party had split up, and were searching all Chinese pedestrians for drugs and pistols. The English officer was on one side of road with two Chinese, and the other two Chinese with a Japanese in charge opposite to them.

Whilst searching a Chinese, this latter party found a small quantity of drugs concealed on his person. Instead of immediately reporting the matter, they threatened to take him to the station, and presumably told him what awful punishment he would receive there. They said, however, that they would release him if he handed over some "squeeze." He was an ordinary working-class Chinese, and he gave up all that he had, which could not have amounted to very much. It was quite insufficient to appease the Chinese police, and they told him to pawn his jacket and pants and give them the money. He did so, leaving himself wearing nothing but a vest and a pair of short white under-pants. But instead of forgetting about the matter, as the police hoped that he would, he reported it to the police station. Inquiries were made, and the British officer was arrested and tried at the British Court. He was acquitted, as it was proved that he had been completely unaware of the occurrence, but the Chinese police received a gaol sentence. It was fortunate that the British officer's innocence could be proved, or the affair would have lowered our prestige.

As usual abroad, the British are very jealous of their honour and prestige in Shanghai, and it generally stands very high. But mistakes are often made, and consciously or unconsciously our reputation suffers. I doubt whether some of the superiors who make these mistakes are fully aware to what an extent they damage us in the eyes of the Chinese and the foreign public in general. For instance, when the British police officer lost his seniority on account of doing his duty with regard to the prostitute and the two Japanese sailors in the case that I have already mentioned, the Japanese considered it a victory for them. Besides an officer being treated very severely and almost unjustly, British prestige suffered a heavy blow, and public opinion in Shanghai said that we were afraid to defend our nationals if the Japanese were involved in the matter.

Then, again, there are times when superior officers throw their weight about, trying to be terribly efficient and merely being officious, and reprimand their juniors in front of the Chinese. Not only is this very humiliating for the person concerned and a reflection on the authority of the superior officer; it makes the

Chinese scornful of the British in the Force. Whenever this happens, we lose "face."

One such case sticks in my mind. It happened during the Sino-Japanese War. One of our British officers from the Reserve Unit had been on duty at some other station, and whilst there had foolishly entered a Chinese fruit shop left deserted by its owner through fear of the Japanese invasion. All the fruit was abandoned in the shop, and this officer took a case of oranges for himself, and even hired a rickshaw to bring them away. Somehow or other the matter reached the ears of his superiors. Looting during the war was considered a serious matter, but he was not taken to court. Instead the police sentenced him to the loss of twelve months class promotion. There was nothing wrong in that; he knew he deserved it and was lucky to escape without a prosecution, although it seemed a small matter compared to the serious events happening at the time.

But this was not all. The whole personnel of the Reserve Unit were paraded on the compound, and his sentence was calmly read out in front of everyone, British, Japanese, Russian and Chinese.

Besides causing him bitter humiliation quite out of proportion to his crime, it laid the whole British branch of the Force open to the covert jeers and sneers of the other nationalities. A little foresight and tact would have avoided this. It would have been so easy for a notice to have been sent round, stating the seriousness of the crime of looting and the punishment it would receive. But no, as so often happens in Shanghai, a British officer was publicly humiliated in front of foreigners over whom he has to exercise some authority.

Top: THE BADLY CONSTRUCTED SANDBAG DEFENCES OF THE CHINESE
Centre and Bottom: BODIES OF CHINESE SOLDIERS SHOT AND THEN
BURNT ON THE BATTLEFIELD

IX

SUCH WAS MY life in the Shanghai Municipal Police Force until the autumn of 1935. All that I have written may give some idea of conditions in Shanghai, the criminal classes, the problems of crime there and the general work of the police in this strange and anomalous city. The end of my career in the Force came with startling suddenness. I was peacefully doing my job and looking happily forward to the future, when completely out of the blue Fate dealt me a blow that nearly destroyed me. As it was, it caused me such anguish and mental torture that I shall never forget it, for it broke my career and my happiness. Even now the world seems strange to me. Will it ever be the same for me as it was before that dark time when everything seemed to forsake me? Try as I will to think that it might well have been worse for me and that I had a lucky escape — all those wise but useless thoughts with which we try to help ourselves when having a bad time — I am really thinking of my shattered career, of having to start life all over again, the cruel force of circumstances, and all the small details and events that seemed to conspire against me. My love and, yes, sometimes my hate, blend to keep in my mind how a tactless mistake nearly ended in tragedy. In December 1935 I was arrested and tried on the capital charge of murder.

Before proceeding further, I must mention a few facts concerning my life and position at the time. I have no wish to bore the reader with my private affairs, and in this case, to put it frankly, a love affair; but although a minor point in the actual trial, it was used in an attempt to besmirch my character. I have treasured it and kept it to myself until now, but it plays such an important part in my own story that it calls for some explanation. It may also take a little of the burden from my heart and soul.

Some time before the event, the brief quarter of an hour that was to change my whole life, I had met a Japanese girl and become very friendly with her. It seemed only a pleasant flirtation at first on both sides. I for one was a strict believer in the saying, "East is East and West is West and never the twain shall meet." But as time went on we saw more and more of each other, and we began to throw aside the cloak of racial differences. I soon realized that her ideas blended with mine. I found that it was no passing attraction for someone strange and foreign to me, and no whim of the moment, but that I loved this Japanese girl truly from the bottom of my heart.

She felt the same way about me. We were quite frank with each other, and reviewed the situation from all angles, as well as the many difficulties that would have to be overcome. I had a long talk with her aunt, with whom she was living, and she wrote to my sister at home, both of us explaining our feelings and our proposed action.

We had finally arrived at the following decision. I was to resign from the Police Force at the end of the year (it was then about June), and we were to get married and return to England. With the money that was due to me from the Superannuation Fund of the police after six years' service, I thought that I had a sporting chance of getting a decent job at home that would enable me to look after my wife.

Before coming to this decision, I had gone over the whole thing many times in my mind, trying to see if I were doing the right or the wrong thing. But I knew that if we liked one another enough to take the risk not only of my future livelihood, but also of our mixed nationalities, then we were doing the right thing. And even now I am not sorry that we came to this decision, and never will be.

At the end of November 1935 I would just have completed my six years' service with the Force. So, after all the necessary arrangements had been made, it was with a light heart that I went early in November to attend my test for the Chinese language examination. I told the superintendent in charge of the Examining Board that it was not worth while putting me through the test, as I had decided to resign from the Force within a month or so.

I mention this to make it clear that, as I had decided to resign, it was obviously to my interest to keep a clean sheet during the brief period that remained; and also to prove that I had made up my mind to leave the Force long before my troubles started.

My future was everything to me then, and I would talk and plan out things for hours with my Japanese girl.

During the month of November 1935 I was charge-room sergeant at Kashing Road Police Station. I was on night duty — that is to say from twelve midnight to eight o'clock the following morning.

In the early part of the evening of November 30th, I was at my girl's house making final plans for our future. This could not be done in five minutes, so I telephoned to a great friend of mine who was charge-room sergeant until I relieved him at midnight, asking him if he would be kind enough to hang on for a short while, as I had some very important business to talk over, and would probably be a little late. This was not a strict breach of police regulations, as such mutual arrangements were frequently made between officers, and they never interfered with police routine. Of course it was against the rules, but in the police, as elsewhere, they are often honoured in the breach as well as in the observance. Certainly the rule of every shift coming on duty absolutely punctual to time was often broken. Anyhow, my friend agreed to do what I wanted, telling me not to be too long.

But making those final arrangements with my girl, I lost all track of time, and it was well after 1 a.m. when I rushed off post haste to duty. I knew that my friend would curse me for being so late, but I was very happy and light at heart because I had promised to place my resignation before the Commissioner about the middle of December.

I had some distance to return to my quarters, and there I changed into uniform and arrived at the police station a little time after 2 a.m. Imagine my surprise to find that my friend had got fed up with waiting for me (I don't blame him a bit, I should have done the same in his place), and had recalled a Russian sergeant off patrol and told him to carry on until I arrived, saying that he was tired and that I would not be long. I immediately took over control of the charge-room and signed on duty. My breach of discipline in being late was now covered, a petty breach considering the number of times that it occurs in the Shanghai Police Force.

The Russian sergeant was then ready to proceed on street patrol again, but I told him to wait in the station, as it was nearly his coffee time. Foreign officers are allowed twenty minutes at certain periods off duty for coffee. His time was between 2.30 and 2.50 a.m.

Just then a message came through from one of the 3 street telephones from a Chinese constable. A Chinese clerk took the message, and interpreted it to me, entering it in a special street telephone book as follows:

"Chinese constable no. — reports that at the corner of Singkeipang and Point Roads, a Chinese beggar is lying seriously ill."

I told the clerk that I would look into the matter.

The question was whether the beggar was really ill or not. In so many cases these beggars in Shanghai feign sickness to gain pity and money, and it is almost part of their profession to do so. Then we worked in close harmony with the Fire Ambulance Brigade. I knew that they would be, as always, very busy, and I did not want them to have a call out for nothing. Unless very seriously ill indeed, there was a hundred to one chance against the beggar being admitted to any hospital. As I have said before in describing these beggars, they are so filthy and such malingerers that none of the hospitals will admit them unless they are almost dying. I don't blame them, either. Unless they had some pretty stringent regulations, they would be overrun by them and would have no room for more legitimate patients. Moreover, these beggars are actually forbidden to enter the International Settlement, but of course they do so, feigning illness, and thus obtaining easy food and shelter.

I therefore decided to send the Russian sergeant along to find out if the beggar really needed medical attention, and, if not, to send him off into Chinese Territory, which adjoined our district. Just at that moment a British probationary sergeant came in reporting for coffee from street patrol. He overheard me giving the Russian some final instructions concerning the beggar, and thereupon stated that a short time before he had seen a beggar lying in an alley-way in the district and had chased him into Chinese Territory.

It seemed probable that it was one and the same beggar in both cases, that he had sneaked back again, and was now lying sick or feigning sickness in the road. I asked the probationary sergeant in what road or near what roads he had seen this fellow. He replied that he could not be certain, as he had only recently been transferred to our district and had not yet learned the names of the roads.

Now, the place where the beggar was reported to be lying was quite close to the station, so I decided on the spur of the moment to see for myself if this was the same beggar as the one whom the probationary sergeant had just kicked out of the Settlement, taking him with me to prove it. Someone had to go with him, as he could not find the way alone, and I also wanted to draw my own conclusions as to whether the man was really ill or only shamming. I had not sufficient confidence in the Russian's efficiency to trust his opinion. Past experience in the Force had taught me not to rely on a Russian when an important judgment was required.

This decision of mine to leave the charge-room for a few minutes was a fatal one for me. Little did I think then that it would form a damning piece of evidence against me and be used by a prosecuting counsel in an attempt to prove that I had deserted my post whilst on duty.

Anyhow, leaving the Russian to finish his coffee, and telling him that I should be away only a short time, I went out with the probationary sergeant. It was then about 2.45 a.m. The station motor-car was called out. When it arrived outside the charge-room driven by a Chinese police constable, the probationary sergeant, his Alsatian dog which he took out with him on patrol duty and I jumped in, and I told the driver to proceed as quickly as possible to the point indicated in the telephone message.

When we arrived, I noticed that there were no Chinese police about. For no reason whatsoever, they had apparently resumed their beats.

So we searched the vicinity, and suddenly came upon a Chinese lying on the pavement at the entrance to an alley-way. We both nudged him, but he gave no response, so I thought he must be pretty bad, although it was a rather dark spot and we had no torches. I therefore decided to take no chances on his looks, and said that I would send him to hospital. Having the station car on the spot, there was no need to send for an ambulance. We simply carried him to our car and laid him on the running-board. (Anyone who has seen and smelled a Chinese beggar will realise why we did not put him inside the car. Diseased and filthy, it was bad enough having to handle him, and anyway we made him quite comfortable.) My fellow-Britisher jumped into the rear of the car, while I stood on the running-board to see that the beggar did not roll off.

Then I told the Chinese police chauffeur to drive very slowly to St. Luke's Hospital, which was quite close to our station. Whilst on our way, the beggar began to move about, and I often had to tell him to "tong sing" — that is to say, to take care. I was in a pretty rocky position myself, holding on like grim death to the car whilst standing on the running-board.

On the way to the hospital we passed over a bridge across a creek that separated our district from another district in the International Settlement. It was quite in order for us to enter this other district because we were taking a man to hospital, but otherwise it would have been against regulations. This again is an important point in the sequence of events that provided such circumstantial evidence against me.

When we had gone only about two hundred yards into this other district, I gave the chauffeur the order to stop. The other officer jumped from the car, and I explained to him that the beggar was recovering. He was now struggling to get into a sitting position, and it would have been foolish and quite useless to take him to hospital, as he certainly was not sick enough to have any chance of being admitted.

If only I could have foreseen the future, I should have taken him off the running-board, sent him off into Chapei (Chinese Territory), and there the matter would have ended. But the wheels of chance turned in another direction, and yet another link was forged in the evidence against me.

But to return to what we did then. I talked it over with my brother-officer, and we decided, out of pity, to drive along the creek side until we sighted a beggar-boat and then to put our beggar aboard it. Numbers of these boats always infest the waterways in Shanghai at night, the beggars mooring them along the creeks in the evening, practising their profession in the streets of the city during the night, and then slipping away in these boats next morning. We thought that our beggar would be cared for by his own kind in one of these boats. It also seemed quite a satisfactory way of getting rid of him and finding him some sort of a home and refuge, besides causing the least trouble and inconvenience to my routine work at the station.

So I gave the chauffeur the order to turn round. At first he took no notice, and still proceeded towards the hospital. I had to repeat my order and sign to him most emphatically to turn about. Then I directed him along the creek-side, which, it must be remembered was not in our district, but in that in which the hospital was situated. After proceeding some short distance, from my position on the running-board I noticed a beggar boat tied up near the shore. I told the chauffeur to stop, and he pulled

up just a little ahead of the beggar boat, with the right-hand side
of the car facing the creek. From there it was quite impossible for
him to see the boat, as it was definitely concealed from his view
by the embankment, the top of the boat being four or five feet
below it.

We both dismounted and half-walked, half-carried the beggar to the low iron railings that separated the roadway from the
creek. The place was pretty well lit. This part of the road was
not far from two bridges, with their usual lamps, and behind
us a few yards away there were some dwelling-houses. Without
any difficulty or effort whatsoever we leaned over the railings
and lowered the beggar into the boat. When his feet touched the
boards at the rear, we let him quite gently on to the boat, and he
seemed perfectly comfortable. He certainly made no attempt to
move or run away, and we thought that he would remain there
until the occupants of the boat returned from their begging expe-
dition in the city and attended to him.

We waited for a few seconds to see that he was quite safe, and
then left him with the sure knowledge that he was lying on that
beggar boat. We returned to the station without passing any Chinese policemen on the way, and reached there just before three
o'clock. We had been away about a quarter of an hour—no more.

We both entered the charge-room, and I told the Russian sergeant to resume his patrol duty and the officer who had been
out with me to get his coffee. During the whole time from when
we left the station to when we returned neither of us had entered into any conversation with the Chinese chauffeur apart
from the remarks that I have mentioned. Nor did we when we
returned. As far as I know, he put the car away in the garage and
then went to bed.

The Chinese clerk asked me what had happened, and I replied,
"Everything is all right, O.K." I knew that we had committed a
minor breach of regulations in dropping the beggar in a district
other than our own, but it had been the most convenient (and
the kindest) thing to do. To save a lot of bother and questions,

however, I put a final remark in red ink in the street telephone book: "On arrival the beggar had left."

I thought that this would be the end of the whole matter so far as I was concerned; and it seemed to me, in so far as I continued to think about it at all, that I had acted in a sensible and humane manner. The covering of small reports of this kind is a recognized practice in the Force, and although not strictly adhering to police routine, such arrangements make for the smooth running of things in general, and no one troubles about them ninety-nine times out of a hundred. But this happened to be the hundredth time, to my cost.

But who would ever have thought then that anyone was going to bother about a Chinese beggar being placed on a boat? He was in Chinese Territory, for in Shanghai all the creeks and waterways are officially considered to belong to them. And, as far as beggars are concerned, all that worries the authorities in the International Settlement is that they should be expelled, forcibly if necessary, and driven into Chinese Territory. This is what had happened in this case; the beggar had been turned out of the Settlement and placed in Chinese Territory, only by much gentler means than usual.

After a round-up of beggars in certain districts, it is a recognized thing for them to be bundled into a police raiding van, taken to some outlying point of the Settlement and turned out into Chinese Territory.

Anyway, in the early morning of December 1st, 1935, I was happily thinking about my future, and not about a beggar who, as far as I knew, was being fed by his colleagues and was getting ready to start out on more begging expeditions the following night. But if there is such a thing as fate and destiny, that beggar was marked down to play a pretty important part in mine. I sometimes wonder whether I was fated to suffer all the trouble and sorrow which my mistake in leaving the charge-room that night has brought me.

I went off duty at about 8 a.m. As it was December 1st, and thus the beginning of a new month, duties were now being changed round, and I went on duty again at 8 p.m. until midnight. That day passed without any incident, and when I came on duty again on December 2nd for a full term from 4 p.m. until midnight, I had forgotten all about the beggar, for it was fully thirty-seven hours since we had placed him on the boat. It came as a complete surprise to me when the inspector in charge of our station came into the charge-room and began questioning me about the station car going out on the morning of December 1st.

I told him that it had, but I became rather evasive in my replies to some of his other questions, as they seemed to have some secret intention. I thought that news had somehow got round that we had taken a beggar and placed him in Chapei, going into another district to do so. I was afraid that they were now out to fix me for breaking the various minor police regulations of which I have spoken.

Then the officer who had helped me to put the beggar in the boat came in and said that he too had been questioned by our Divisional Officer. I was called in after that in my turn, and told that serious charges might be preferred against me, but that I need not make any statement yet unless I wished to do so. My Divisional Officer told me that he had received information that I had thrown a man into the Hongkew Creek. I told him that this was a lie, and thought that he was trying to trap me into confessing that I had been into another district. Then I made my first statement. I said that having found a sick beggar, I had decided to take him to hospital, but that he had recovered on the way and so I had let him go. I managed to avoid disclosing that we had dropped him in another district, as it was still in my mind that they were trying to fix me for that. But when the other officer wrote a statement later, he went too far in trying to cover our tracks in this respect, and mentioned an actual road in our own district in which he pretended that we had let the beggar go. This was a pity, but we still thought that we were involved in a minor disciplinary investigation, and thus had the right to a slight prevarication in order to avoid penalties that at the most would have been the loss of a few months' seniority. Even that would have been particularly severe and unusual punishment for the breaches of regulations that we had committed.

Naturally we wanted to avoid this if possible, and so made our respective statements in the belief that the mistakes that I have mentioned were our only crimes. Otherwise we certainly would not have made them. If I had thought that they meant what they said when they talked about throwing a beggar into a creek, I should have made no statement then. If I had imagined for one moment that it was a serious matter, I would either have told the whole truth or have said nothing at all, reserving everything until I had obtained legal aid. It was only after we had both made these initial statements that we had the slightest suspicion it was a serious matter. This was when we were both told that we were suspended from duty and confined to our quarters.

When we reached our rooms, I suggested that we should make fresh statements, saying that as the case against us now seemed to be assuming serious proportions, we both wished to correct various inaccuracies in what we had previously stated. This we did, stating the facts of the case from our point of view very much as I have told them above.

The following night—that of December 3rd—the creek was dragged for the body of the beggar, which could not be found. Then on the afternoon of the 4th we were taken to the St. Luke's Hospital under escort and confronted by a patient in bed. I did not recognize him, but he was the beggar.

In this small ward were several officials of the Police Force, both foreign and Chinese. I found out later that they were taking down the man's dying declaration. They asked him if he recognized us. He shook his head and feebly murmured, "No," in Chinese.

I was now beginning to wonder what the whole thing was about and what it all meant. I knew that there was some explanation—I feared serious explanation—for our suspension from duty, but we were both absolutely in the dark at that time as to the exact nature of the charges made against us.

Question after question flitted through my mind. Why had we both been brought to this beggar's bedside? How had he got into the creek? Had someone pushed him in, or had he fallen out of the boat into the water? In either case, who had pulled him out? Everything was a maze in my mind without a break in the clouds to enlighten me.

We received no aid from our colleagues; we could hardly expect any, perhaps; for, after all, they were policemen, and it was difficult for them to give even a word of friendly advice or sympathy to men obviously suspected of some crime. But for us the suspense and uncertainty only made our position worse. I felt that I would much rather know the worst at once than go on waiting with the terrible anxiety of some unknown charge hanging over my head.

At about half-past four that same afternoon, while we were still confined to our quarters, a telephone call was put through from the Police Station for me. It was to inform me that my fellow-officer and myself were to report right away at the station in mufti, bringing our overcoats.

I knew then what was happening. Overcoats! We were to be arrested. So it had come at last. Were we to be sent to gaol? It wasn't true, it couldn't be!

Well, it was no use talking about it, we had to do something. We must obtain legal advice. Having got in touch with a lawyer, we told him what we were expecting, and that we would communicate with him again after we had been to the station.

Disaster seemed to be looming ahead. All my happiness was in danger. Until now I had simply told my future wife that I was in a little trouble. So I quickly had to tell her that I expected to be arrested for something about which I knew little. She was very brave, and told me not to worry and to expect all the help that she could give. So, with a parting goodbye, we both made our way to the station.

We were taken to the inspector's office, and there found the Divisional Officer and detective officer and the inspector, besides

Top: A Typical Chinese Beggar
Bottom: One of the Creeks in the Settlement, but without the
Modern Embankment and Railings of the One Mentioned

the detective in charge of the case. We were cautioned in the usual manner and the charge was read over. We were charged with assault, with causing grievous bodily harm to a Chinese one Mau Teh-piau of the beggar class, by throwing him into the Hongkew Creek. We had nothing to say, and were then taken to another police station.

In the charge-room the usual formalities were gone through, our names were taken and the charge was entered. Then a thing happened that I shall always remember. The sub-inspector on charge-room duty asked us whether we would sleep in the cells that night, or would prefer to go to a spare room that had been fitted up for us with nice beds, a fire and some books, on condition that we did not abuse the privilege.

As a Britisher and fellow-officer, I felt like asking him what he would do in my place. Finally we were taken to this room, with a uniform and detective sub-inspector as escort. We were very well treated there, receiving a good meal, cigarettes, books, and even a cup of tea in bed the next morning.

Then the lawyer arrived. A barrister and a gentleman, he did everything he could to help us, not only as counsel for our defence, but also as a man. Explaining our case, he said that he would see us in court the following morning.

My companion in distress was comparatively unknown to me then. I had seen a bit of him on the football field, and knew that he was a good fellow and a fine sportsman. But as the case became darker and darker against us, we naturally got to know each other very well in this terrible fight of ours. He proved to be a very intelligent man with a most pleasing personality — the sort of fellow you felt sure would not lose his head and panic in an emergency. He didn't do so then, but kept extraordinarily calm. I know he helped me; I hope I helped him. Like me, he was fighting not only for his honour and his life, but also for a girl who deserves every praise for the encouragement and real sympathy that she gave him then. But at first he felt about it all as I did — "We are not guilty, so what harm can befall us?" But as time went on and things looked blacker than ever, he realized that we had our backs to the wall and that it was a fight to the finish. He remained a brave and courageous fighter to the end.

On December 5th, 1935, I entered court for the first time as a prisoner. The court registrar read the charge over to us, and the proceedings were adjourned owing to the condition of the beggar. Bail was granted, which was a problem; for we were first of all not allowed to have police friends standing security for us. Later the Court decided that they could do so, the reason being, I think, that the British court did not recognise the Shanghai Municipal Council police as British policemen.

Bail being granted and arranged, we were still confined to our quarters, but were told that we might leave to do business with our lawyer when it was necessary.

Our next difficulty was finding the money with which to pay our lawyer. Being a barrister, it was etiquette to pay him before the case started. Our money in the Superannuation Fund was all tied up, but a good friend who had previously helped me out of various little difficulties came to my aid and kindly paid my first instalment. My Japanese girl also came to my assistance. Little requisites and aids that I needed were ever at hand and also words of encouragement, which I think helped me to keep level-headed during this absolutely unfair trial—unfair in the sense that it ought never to have been brought, not of course with regard to its procedure once it had started.

On the day following our first appearance in court, the beggar died in hospital. Our lawyer immediately called us to his office and told us that now the man had died the case was assuming an extremely serious aspect. He said that it now depended on the evidence submitted in the police court by the prosecution as to whether we should go for trial in the Supreme Court. If we did, the charge would be one of murder. He told us to try to get as much information as possible concerning the evidence that would be used by the prosecution. He wanted to be prepared for it, and to know how to deal with it when it was subsequently submitted once the case had started in the police court. By methods that rather mystified the police in charge of the case we did obtain highly important information in this respect which was extremely useful to our counsel.

We took our lawyer through the same ride as we had taken on that fateful early morning, going over every detail with him with such minuteness and care that he finally had as much, if not greater knowledge of our case than we had ourselves.

We were again brought before the court on December 10th, and further charged with unlawfully killing the beggar.

The police-court case dragged on throughout the whole month of December. The case for the prosecution seemed interminable; witnesses and exhibits followed one another in endless succession. From the evidence of the various witnesses for the prosecution, the following story can be outlined as to how the beggar was finally taken to hospital.

First of all, what occurred at my station was this. Nothing had happened there until about thirty-six hours after we had put the beggar on that boat. Then information had been received from some unknown source at the station, which had led to the questioning of the Chinese police chauffeur who had driven us. He finally stated that we had told him to drive nowhere in particular that morning, and that he had gone in the direction of the hospital simply because he surmised that we wished to go there. (This was completely untrue. I had told him definitely to drive to St. Luke's Hospital.) He went on to say that after he had been ordered to stop at a certain point alongside the creek, he had seen the two foreign officers walk with the beggar to the railings and deliberately *throw the beggar into the water.*

According to him, the reason that he had not reported the affair on returning to the station nor during the next thirty-six hours was because we were his superior officers.

After such a statement, it seems curious that the authorities continued to rely on such a witness. Was it credible that he should see one of his fellow-countrymen thrown into a creek to certain death from drowning as stated by him, and that he should fail to report the attempted murder simply because it was committed by his superior officers? And if we had been murderers, should we not have tried to intimidate him to keep silence before or after the supposed crime? Was not that more feasible than that we should not have spoken to him except to give him brief orders throughout the whole journey? Did it never strike the prosecution that there must have been some explanation for our not entering into conversation with him or attempting to suborn him as a witness — the perfectly natural explanation that it never entered our heads for one moment that he would ever be called to give evidence against us?

Nothing caused and still causes me more bitterness than the apparent zest and gusto with which our fellow-countrymen and colleagues did their duty and tried their hardest to bring about our downfall. Tooth and nail they went at it; not for one moment did they seem ready to give us the benefit of the smallest doubt. I positively hated them at the time, and still do a little for their sudden attachment to duty that seemed only too ardent. Such is, I know, the law, and I suppose I should not worry or fret about the conduct of the case. But we were on opposite sides in a battle in which our lives, not theirs, were at stake; and innocent as we were, I remember thinking that instead of trying so hard and with such apparent enthusiasm to convict us, they might have paused for one moment to consider the possibility of the beggar's suicide.

The evidence went on to relate how a Chinese hawker had seen a motor-car outside his house early on the morning of December 1st and had seen two policemen looking into the creek. Being a most marvellous sight, as he naïvely expressed it, he ventured in his turn to look into the water when we had driven off to return to the station. At the same time he had thoughtfully noted the number of the police motor-car. A most intelligent and observant hawker this! Had he foreseen the whole course of events and how valuable his information would be to a prosecuting counsel? As a witness he was not quite so useful or reliable, however, for he was proved to be a "pimp," and living with a prostitute at the time.

He went on to say that when he looked into the creek, he saw a man floating in it. He immediately shouted "Save life," and, rushing up, he had obtained a boat-hook from a boatman near by. Then a next-door neighbour came on the scene, and between them they managed to haul the beggar out of the water on to the side of the creek.

Just then a policeman from the district in which we had placed the beggar — that is to say, not our own — hearing the shouts of "Save life!", dashed up, and he immediately telephoned to his station for an ambulance.

Now, why did not the hawker report to him that he had seen us standing on the edge of the creek, as he afterwards stated in court? Was not that the obvious thing for him to do? Again a fellow-countryman had apparently been drowned, and yet the witness made no accusation against the supposed murderers until some days later!

The ambulance came and removed the beggar to the hospital. A Chinese detective, a man from this other station was ordered to sit by the beggar's bedside to try to obtain a statement from him if he recovered consciousness, as to how and why he came to be in the Hongkew Creek. From the hawker's story onwards this was of course all happening unbeknown to my station at the time.

The beggar finally rallied and regained consciousness. It was then discovered that the detective could not understand his dialect very well, so he got a Chinese patient in the next bed to help him to translate his statement. This was the only true and perfectly coherent statement ever obtained from him.

The detective said, "How did you come to get into this creek?"

The beggar replied, "I jumped into the creek because I was cold, hungry and homeless."

In this first statement of his he never mentioned the word police, and never made any direct or indirect suggestion that any policemen were in any way concerned with his being found in the water.

The detective made his report at his station, and it was treated as a case of attempted suicide.

Now, it must be remembered that up to this point there had been no communication between this station and mine, and that neither knew what had happened at the other. They became linked up in the following manner.

As the result of what the unknown informant had said at my station, together with the statement of the Chinese chauffeur and further investigations on the part of the police, it was decided to drag the creek.

This took place in the early morning of the 3rd of December, a Chinese detective and a foreign sergeant being in charge of the dragging operations. While waiting for any developments, the sergeant noticed a young Chinese woman speaking to the detective. He joined them, and learned that she had been asking why these people were dragging the creek, because on the morning of the 1st she had seen two Chinese pull somebody out of the water.

On this dragging operations were immediately suspended and my station was informed. Direct communication was thus established between the two stations, and then things began to move quickly. The hawker, his neighbour and the various policemen connected with the affair were questioned, the beggar was visited in hospital, and on the doctor in attendance stating that he was in a serious condition, a dying declaration was obtained from him.

I know nothing of the law in such circumstances, but in my opinion both my fellow officer in the case and I should have been in attendance at that declaration, instead of being told to wait outside the ward after the beggar had failed to recognize us. A certified official of the British authorities took it down through the medium of a Chinese interpreter. But was it fair for this interpreter to be a Chinese police sub-inspector who knew all about the investigations being made? With such an important state-ment, and so much depending on it, why wasn't a neutral interpreter employed — someone with no knowledge of what was going on, and consequently with a completely unbiased opinion?

The prosecution based a tremendous amount of their case on this dying declaration. It was not known until after the whole case was over that it was not worth the paper on which it was written, for the beggar had never *signed* it, or even made his mark.

It seems strange that the prosecution should have based so much of their case on a completely worthless document.

Furthermore, does it not point to the fact that the beggar was not in a fit state to sign it, and was therefore not in a condition to make it? To drive the point further home, does it not mean that he was so ill that he was particularly susceptible to any sugges-tions made to him, and might agree to statements which, if he had been stronger, he would have denied?

Why, even when he was confronted by me, he could not speak, but only shook his head and mumbled something. Yet according to his declaration he is supposed to have stated some-thing like this: "I was taken in a car by two men in uniform and thrown into the water by these two men."

But what seems to me conclusive is this. Why should he con-tradict the first statement that he had given of his own free will to the detective and the man in the next bed, who was a completely independent witness, when he told them that he had *jumped* into the creek because he was destitute?

Throughout the long sessions held in the police court during December, the case for the prosecution was very patiently and minutely presented. We sat there day after day listening to the statements of the various witnesses brought by the prosecution.

Strong legal points were argued out by our counsel and the prosecution, one being the legitimate use of the dying declara-tion, the fact of its being unsigned being unknown to us then. Our very able counsel was a man with tremendous knowledge of the Chinese, and his cross-examination often found them out in contradictory statements and mis-statements.

Throughout this time we were making every effort to get in touch with our independent witness, who had by now left the hospital. We sought the aid of a private detective agency, who promised to do their best to trace him. Our bad luck pursued us even here, for we found that he had left Shanghai; but the agency received information by which they hoped to find him within a few days. Shortly afterwards we heard, to our relief, that he had returned to Shanghai. Our lawyer tackled a Chinese lawyer friend of his, and they both sounded the witness concerning his knowledge of the statement made by the beggar to the detective in the first instance in hospital. He said that he would willingly attend court at any time when called upon, on the understanding that he received the cost of the time lost from his employment by his attendance.

We immediately agreed to this with great relief, for he was our only witness, but in our opinion a star witness.

The clock was also playing a very important part in this case of ours. The prosecution tried to destroy the reliability of our statements concerning the time at which we left and returned to the station. They tried to make out that we must have been away from the station more than fifteen minutes. The Chinese clerk had entered his message from the policeman reporting the sick beggar at 2.45 a.m., and we had stated that we had returned to the station quite by three.

To substantiate this, we had the evidence of the Chinese policeman who went to the scene at the creek on hearing the hawker's cry of "Save life!" This was a very big point in our favour. His beat that morning brought him to a bridge which we had to pass on our return to the station. Moreover, it was not more than fifty yards from the spot where we had placed the beggar in the boat.

He said that he arrived at that bridge at two minutes to three o'clock. He had apparently looked at his watch then, as that particular point was the end of his beat and he was timed to walk it in an hour.

No car had passed while he was there. This meant that we must have passed the bridge before his arrival, as it was only two or three minutes away from the station by motor-car. We were therefore able to settle that point.

Then the hawker declared that he saw the beggar in the water and shouted "Save life!" immediately after our departure. But the Chinese policeman again came in useful. He declared for his part that it was seven minutes past three when he heard the shouts, because he was just going to resume his beat. He had looked at his watch before doing so, and heard the cry just afterwards.

The time factor was tremendously important, as these creeks are tidal, and the tide at that time in the morning was flowing in. If ten minutes had elapsed after we were supposed to have thrown the beggar into the water, his body would have floated a considerable distance. Instead of that, he was found only about ten yards from where we had placed him on the boat. Now, the Chinese policeman never saw us, and yet arrived on the scene when the beggar had *just* been pulled out.

The probable explanation seems to me that the beggar, recovering a little and finding himself alone, decided to jump into the creek from the boat about seven or eight minutes after our departure.

The policeman's time corresponded with his station's official time, and the clocks there are synchronized by the central control-room. As soon as he had seen the beggar, he hurried to the nearest street telephone, which was no more than a hundred yards away, and reported the matter to his station. The message was received there at twelve minutes past three o'clock.

When we heard that an autopsy was to be held on the beggar, we decided to have a doctor of our own in attendance besides those of the police. With some difficulty we obtained the services of an American doctor. A rather amusing incident occurred in connection with this doctor when we were trying to find his address, although I did not see its comic side to its full extent at the time.

He lived in the French Concession at an address unknown to us, so we — the two accused in the Beggar Case, as it was called — went to a French police station to ask for help.

We were naturally still suspended from our Force, but as we were pressed for time, my companion, after asking the direction from a French policeman in the charge-room, calmly turned to an officious-looking officer and asked if he would lend us their police car as we wanted to see this doctor on very urgent business. He said that we were both International police officers, showing his driving licence to prove the fact. True as it was, what a position we were in at the time! It hardly seemed something to boast of. The French officer looked rather dubious, and I didn't blame him. Even with the driving licence to back him up, my companion's request seemed a bit fishy on the face of it. I tremble to think of how that pompous Frenchman would have spluttered with rage if he had known who we really were — the notorious policemen accused of killing a Chinese beggar. His pride would never have survived the shock.

As it was, he began to argue with the other man, who seemed quite agreeable, until I thought there would be a free fight. On this, having received the direction, I hurriedly left, dragging my reluctant and unrepentant companion with me. He even had the cheek to curse me for losing a chance of a free ride. I have often thought since what would have happened if we had taken the car and been involved in an accident. At that time we had all the trouble we wanted.

The result of the autopsy had very little bearing on the case.

The proceedings in the police court were now drawing to a close, and one of the worst parts of the whole thing began for me. It hurt me terribly.

Our lawyer gave us the impression that the case would have to be tried in the Supreme Court on account of the amount of evidence submitted by the prosecution. He told us not to get down-hearted, however, whatever the charge should be.

I had told my Japanese girl and her aunt not to worry, and at first they could not quite understand the seriousness of the affair. I had been building my hopes on the case coming to an end in the police court, and I tried to worry them about it as little as possible. But I began to realize then the awful position into which we were slipping, although it still seemed impossible for us to be found guilty. But I had to face every possibility, even the worst, and the only thing to do was to keep a level head and not get frantic. But the unbelievable nightmare was materializing into a cruel, grim reality. A stiff upper lip was certainly required, and it was with that thought uppermost in my mind that I attended court on the day on which the case for the prosecution came to an end.

The police-court registrar stated that on the evidence submitted he had not the power to deal with the case, and it was his duty to send it for trial to His Britannic Majesty's Supreme Court for China. We reserved our defence for this court, and the registrar then said that he would adjourn the case until a certain date so that the charge could be framed.

This meant that strong circumstantial evidence was pushing us down, and that we should have a hard fight to prove our innocence. Whatever the charge was going to be, it meant either innocent or guilty. The thought that we couldn't be found guilty, as we hadn't done this thing, was a consolation, But, then, if justice miscarried and we were found guilty. . . . It was a thing hardly to be thought of. I tried to push it from me. Probably I should not have done as much as I did if I had been alone in my trouble.

It was with a heavy heart that I went to my girl and told her the situation. I told her that my next appearance in court meant the charge being read, and then my probable remand in custody until the trial began, so that I should not see her until it was over, and if the worst came to the worst and I was found guilty — I had to tell her everything.

It nearly broke her heart, poor girl, and mine also. But I told her that we must both be very brave, and she was, thank God! She promised that, whatever happened, she would always be waiting for me. And she promised to visit me whilst I was in custody. I shall never forget those cheery and heart-felt words from the girl who stood by me with such courage and love in my darkest hours. My thoughts will always be with her. No one else will I ever treasure in my heart.

At that time my companion and I needed a little help and a little courage, and, thank God, we both received it, he from his girl and I from mine. God bless them both.

Perhaps I am dwelling too much on what she was to me then, but it eases my heart to speak of how that dear girl gave me hope throughout those weeks of mental torture.

Every day she went with her aunt to their place of worship to pray for my acquittal. On the night before I appeared in the police court for the last time she gave me a talisman which meant that no ill luck could befall me.

With this good luck and "I shall never forget" ringing in my ears as I said good-bye to her, I left, not knowing if there was going to be a future.

At court next day the registrar read the charge out to us individually before a large crowd. One sentence sticks in my mind — "that we did murder the said beggar by throwing him into the creek." Other formalities over, we were asked if we had anything to say, to which we both pleaded "Not guilty." We both made short verbal statements, being the true story of what we did that morning of December 1st, 1935.

I said:

"I am not guilty. On the early morning, of December 1st, 1935, I accompanied the probationary sergeant to Sing-Keipang and Point Road corner, a report having been made that a beggar was lying there. I had accompanied him because he had recently been transferred to the Kashing Road district and did not know the roads. We were taking the beggar to St. Luke's Hospital. Before we arrived at the hospital, the beggar appeared to have recovered. As the hospitals will not admit beggars unless seriously or dangerously ill, I decided to place the beggar on a beggar boat, several of which lie in the Hongkew Creek.

"I ordered the car to turn back, and on Fearon Road placed the beggar on a beggar boat. I did not throw him in, but put him on the boat, and when I left he was on that boat. I proceeded back to Kashing Road Station and arrived there a little before 3 a.m.

"That's all, your honour."

My companion said:

"I am not guilty, your honour. At about 2.30 a.m. on December 1st, 1935, I reported for coffee. At that time a message was received reporting a sick beggar on Sing-Keipang and Point Road. I then said to Sergeant Peters probably it was the same beggar I had seen previously. Sergeant Peters detailed me to go and see to this beggar.

"Being new to the district and not sure of the road, he said he would accompany me. We picked up the beggar and were taking him to St. Luke's Hospital. Before we arrived at the hospital, he appeared to have recovered, so we decided to put him on a beggar boat on the Hongkew Creek. We did not throw him into the creek, but lowered him into this beggar boat. When we left, he was still on the beggar boat. We returned to Kashing Road Police Station, arriving there sometime before 3 a.m.

"That's all, your honour."

We were told that we would be remanded in custody until such time as the date was arranged for our trial. We were then taken under escort to our quarters, where we packed a few of our personal belongings.

We were then rushed off to what was to be our home for the next five weeks — the Foreign Section of the Shanghai Municipal Gaol.

X

IT WAS AFTER midday when, having packed a few things, we were ready to proceed to the gaol. People are not normally admitted there between noon and two o'clock, but the officer-in-charge of my station telephoned to the prison authorities and was told to bring us along at about two o'clock. If this had been done, we should have had a little respite and a chance of a decent meal before entering the prison. As it was, however, we started at once. With a look of sympathy this officer said:

"Everything will be all right when you get to gaol; the warders who are your friends will give you a good feed and a smoke."

We might have been going to a charitable institution, not to prison.

When we arrived inside the gaol, we were told to wait until two o'clock, when a certain official would see us. Still trying to be considerate in a completely ineffectual and officious way, our officer asked the warder who received us if he could get us a decent feed and a smoke. The latter replied that it was more than his job was worth to do so, which was certainly the truth.

So we were left to wait with an empty stomach, thankful at last to say good-bye to our escort. He went off with a cheerful "Good luck" on his lips. I'm afraid I didn't wish him the same.

Two o'clock came round, and a Russian medical orderly took us to a room where we stripped and were weighed. In an adjoining room we were examined by a Chinese doctor (this seemed to me an unnecessary indignity) and declared fit for our incarceration in the cells. The gaoler in charge of the Foreign Section of the gaol then interviewed us. He was a good sort, straight, just and lenient and fair in every respect without any favours. I knew him slightly, as we had both been members of the police bowling team. I think this made him extremely careful not to pay me too much attention, which I quite understood. He told us to remember where we were, to abide by the gaol regulations, to tell him any complaints or requests, and as a man he wished us the very best of luck. I know he meant it. After that, we were prisoners awaiting trial and he was the officer in charge of us.

Then we were both taken to our cells, right apart from each other. I was told to hand over my collar, tie, shoe-laces, belt, braces, razor and anything else with which I could possibly commit suicide.

I looked round my new home. The cell was about ten feet long and six feet broad. At one end there was a double-locked grilled door, an absolutely open door of cross-bars that looked straight out on to the corridor. This meant that any passing warder looked straight into the cell and could see the whole of it. Outside this, there was a double wooden door that was closed and locked at night.

Then there was a wooden bench, a mattress about two inches thick and four blankets. It was winter time, and we needed them. A board secured to the wall served as table, and there was a stool secured to the floor. A lavatory completed the cell's equipment.

At first it was terribly cold — so cold, in fact, that I would wrap myself in my overcoat and walk continuously up and down my cell to keep my blood circulating.

About four o'clock in the afternoon of our first day we were brought a cup of something that looked like coffee, smelt like tea and tasted rather like cocoa. We were also given half a loaf of dry bread. Thanks to my friend the escort, that constituted my sole rations that day.

I gazed along the corridor from my cell. It consisted of six cells on either side containing several British subjects and one American. By screwing my neck, I could just glimpse my fellow-officer, and waving my hand, I settled down to my steady tramp, tramp of the cell. At five o'clock the wooden doors were closed and I saw nothing outside until six-thirty next morning. At eight o'clock at night the lights were put out and we tried to sleep.

At six o'clock I was up; and, having neatly folded my bedding as I had been instructed, I stood waiting to go for my wash. This consisted of going to communal wash-basins and having a quick swill. I noticed the other prisoners particularly that first morning. There were Russian vagrants, thieves, pickpockets, a few Britishers and a few other nationals. Later on I found out that my companion had himself often arrested some of the vagrants who were there. This now put him in rather an uncomfortable position. Then I went back to my cell and awaited something to eat.

It came at last — a tin mug of the so-called tea, another mug of gruel and half a loaf of dry bread. A little later we were allowed a library book and an illustrated magazine to read. At first I was delighted to have these, but I soon found that it was too cold to sit and read, and I continued my pacing of the cell until a Russian warder came along and grunted that we were to go into one of the prison yards for an hour's exercise.

What a relief it was, after being cooped up like a chicken in that cell for so many hours, to be able to walk around a large open exercise-ground, breathing some good fresh air! We were strictly forbidden to talk, but I occasionally got a word or two with my fellow officer. On one thing we both agreed: we hoped that we should not have long to wait in this place before our trial.

We were locked in our cells again afterwards, and received a meal about eleven in the morning, consisting of a little meat and vegetables. The superintendent of the gaol visited us at about this time, asking for any complaints. At about four o'clock I received a cup of tea and half a loaf of bread.

This routine went on for a couple of days, and then we were both taken to the civil section of the gaol and put in cells facing one another. We much appreciated this favour, and I believe that the gaoler had a lot to do with it. Anyway, there was a fairly decent bed, a wash-basin and a mirror in these cells and they were an enormous improvement on the previous ones.

We inquired about food, and were told that we were entitled to food from outside if we paid for it. Unbeknown to us, the warders, many of whom were friends of mine, had been trying to get food for us from their own kitchen, but this had been refused.

Although in need of every penny I could muster, I was thinking of buying my food from outside when we were told that a special grant had been made enabling us to receive food from the warders. And what a change it was from prison diet! We had coffee and eggs in the morning and good meals during the day. It helped us a great deal in forgetting our troubles.

From the time that we were charged with murder, our lawyer had obtained the advice of another counsel. He suggested that they should represent us individually, but of course working together. It was agreed that the new lawyer should represent me. I had not seen him yet, but he was going over the case very thoroughly with our first counsel, who was to represent my friend. We had heard nothing as yet concerning the proposed date of the trial. Meanwhile, we would both sit for days writing notes in our cells.

We were allowed to write letters and to receive them, but they were all censored by the gaol authorities. Until then I had not wished to worry my family and relations by telling them of my predicament, but now I decided to write to my sister in England. I didn't want her to learn of it from other sources.

While I was in that gaol, the strict censorship of letters became rather unstuck owing to linguistic difficulties. A Jew who had been born not far from Arabia was in prison for debt. He was a most peculiar fellow. For instance, when being shaved by the prison barber he asked him how much he was in *his* debt. Now, he could speak and write English, but when he wrote to his father he wrote in Arabic. The letter was immediately returned to him by the warder in charge, who said that he couldn't send any communications in cipher. But the man protested that his father could not understand English, that the regulations allowed a prisoner to write to a relation, and that it was up to them to translate his letter. The authorities were in a fine fix. There was no Arabic interpreter at that gaol, and finally they had to let the letter pass.

I had been in prison about five days, and was on exercise in the yards, when I was sent for and told that there was a visitor to see me. I felt that I hardly looked my best, without collar or tie, I had not been shaved since my admittance, and I must have looked a regular tramp.

I was taken to a corridor that was divided in the middle by two strips of fine wire netting, stretched right across from top to bottom, about three yards apart. In between there was another corridor running at right angles, and here a warder paced up and down throughout the interview. Looking across to the other side, I saw my Chinese boy with rather a doleful expression on his face. Perhaps he had come to like me — he had been with me for some years — but I make no pretence of reading the Chinese mind. He would now certainly lose his job. Anyhow, he had brought along some change of clothing for me, and, with surprising and touching forethought, he had gone to my Japanese girl's address and had escorted her to see me. His sympathy for us must have been very real and genuine, for few Chinese would go out of their way to do a kindness to a Japanese. I am happy to think that I must have been a good master for him to do this.

Tears accompanied my girl's first visit, and I suggested that she should not come again; but, with good Japanese spirit, she promised to be brave when she returned next time.

Each week she paid that visit. She talked to me about her aunt and things in general, and always left with a smile. I sometimes had to make a very hurried farewell. But those visits of hers did me more good during those almost unbearable weeks than if a thousand other friends had visited me. My friend also had his girl to see him. The look of happiness and contentment on his face when he returned from seeing her was as good as having a visitor of my own. It made me feel that our imprisonment was an absolute farce, that being behind those bars was simply a bad dream. Then again I would realize the grim reality of it all when one of the detestable Russian warders would come along and say in the harsh official voice which he gloried in using, especially to two British policemen, "Get your overcoats on; exercise in five minutes."

Then we would walk round that large square close behind one another and sneak a few words whenever we could. This helped tremendously; for, leaving the case out of it, we used to talk quickly and slyly about other things, such as what we would do when we were released, of how nice it would be when we were no longer treated as criminals and were free again to talk and smoke just as we liked. Our great anxiety then was how long we should be cooped up in that awful gaol. But we were still quite in the dark about the date of our trial.

Our first lawyer came to see us after we had been there two days, bringing with him good cheer and, thoughtful man, a quantity of magazines. He told me that my counsel would be along to see me later on; meanwhile he was busy studying the case in general.

No other visitors had been to see us, but we could hardly expect to see many of our police friends. Etiquette would not quite allow them to pay a friendly visit to a gaol. In spite of this, however, one of my friends in the Force—an Australian whose care-free colonial manner did much to encourage me—did visit me later on.

When we shaved, we were walked from our cells to a small room, where we were kept under observation. We were also allowed a bath once a week, which was a great luxury.

A Russian prisoner, whose duty it was to keep the baths spotlessly clean, had prepared our first baths. Although it was like sitting in a very large pudding-basin, they were most comfortable. I was very surprised when this Russian came sneaking up to me when I was in the midst of my ablutions, and, making sure that there were no warders near at hand, said, "Give me a cigarette." I told him that I had none, and then he said that he knew we were policemen, and therefore expected us to have such extra privileges as cigarettes.

The curious point was how he had discovered that we were police. But it is amazing the way prisoners find out who everyone is in gaol, and also the happenings in the outside world. I discovered this when on another visit to the bath-house. I had read that day in one of the Shanghai newspapers (which we were allowed to read) of the sad news of the death of King George.

The same afternoon I was thoroughly enjoying my weekly scrub when I heard a soft tread near my bath. Looking up, I saw the prison cook, an Englishman serving a three years' sentence for embezzlement. He seemed very nervous and worried. He hurriedly asked me in a whisper:

"I hear the King has died. Is it true?"

On my reply, he went on:

"Could you tell me when the new King will be coronated?"

Funny as it seemed then, his curiosity had some serious reason in it. He wanted to know the date of the coronation, as the King often grants a kind of amnesty then to various classes of prisoners. But he had forgotten that the mourning had only just begun, and no one had yet thought of the possible time of the coronation.

One day we were told that there was a visitor to see us both. Wondering who it could be, we were taken to a small room adjoining the prison chapel, and there saw the Rev. Dean Trivett from the Cathedral.

I was very thankful when he began to talk about general things, and not of religious matters, as I had expected. We had a very interesting talk with him for quite half an hour. Then he gave us a little spiritual help and advice, and with a parting "Good-bye and be brave," he left. He came to see us again later on, and I thoroughly enjoyed his visits. He was a Canadian, and one of the most popular men in Shanghai amongst the British residents. He was a man, besides being a clergyman.

I have since learnt that persons awaiting trial or on remand in English prisons are allowed to smoke. Not so in Shanghai. Soon after our arrival we asked if we could smoke, and were met with a stern refusal. On repeating our request later on, the gaol superintendent told us that we were not permitted to smoke, but could have a pint of beer a day. Strange as this may seem, it was true. When we complained about it to the visiting board who came round the gaol every fortnight to hear any complaints from the prisoners, they too refused us the privilege to smoke. We also tackled them about the manner in which we were allowed to see visitors. The strips of wire netting between us and our visitors made us feel like monkeys in a cage, and it was a bitter grievance of ours. After a little debate amongst themselves, they said that in future we would be allowed to receive visitors in a small room.

We had to sit on opposite sides of a table, and the warder always made sure that my visitor and I sat at either end, so that it was quite impossible for us to pass anything to one another. I laughed heartily one day when, just as the visit was over and my Japanese girl was leaving the room, I shook her hand. This in itself was a serious crime in the eyes of the warders, but when I snatched a kiss I thought he was going to cry. He besought us not to do anything so drastic again, and I promised not to, and kept my word, otherwise I suppose I should have been refused a visitor again.

About twice a week the foreign section of the gaol was paraded and inspected by a prison doctor. But we were exempted from this parade, and just stood outside our cells, and were questioned by the doctor there.

During those weeks in that Shanghai prison I would lie awake sometimes the whole night, wondering what the outcome of the affair would be. Being innocent, I was not very worried about the verdict, although until we were proved innocent everything seemed uncertain. The prosecuting counsel had built up a very strong case against us, and we knew that we should have to fight tooth and nail to clear ourselves of this outrageous charge.

I also thought about what would happen once the case was over. I knew that, whatever its outcome, my career in the Shanghai Municipal Police Force had come to an end. It was a recognized thing that if a British police officer was charged at the British Court and his case in any way involved the Chinese, there was no hope of his ever being reinstated in the Force. It was generally said that you were cleared of your charge in court, but told to resign.

So all the plans for happiness and marriage, all the castles that I had been building in the air, seemed doomed to fall in ruins whatever the result of my trial. But I thought I saw a silver lining to the clouds. Even if I were compelled to resign from the Force, it was only what I had made up my mind to do six months before this accursed business had started. I thought that I should be able to draw my superannuation money just the same. I knew that I could not expect to get off scot free for my infringement of police regulations, but at the most such petty offences as mine were generally punished by loss of seniority and nothing more. I had never heard of anyone being punished more severely for such "crimes," and I thus thought that I should be deprived of three or six months' seniority. Anyhow, I knew that I should have to resign from the Force, and I expected to be given the usual second-class passage home.

Such thoughts prevented me from worrying too much about the case. Sometimes I would be very happy in my cell, thinking that I should soon be able to carry out my plans of getting married and either going to Japan with my wife or returning home to England.

Although my mind was a little topsy-turvy from thinking of all these plans, I realized that I had to concentrate on one thing, and one thing alone: that was the clearing of my name and the regaining of my honour in the eyes of the law and the public.

With a copy of the case-papers I would sit for hours in my cell with pencil and paper, taking notes and trying to find some means of smashing the prosecution when the test came.

I studied all the evidence, especially that of the principal Chinese witness, the chauffeur, and I noticed many contradictory statements that I brought to the notice of our lawyers. Many of the points that I noticed then came in very useful in court later on.

My friend was not idle either. We used to study a particular part of the case every day. Then we would examine a piece of evidence for an hour or so, jotting down notes and observations. Finally we would check our notes, and at the end of a few hours of such work we felt that there was little need for us to worry about most of the evidence submitted against us. As far as I could see, it was the chauffeur's evidence that formed the most formidable aspect of the case against us. We thus concentrated all our energies on trying to think of means of smashing it.

He had already made various statements in court that contradicted his first written statement. But, from what I could see, if he still doggedly persisted in stating that we threw the beggar into the creek, then the whole issue depended on the interpretation given by judge and jury to the various times of which I have already spoken, and on our word against his.

Then my own counsel came to see me, the new lawyer, Mr. McDonald, whom our first counsel had called in. He told me that he had studied the case very closely, and now wished to impress upon me not to hold anything back. I had nothing whatsoever to hide, nothing that I considered concerned the case and the charge against me, and I told him precisely what I have now written from the time when I reported for duty at 2.30 a.m. on that fateful morning. I did not tell him, however, any more than I had told our first counsel, the real reason why I had been late. I considered that a private matter having nothing whatsoever to do with subsequent events. Perhaps I did wrong in making this reservation, but I wanted to keep my girl's name out of the whole thing, and in a way I didn't realize then how serious it all was. I certainly didn't foresee how the prosecution would twist and distort the truth in this respect, or perhaps I should say how they would give an unpleasant interpretation of the facts owing to my silence.

Anyhow, on my telling him that I had nothing to hide, Mr. McDonald looked me very straight in the face for a few moments and then he finally said:

"Look here, Peters, you must understand that this is a very serious business, and as your counsel I wish, with your permission, to ask you something."

For one moment I thought that he was going to ask me why I had really been late that night, but he went on:

"When we are in court, I want to stick out for murder or nothing. That is to say, if you killed this man, then you must pay for it; but if you did not, then I as your lawyer for the defence will do all in my power to see that you are acquitted."

I agreed with everything that he said, because I knew that I had not done this thing, and I did not wish to cringe behind any pleas of manslaughter. So after a long talk about my character in the Royal Tank Corps and the case in general, he left me, and I returned to my cell with the words "*Murder or nothing*" ringing in my ears.

Then at last it came. One day the inspector in charge of the gaol brought an official letter from the Supreme Court stating that we were to attend court on February 5th, 1936, to stand our trial on a charge of murder.

Somehow I felt very happy now that I knew at last something definite. I think that we received this news about a fortnight before our trial.

I know I used to count the hours from that time onwards, and to keep myself busy and warm (it was very cold in those cells) I asked for some floor polish and a cloth, and I soon had the stone floor of the cell looking quite respectable. Having nothing to do physically, cooped up in that cold and cheerless cell with only that one hour's exercise a day, it was a pleasure to polish away at that floor.

One night after we had all been shut in by the warders and the outer wooden doors had been closed, I heard a loud conversation taking place between some warders and a newcomer to the prison. After a while I heard the doors click, and knew that another prisoner had been locked in. This was just opposite to me, and although I could not see, I could hear him pacing up and down his cell and muttering to himself.

There was silence for a while. He must have been in bed for a few minutes when he began to moan. I thought he must be ill, but then he began to sob and to repeat over and over again the words, "It's cold! Oh, it's cold!"

The warders came to attend to him, and I think they gave him an extra blanket, but this groaning went on throughout the night. Not being at that time a very heavy sleeper, it kept me awake, and finally I shouted out to him to go to sleep and stop crying like a baby, that he would get used to it and that the first ten years were the worst. Next morning I found out that he was a Russian in gaol for debt.

At about this time a president and vice-president of a large bank in Shanghai were on remand in gaol awaiting trial for fraudulent conversion. It was rather a sad case, particularly for the investors. The life savings of many poor people were involved, and I remember noticing later that only a very small dividend was ever paid out. The president was an oldish man, an American, who had once been Chairman of the Shanghai Municipal Council. It seemed strange to me that the man who might well have been my employer was in the same prison as myself. I think it must have been a severe blow to him, and he was somewhat ill. Reading the newspapers in my cell one morning I saw that both he and the vice-president were said to be in very comfortable rooms, the very ones which we had occupied for our first two or three days. The report went on to say that they were being well looked after and had private bathrooms allotted to them near their cells. I could have given that newspaper a very different version of their position, and the true one. For instance, their private bathrooms were nothing but the communal bath-house with the large pudding-basin baths in which all the prisoners washed. Perhaps these inaccurate newspaper reports prevent relatives worrying about such people. But if they knew the truth, some protest would be made, and something done to improve the prisoners' conditions there.

I felt nearly mad at times from the monotony of that gaol life, with the uncertainty of all things pounding away inside me, except for those weekly visits that never failed to put fresh hope and courage into me.

Then one morning my Chinese boy brought me some decent clothes. Until then I had been wearing some old flannel trousers and an ancient jacket. It was the day before our trial was to begin. A good hot bath, shave and general clean up the next morning, and we were dressed and ready long before our escort arrived. Then at about nine o'clock a warder called us, and we were taken and handed over to two foreign sergeants who were waiting to escort us to Court. The one in charge advanced with handcuffs, but he put them away when I spoke to him as a friend (they were both friends of mine), and told him not to be silly, as I should not run away nor abuse any privileges.

We all jumped into a police car and drove out of the gaol. It was a real pleasure to again breathe what seemed fresh pure air, and we both heaved sighs of relief at even this few moments' respite. As we had a ride of about fifteen minutes to the court, we were offered cigarettes. They were a bitter disappointment. I know mine tasted like a burnt rag. I survived it, however, but my companion felt ill all that day.

Our escort started to ask us innumerable questions, but I'm afraid that they didn't interest me very much. The feeling of freedom after that prison was all I needed. It excelled everything else.

Arriving at the court, we were taken up a large flight of steps into a corridor outside the court-room.

About ten minutes before the trial began, we entered and became the subject of the murmurings of a crowded court. Looking round, I noticed a large crowd of policemen, friends of us both. This in itself was a pleasure, but more so than ever when they tried to encourage us by gestures and whispers.

The British community were there in force — a large gathering of men, women and young girls. It was a pleasant feeling to think that you had some people there helping to share your troubles.

In the front row of the court sat the proprietor of the "Dutch Village Inn," an establishment which was patronized by many members of the Police Force. You could always get good music, good food and last, but not least, good beer there. We called the proprietor Mr. Van and I shall never forget with what feelings of gratitude I heard him say, "Hallo, Peters; good luck." Those little things helped an awful lot. There was only one face that I missed — I had told her to keep away during the trial.

We both went into the box, and a little later the judge entered. Everyone stood up and then sat down again, but my companion and I remained standing.

We were, of course, being tried by the British Supreme Court with a British judge and jury. Certain men of the British community were there in court, and from among them the jury was to be chosen which would finally decide our fate. Our counsel told us that if we disagreed with any choice, we could say so, and they would be stood aside until twelve were picked. This was at last done.

The opening proceedings then followed their usual course. The judge explained their duties to the jury, and told them how they would have to live together in an hotel until the case was over.

From where we stood we could see the exhibits. There were our statements, various official books from the charge-room, some photographs, some medical bottles and jars containing portions of the beggar's lungs, his clothes and several other items.

The atmosphere seemed quite different from that of the police court. The judge and the counsels all looked very severe in their robes. Our own counsel, in whom we had every confidence and who had given us faith and courage, now looked just a spoke in the wheel that was beginning to turn to happiness or despair. The jury who had the task of deciding our fate looked very grim and business-like. Then there were the set, intent faces of all the people who had come to witness what was already beginning to be called one of the most sensational cases involving Englishmen in Shanghai of recent years.

Then the trial began, and the routine of the police court started all over again, only in a far more severe and strictly judicial atmosphere.

The Crown Advocate summarized the case for the Crown and the facts for the prosecution in the following words:

"On the night of November 30th last year, or I should state, on the night of November 30th and December 1st, because it was shortly before three o'clock on the morning of December 1st that the first scenes of this trial were laid, two police constables, Nos. 1728 and 1193, were patrolling along Point Road. Point Road is in the area which is under the jurisdiction of Kashing Road Police Station, and is situated in the Northern District of Shanghai. As they were patrolling, they came across a Chinese male person whom they described as being of the beggar class, who was lying at the side of Point Road, where Sinkeipang Road runs into it.

"They will tell you that they endeavoured to rouse this man and to get him on his feet, but that they were unsuccessful in this, and that they formed the opinion that he was very sick, inasmuch as he was groaning and foaming at the mouth. Therefore they betook themselves to a street telephone-box and put a call through to the Kashing Road Station. That call was received by a Chinese clerk who is employed at that station, who passed the information on to the accused Peters. Now, I must pause here, gentlemen, to tell you what the organization of that station was at that time.

"Inspector Bennett was in charge of the station, and under him were a number of subordinate officers. On that evening in question, Sergeant Peters was not very prompt in appearing for charge-room duty, and his place was taken by a Russian sergeant. He came in later. The probationary sergeant, who was on patrol duty, came in for a cup of hot coffee, and some little time before 3 a.m. a telephone call was received, as a result of which Peters told the Russian sergeant to proceed to the creek on Point Road to pick up a beggar. This order was countermanded when the probationary sergeant remarked that he had seen a beggar there, and Peters said he would accompany the other accused to the scene in a station motor-car. It was strictly against orders for the accused Peters to leave the charge-room.

"The chauffeur will be called, and will testify that he drove the accused to Sinkeipang and Point Roads, where they picked up a beggar and placed him on the running-board of the car. They then entered the car, but after he had driven them as far as Fearon Road, he will tell the court how they ordered him to return to Fearon Road, near the Yuhung Road Bridge, where he saw the accused throw the beggar into the creek. They then returned to the station.

"Evidence will also be given by a hawker, who lives in a house at this point and who, rising early as was his wont, saw the car in the middle of the road, and two foreigners near it, flashing their torches into the creek. Suspicious, he mentally took the number of the car, and after they left, went over to the creek, where he saw a man going through the actions of drowning. He got help and rescued the man, who was taken to St. Luke's Hospital in a Hongkew Fire Station ambulance.

"The beggar was subsequently identified in hospital by Police Constables 1728 and 1193.

"Inquiries were subsequently started by the Hongkew Police Station, as a result of which these proceedings were instituted."

Those were the main points in the opening summary of the case for the prosecution. Everyone seemed to follow it very closely. I know that a judge must understand every point in the case that he is trying, but I must remark what a comprehensive and profound knowledge the judge at our trial had of the whole case. It was quite extraordinary how he would remember small points. He also conducted the whole trial in an absolutely fair and impartial manner.

All that first morning we were left standing. In the circumstances it was a great strain. I began to wonder if we were going to have to stand throughout the whole trial, but in the afternoon the thoughtful foreman of the jury asked the judge if we might both be allowed to sit down.

During the tiffin adjournment we were taken back to our old station, and were given lunch under police escort at our fellow-station-officers' expense.

This being our first appearance there for over a month, we were bombarded with questions throughout the meal, but our motto was to say as little as possible then. I particularly noticed the attitude of the Chinese personnel in the charge-room that day, when I went to see a friend of mine who was on duty.

As I have said before, the Chinese are an extraordinary race, and their minds are a complete mystery to me even now, after years spent in the country. In spite of the charge against us of having murdered one of their countrymen, they seemed genuinely sorry for us and for our troubles. I was greeted almost at once by the Chinese interpreter, who said:

"Hullo, Mr. Peters. This trouble very sorry."

This remark voiced the sentiments of all the Chinese in the charge-room. So spontaneous and unaffected seemed their expressions of sympathy then that I was convinced they had nothing to do with the whole business. I was struck more than ever by the thought that some outside forces had been at work.

Back to court after lunch, the monotonous proceedings of the trial commenced again. The prosecution began to call their witnesses, the chauffeur being one of the most important.

This man, Doo Sung-foo, the driver of the station car, testified to seeing us throw the beggar into the creek. After describing the route taken from the station to Point Road, near Sinkeipang Road, he said that we alighted from the car and walked behind it.

He spoke in Chinese, of course, but his evidence can be summarized thus:

"A moment or two later I saw them carrying a beggar towards the car. So far as I could see, they picked the man up at the entrance to an alley-way in Point Road. They drove slowly towards Nanzing Road, and I thought they were making for Hongkew Police Station, where beggars are usually taken. At Nanzing Road corner, however, Peters suddenly asked me where I was going, and ordered me to turn round. I drove towards Fearon Road, and between Yalu and Yuhung Roads was ordered to stop.

"They then got out of the car, and taking hold of the beggar's arms and legs walked to a point in front of the car and threw him into the creek."

Using the interpreter as a dummy, he then demonstrated to the court and jury how we had done this. Asked whether he had heard anything after this, Doo replied that he heard the water make a noise which sounded like "wah" and "pah." He said that he felt "sorrowful in the matter," and turned his head away, as he did not like to see the man thrown into the creek. His evidence ended with a description of how he had heard the door of the car close behind him and had driven back to the station.

He never attempted to explain why he had not tried to prevent us from drowning his countryman or why he had not reported the matter until questioned days later. His only excuse was that we were his superior officers! Our high rank was supposed to cover everything.

During the trial both at the police court and the Supreme Court, the prosecution laid particular emphasis on the beggar's dying declaration as evidence against us. Our counsel strongly protested against this, and said that it was quite unjustifiable for it to be used at all. The registrar in the police court had left the final decision on this matter to the judge, and he, after quoting various legal authorities on such questions, declared the document void.

This was not entirely to our benefit. The whole time that this legal battle was going on our only witness, the patient in the hospital who had heard the beggar's first statement, was standing by ready to give evidence on our behalf. But permission for him to be used as a witness entirely depended on whether the dying declaration was allowed or not. When this document was declared invalid and entirely wiped out by the judge, we were deprived of our one and only witness.

The case dragged on throughout the week until Saturday. Innumerable witnesses were called and questioned, and we now had another week-end in the cells to look forward to. The jury too began to look rather unhappy, as they had all been away from their homes for a week, and they had hoped to get back to them on Sunday.

It was rather a joke when some of them asked if they could attend a football match that afternoon, and others asked if they could visit their homes. The judge replied that they could all go to the football match or all go to their homes—that was their respective homes in a body—as they must all be together whatever they did. This was considered rather inconvenient in some cases.

Another incident that seems rather funny to me now, although it didn't then, occurred towards the end of that week. I was standing outside the court building, waiting for the afternoon session, under police escort as usual, when I saw my counsel coming towards me with an air of some secrecy.

Following on behind was my good friend the inspector in charge of my old station, looking like a sleuth following a good clue in the illustration to some detective story. The case for the prosecution was now nearing its end, and it was thought that I should probably be cross-examined that afternoon. My lawyer asked me how I was feeling, and I replied, "O.K." He then stealthily brought out a flask of whisky from under his court robes. Having obtained the rather dubious consent of the inspector, who would have objected if he had dared, he handed it to me and told me to share it with my companion if we felt like it. But he made me promise to return the flask to him, as it had once saved his life when in France in 1916. I took it, feeling that I did not require any whisky to keep me going, but as the trial went on, it turned out that I should not be cross-examined that afternoon. However, we drank the whisky. When the session was over, my counsel came dashing up, afraid of losing his flask, and I fear he thought that we had consumed the whisky rather on false pretences, as I had not given any evidence. Anyhow, I noticed that I did not receive a fresh supply when I finally went through my cross-examination.

I started off by making the following statement:

"On the night of November 30th and December 1st, I went on duty at 2.20 a.m., although I should have done so at midnight."

Here the prosecuting counsel asked:

"Have you anything further to say about this?"

"I had business to contract and was late on duty. Clerk Yuan reported to me that a beggar was lying sick in Sinkeipang and Point Roads. I had had previous reports of sick people requiring ambulances which turned out to be fictitious. I decided to send someone to find out if it was a genuine case. I first detailed Sergeant Makovetsky to this duty, but on the probationary sergeant remarking that the man was probably one he had seen on his rounds, I told him to go instead, and said I would accompany him, first, because this man, who was new to the district, was not sure of the way, and secondly, because I wanted to satisfy myself that it was a genuine case. I wanted to make sure whether I should have to send for the ambulance or not.

"We alighted from the car and looked around, and saw a man lying outside an alley-way on Point Road at the rear of the car. We looked at the man and nudged him. He made very little response. We assisted him to the car. I told the chauffeur to drive to St. Luke's Hospital. On the way there the man appeared to recover slightly and to move about, so we decided to place him in Chinese territory somewhere.

"I gave orders for the car to turn round, and we proceeded north along Fearon Road until we arrived somewhere between Yuhung and Yalu Road bridges. There I saw several boats lying in the creek, one of them, I knew, being a beggar boat.

"A beggar boat is a boat about twenty feet long, of a dirty and dilapidated appearance, with a cloth cover in the centre.

"The car stopped in the middle of the road. My companion then got out. The beggar was then sitting on the running-board. The probationary sergeant came round the rear of the car and I got off the running-board. We then walked to the creek, looked at the boat and decided it was quite safe to put him there.

"We then went back to the beggar. I held his left arm and my companion his right, and we walked him to the railing alongside the creek. There we sat him down. We then lowered him on to the rear portion of the boat.

"We went back to the car and returned to the station, where I returned to the charge-room."

That is the essential part of my opening statement. Then the following cross-examination ensued.

"Why did you enter the words 'On arrival, the beggar had left' in the station's telephone book?"

"Because I had committed a breach of police regulations by going into the Hongkew District. It is the usual custom to place beggars in the Chinese Territory."

"You admit that your proper hours of duty on November 30th and December 1st were from twelve o'clock midnight to eight o'clock in the morning? — "I do."

"You admit that you turned up for duty two and a half hours late?" — " Yes."

"You told us you were delayed over business?" — "Yes."

"What was that business?" — "Private business." (After some hesitation.) "I had business with a girl friend."

"When you arrived at the station, you were a little elevated?" — "What did you say? I was normal."

"I put it to you, you were not?" — "I was normal."

"Is it true that it is absolutely essential for the charge-room sergeant not to leave the station?" — "That is the order."

"And you will agree with me it is absolutely contrary to regulations for you to leave a patrol sergeant in charge of the station when you are on duty?" — "Yes, but this particular time was Sergeant Makovetsky's coffee time."

I have quoted this part of my cross-examination just as it stands in a report of the case. Of all my trial, it was the hardest and cruellest part for me to bear. I knew I had done wrong in breaking police regulations, and was willing to pay for that mistake. But because I had kept silent on this point, the prosecution made quite unjustifiable suggestions and insinuations and, I admit, blackened my character out of my own mouth.

But why should they have adopted such a conception of the truth simply because I said nothing about it myself? As I have mentioned, I also refrained from telling my own counsel the reason for my being late that night, and it is only now that I have thought it right to tell the whole truth, now that I have been acquitted of that terrible charge, now that I have won my battle for my life, my freedom and, I hope, my honour in every sense. My only reason for not speaking more openly then was that I wanted to keep my future wife's name out of the court proceedings. Probably in the circumstances I was wrong, and people will say that only in novels do these things happen; but if they would put themselves in my position then, burdened with so many troubles, I am sure they would have done the same thing.

It was pretty heart-rending thinking what the public would surmise from reading my version of why I was late — "business with a girl friend." How different was the pathetic truth! I should not have been late if I had not lost all sense of time in planning my future life and happiness with my intended wife. I can hardly bear to think even now what those moments have cost me. But

I have thought and pondered since. I wonder, had the prosecuting counsel known the true reason for my being late and why I refused to mention it, if he would have dealt with the subject in the same way, lowering my character in the eyes of everyone and trying to destroy my self-respect. I hope for his own sake that he would not have done so.

But to resume the cross-examination:

"You admit you were told there was a beggar in a very serious state on the corner of Sinkeipang and Point Roads?" — "No, merely a sick beggar."

"I put it to you, you were told the man was in a very serious condition?" — "I was not."

"You are suggesting that this man, a police sergeant out on patrol, didn't know the way back to the station?" — "He had only been in the district for five days. He was not sure if he could find Sinkeipang and Point Roads. A Chinese sergeant was with him on patrol."

"You seriously suggest that you found it necessary, in contravention of your orders, to leave the station in charge of Makovetsky and to take the probationary sergeant to find a man at a point on his own beat?" — "I did not only go to show him where it was, I wanted to go to find out if this beggar was really sick. When the man appeared to recover somewhat, I decided to place him in Chinese Territory; the Hongkew Creek was the nearest and most convenient, so I placed him in a beggar boat."

"I put it to you that the Hongkew Creek is not Chinese Territory?" — "As far as I know, all waterways in the Settlement are Chinese Territory. That is what I have been taught."

"Why did you write 'On arrival the beggar had left' in the telephone book instead of 'The beggar was placed in Chinese Territory'?" — "The latter entry would have given rise to questions being asked as to when, where and why this was done, in the course of which it would have transpired that I had left the station. I made the entry 'on arrival, the beggar had left' because it would automatically stop any questions which might lead up to a discovery that I had both been out of the station while on charge-room duty and out of the district. I admit making false entries in the Occurrence Book in order to hide the fact that I had been late in coming on duty."

The only other part of my cross-examination of any importance now is my final statement:

"I can ascribe no motives to the chauffeur's having stated that he saw us throw the beggar into the creek."

My companion was cross-examined later, but not subjected to such gruelling questions as I had been.

Then the Crown Advocate finally summed up the case for the prosecution. After a little of the usual stuff about its being his painful duty and so forth, he said:

"I submit, gentlemen, that you can come to only one conclusion—that Peters was in the charge-room that night and that he came, in dereliction of his duty, two and a half hours late, and that on his arrival he proceeded to break all the rules and regulations which he possibly could."

He then took the jury over the evidence of the prosecution, laying particular stress on the evidence of the chauffeur and the hawker. Regarding my explanation of why I had made the entry "On arrival, the beggar had left" in the telephone book, he went on:

"You cannot believe that he wrote a deliberate mis-statement in that telephone book for the reason he mentioned. You have seen him in the box under examination which, I submit, necessarily must be closely put. . . . I submit that the attack of pneumonia had materially assisted in bringing about the man's death. . . . Therefore, gentlemen, although there is much more that I could say, my time is limited, and I do not want to keep you here listening to me too long. I submit that, however painful it may be to you, you will—as I know you will—come to the only reasonable conclusion, that both the prisoners at the bar are guilty of murder."

Knowing that I had not done this thing, these terrible words left me cold and stunned, but in some way their full import did not reach me.

At last my counsel made his speech in my defence.

"If you believe the case for the prosecution in its entirety, then my client committed murder, and he must suffer the penalty which murder entails—he must forfeit his life, and that life is now in your hands.

"There is no halfway street, no question of manslaughter or assault. It is murder or nothing. If you disbelieve or are not satisfied beyond all reasonable doubt of any material point in the case for the prosecution, you have only one course open, and that is to find my client not guilty.

"Who the sinister figure or figures in the background of this prosecution are, none of us know."

The Judge: "Do you suggest the police? What are you suggesting?"

My Counsel: "No foreigner. No one in this court. No foreigner."

"On November 30th, Peters was like Samson of old. He dallied too long with some Delilah that night, and then attempted to cover himself. (*Even my own counsel, you see, had by then accepted this distorted version of the truth.*) He not only attempted to cover himself, but also attempted to shield others, and has suffered for it more than any member of the jury would in similar circumstances in the normal course of events."

My companion's counsel, in speaking in his defence, made several important points.

He submitted that it was not reasonable to infer that we, the accused, bore any malice towards the deceased beggar. It could not be suggested that we committed a crime of this nature, which could only be committed by a man or men deprived of all sense of social justice and a total disregard of the laws of humanity.

"Throughout the whole affair the two accused have acted openly. It is suggested by the Crown that they committed the murder under the eyes of another policeman of the same race as the deceased, and have yet never said a word to the chauffeur either then or since.

"It is a psychological fact that whenever anyone sees something happen and reports it, he almost invariably embellishes it in the course of his story. The more uneducated a man is, the more he calls his imaginative powers into play. He even comes to believe in it himself, and then deliberately creates those links of evidence necessary to carry conviction in the mind of another person."

Then at last we came to the judge's summing up of the whole case.

He started with a long introduction on various legal points for the benefit of the jury. Then he went on:

"In order to put the facts of the case clearly before you, I propose in the first place to give you, from my notes, a time-table of the events alleged to have happened, commencing at 2.30 a.m. on December 1st, and taking you up to 2.45 p.m. on December 6th.

"You can take it from me that November 30th was a Saturday.

"On Sunday morning at about 2.30 two Chinese policemen were walking along Point Road on their beat. There they found a beggar on the ground—a Chinese beggar. The two policemen went to a telephone-box and put through a call to the Kashing Road Police Station, which was their station in their district.

"Now, the next time on the time-table is given in the evidence of Clerk Yuan; he was the interpreter on duty at the Kashing Road Police Station. He was the person who received this telephone message. He says, '2.45 was the time I entered the call in my book.'

"The next time is found in the evidence of Sergeant Makovetsky. You will remember that Sergeant Makovetsky went on duty at 12.30 a.m.—charge-room duty. He should have been on patrol duty, but he was called in. He says, 'I saw the probationary sergeant come to the station about 2.35 a.m. About five minutes later Sergeant Peters came to the station.'

"Makovetsky says that it was nearly 2.45 a.m. when Peters took the key of the car and went out. The probationary sergeant left after Peters—maybe ten or fifteen seconds after. They came back to the charge-room about 3 a.m.

"The chauffeur—Doo Sung-Foo—says, 'I drove the car out at 2.45. I was away from the station until about 3.05. I think we were about twenty to twenty-one minutes in all.'

"The hawker, Zung Ching-Sung, says, 'I left my house just at 3 a.m.'! The policeman says that he was on patrol duty, and that Haining Road and Fearon Road corner was his 'hour point.' He stood there until 3.03 a.m. He then walked on. At Haining Road near Fearon Road he heard shouts of 'Save life.'

"He thinks it was then about 3.07 a.m. That constable heard the cry and ran towards Fearon Road. He saw a man lying on the ground and six people standing by. He spoke to Zung Ching-Sung, and then went back to Haining Road Bridge and put through a telephone call. He says it took five minutes to telephone.

"Now C.P.C. 1665 was then on duty in the charge-room of Hongkew Police Station. He says he received a telephone message at 3.10.

"Mr. Hourihan, Fire Officer of the Shanghai Fire Brigade, who was on duty at the Hongkew Fire Station, tells us that the call for the ambulance came at 3.12.

"Dr. Lum of St. Luke's Hospital, and also Student Nurse Hoo Ching-Sung, can only give their times approximately. They both say that the ambulance arrived at St. Luke's 'about 3.30 a.m.'

"*Monday afternoon, December 2nd.* Patient was shaved and had his beard cut, while he was unconscious.

"Inspector Bennett received a report from Chinese Inspector Tsau Ching-van. As a result he made inquiries, examined the station's books, sent for C.P.C. 3067, the chauffeur, took a statement from the latter and reported to Captain Kennedy. Captain Kennedy came to the station about 7 p.m. and also made inquiries.

"It is important to note that the chauffeur's statement was given to Inspector Bennett and to Captain Kennedy before the accused had been asked to say anything or were interviewed in any way.

"*7.30 p.m.* Captain Kennedy said Peters made a statement which was taken down and he signed.

"*8 p.m.* The probationary sergeant came into Inspector Bennett's office with a written statement and gave it to him. Shortly after 8 p.m. Captain Kennedy made certain requests to the River Police.

"*Tuesday, December 3rd, 5 a.m.* Inspector Bennett went down to Fearon Road and spoke to a detective of the Customs River Police. The chauffeur was taken along, pointed out a place, and on this spot dragging operations were commenced. Deaville* was left behind by Bennett, who returned to the creek shortly before 6 p.m. There he saw Zung Ching-Sung (the hawker). Deaville said he saw the Customs officer conversing with a woman and a man (the man was Zung Ching-Sung). Dragging operations then stopped.

"Again it is important to note that Inspector Bennett interviewed Zung Ching-Sung some hours before the two accused handed him their statements.

"It has been suggested to you by counsel for the first accused that both the chauffeur and this witness, Zung Ching-Sung, had been told what to say in their evidence, and that there were some sinister figures in the background working against the accused.

"Having regard to the fact that Inspector Bennett had interviewed both the chauffeur and Zung Ching-Sung hours before either of the accused had ever mentioned a beggar boat or admitted that they had been on Fearon Road that night, you will probably find little difficulty in arriving at the conclusion that little weight can be given to such a suggestion.

"*8.45 a.m.* McFee** took Zung Ching-Sung to the St. Luke's Hospital, where he, Zung, identified a patient as being the man he had pulled out of the creek.

"*10.30 a.m.* Dr. Tucker examined the patient and found him suffering from double pneumonia.

---

*One of the detectives working on the case.
** The detective in charge of the case.

"11 *a.m.* C.P.C. 1193 and 1728 were taken by Bennett to the hospital. 1728 said the patient was similar to, and 1193 positively identified him as, the beggar they had seen on Point Road.

"12 *noon.* Bennett was back at the station again, and the two accused handed him two new statements. In these two statements were found the first mention of a beggar boat.

"*Wednesday, December 4th, 5 p.m.* McFee arrested both the accused on warrants issued by the court; they were charged with causing bodily harm.

"*Friday, December 6th, 6 a.m.* According to the evidence of Ting Tsai-ling of St. Luke's Hospital, the patient died. That would be twenty-three hours after he was rescued."

When the judge had finished his summing up with a few more remarks, the jury were told to leave the court to consider their verdict. The court was then adjourned until such time as the verdict should be settled. We were taken into the fresh air outside the court-room, and stood at the top of some steps that led into the grounds of the British Consulate. My counsel had said nothing to me after the summing up, and had only made some encouraging signs.

But our first lawyer, who was now my companion's counsel, had taken more than a business interest in the case. He had, I believe, listened to the judge's summing up with almost as much anxiety as we had. But the result was that he said now that although we should be all right in the end, it was always best to prepare for the worst. Then he mentioned that in his opinion the judge had dwelt rather too much on manslaughter.

I know it was all kindly meant and said with the best intentions, but I would rather not have been told this.

I knew that we should be allowed to appeal and probably be acquitted later. But I thought that if we were once proved guilty of manslaughter, an element of doubt might always remain in the minds of some people, innocent as we were.

I think I began to feel a little reaction then from the whole trial. Until that time I had felt no strain at all, but now that the jury had retired, I began to realize the grim reality of all that I had been through. And still the issue was uncertain. My great fear was manslaughter and a sentence of imprisonment.

I cannot describe my feelings as we waited. My friend and I kept our thoughts to ourselves and spoke encouraging words to one another.

While we were waiting, a young man climbed the court steps towards us. He was an American reporter from a newspaper, the *China Press*. He went up to my companion, and after expressing his sympathies, said, "Have you got any people or relatives in England?"

I was flabbergasted. Although I knew that reporters were always after sensation, I had never expected them to go as far as that. After a few words from us, he soon learned that no information was forthcoming and left. It was about time, or he might have received a little help down those steps.

After waiting for exactly forty-one minutes, we were brought into the box again. The court-room was packed with people to hear the verdict of "the most sensational trial of recent years in Shanghai," as the newspapers called it.

The jury filed into their places with grim faces that gave not a hint as to whether they had found us innocent or guilty.

In intense silence the judge told the foreman of the jury who was standing that a separate verdict was to be given for each of us. Then he said:

"Gentlemen of the jury, how do you find the first accused, Ernest William Peters? Guilty or not guilty?"

Without a pause or a tremor in his voice, the foreman replied: "Not guilty, My Lord."

Amidst the cheering and the shouting that broke out from the whole of that packed court, we quietly shook hands behind the box in which we had been for a week. It was only after repeated demands for silence that the verdict of "Not guilty" for my companion was given out by the judge. Then again the court was in an uproar.

We immediately shook hands with our counsels and thanked them very much for all that they had done for us. Then we shook hands with the jury and received the congratulations of the Assistant Commissioner in charge of the case. After that it was rather a nightmare. Crowds of my police friends gathered round us. My companion was immediately dragged from the court by his girl, and, as one newspaper put it, he was last seen disappearing along the road with his coat-tails flying out behind him.

I was still in court surrounded by crowds of people, all wildly congratulating me. It was a good thing that my girl was not there, as I received sympathetic kisses from some of the girls. But what touched my heart most was the remark of a dear old lady who had waited patiently throughout the whole trial. She came up to me with tears in her eyes and said, "My boy, I am so pleased and so happy. Good luck, my boy!" I treasure that remark.

But there was someone waiting for me with her heart nearly breaking. We had made our plans, and it rather hurts me even now to think that I did not keep them then. I had, of course, agreed to go to her right away if I were acquitted.

What happened was this. I was half dragged out of the court by some police officers, who suggested that I should get away out of the crowds. They took me along to an hotel and gave me a very large whisky and soda. Now that the ordeal was over, I was in a half-dazed state, and I hope I can be forgiven when I say that I did not leave them at once. From there I was taken to a police canteen, where, after receiving more drinks and congratulations, I came to my senses.

It was then about nine o'clock at night, about five hours after the trial had finished. I now realized the terrible suspense that I had been fool enough to cause the sweetest and bravest pal I had. I rushed off, and although we had a wonderful reunion, she certainly reminded me of my promise. She forgave me at last, however; but, woman as she is, she could not forgive the two kind friends who had taken me for that drink.

XI

I HAVE TRIED to tell the true story of this case as far as I, one of the accused, know it. But looking back at the whole thing now, much still seems very strange and uncertain.

But of some things I am quite sure, and about them there is no doubt in my mind. It was unquestionably a case of circumstantial evidence, piling up until by its very magnitude it looked very black against us, and made investigation and action on the part of the authorities inevitable. It was also a case in which coincidence played a large part, so much so that it leaves me stunned at the way apparently unimportant events and thoughtless actions can combine together to cause such tragic results. Then the complicated conditions of police work in Shanghai entered into it. For instance, I doubt whether it could all have taken place in precisely the same way in one of our colonies or dependencies. And finally, there is the Chinese element. The fact that we were English and our supposed victim Chinese created an awkward situation for the authorities, and doubtless made them particularly strict in their treatment of the case. For the sake of British prestige in Shanghai, it was impossible for them to do otherwise. But I feel sure that in the obscure workings of the Chinese mind — that Eastern psychology so difficult for us to understand — lies the explanation of whatever peculiarities it still has.

Of the actual trial itself and its happy result, I will only say that what proved our innocence was obviously the time factor. The judge directed the jury's attention to that, and that is what saved us. Apart from those matters of time, we had so few facts in our favour and, as I have shown, all the witnesses were against us. It says something for the accuracy and attention to minute detail of British justice that we were acquitted by the hands of the clock.

But returning to the case itself, the source of the first scraps of evidence against us is still a mystery. They started the whole train of events that involved us, but what they actually were or who supplied this information we never knew. When preparing our defence, we did our utmost to trace things back to their origin, but we always reached a certain point that brought us up short like a brick wall. We knew that there was something beyond, but we could never discover what it was.

As far as the actual facts went, we knew practically everything after the Chinese Detective Tsau Ching-van had made his first remarks to Inspector Bennett and led him to start inquiries. But we never knew what he said to him, what information he then had, nor how he had obtained it. But as this conversation between him and the inspector was what brought us into the picture in the first place, it was the big point that we puzzled over while in prison, and it still remains a mystery to me.

I shall probably never know the truth about this. I doubt whether anyone will ever find out what actually happened then. We are left, however, with surmise and conjecture. I am going to suggest, therefore, a possible theory.

In my opinion, the whole case started from the chauffeur. I do not mean simply when he was questioned at the station and made his first statement that he had seen us throw a beggar into the water. I am suggesting that he was the source of information against us in the first place—in fact, that he played, perhaps unconsciously, a part in the drama in the very beginning during that fatal quarter of an hour.

Starting from the moment when we actually left the Kashing Road Police Station in the motor-car with that chauffeur, let us concentrate on him, his mind and actions and possible thoughts.

A study of Chinese psychology is quite beyond me. Even after living and working with them for so many years, the mind of the average Chinese still seems like a bottomless well to me.

However much a Westerner thinks that he is beginning to understand them, he is always having to confess surprise at some
unexpected word or action on their part that reveals his own
ignorance. With regard to our chauffeur's mind, therefore, I will
only say that I have found the average Chinese as cunning as a
fox and yet as simple and as imaginative as a very young child.

With regard to his actions, the only time when I can remember
anything peculiar about them was after the beggar had partially recovered and we had decided that he was not ill enough
to be admitted to the hospital. We had then stopped to examine
the beggar; and, on coming to this conclusion and the decision to
put the man on a boat rather than leave him in the street I gave
the chauffeur the order to turn round. *At first he took no notice, and
still proceeded towards the hospital. I had to repeat my order and sign
to him most emphatically to turn about.*

What was the cause of this hesitation on his part? I am quite
sure that he heard my first order well enough, and yet he pretended not to have done so and tried to drive on. Curiously
enough, he stated in court that he had no idea we were on our
way to hospital in the first place. If this were true, then he may
well have become suspicious as to what we were doing with his
fellow-countrymen from the moment when we picked him up
off the road and put him on the running-board of the car. On the
other hand, it seems far more probable that he knew perfectly
well where we were going in the first instance, and became
suspicious when I ordered him to turn the car in the opposite
direction to that of the hospital.

Anyhow, it is a tenable theory that he was in a suspicious
frame of mind at this point and resented my order, thinking that
it meant some harm to the beggar.

It will be remembered that I then directed him along the side
of the creek until I told him to stop on seeing a beggar boat tied
up near the shore. What were his thoughts while doing this? Had
he already made up his mind that we were planning his countryman's destruction?

If those were his thoughts, then they must have been fully confirmed when he saw us carry the beggar to the low iron railings alongside the creek. In his evidence in court he said that he felt "sorrowful in the matter," and turned his head away at this point, as he did not like to see a man thrown into the water. If he actually did that, then it means that when we returned to the car and drove back to the station, our chauffeur had the honest belief and real conviction that *he had seen us throw the beggar into the water.*

He said later that he did not report the matter on returning to the station as we were his superior officers. A curious statement this, and one most difficult to understand. One would have thought that he would have been only too eager to accuse foreigners if he really suspected them of such a crime. On the other hand, the Chinese have a peculiar dread of police proceedings, and perhaps fear of getting himself into trouble was the real motive in his mind for his silence. Or perhaps his suspicions were not quite as strong as I have made them out. Perhaps in a confused sort of way he thought that we had been ill-treating one of his countrymen instead of taking him to hospital, and that was all.

What I suggest happened then goes beyond my previous theories for which I have some data, such as his refusal to obey my order. What follows now is pure surmise and conjecture, an essay in fiction, but something like it must have occurred.

Whilst off duty the chauffeur goes to a tea-shop. As I have mentioned before, the Shanghai tea-shops are great centres of gossip and scandal. The Chinese meet there for their tea-shop conferences, at which they confer on all manner of topics over their cups of tea. Our chauffeur may very well have mentioned to some of his friends the incident of seeing two foreign police officers drown a beggar. It may have set up quite an argument, and various suggestions and solutions may have been put forward.

My next and final conjecture is this. An informer of Tsau Ching-van, the Chinese detective at the Kashing Road Police

Station, was there in this tea-shop and overheard the whole conversation between the chauffeur and his friends. Unbeknown to the chauffeur, he reports the matter to his superior, Tsau Ching-van. The latter in his turn reports to Inspector Bennett his suspicion that something fishy was going on in the station on the night of November 30th — something connected with the station car, two foreign officers and a beggar.

On receiving this information, Inspector Bennett naturally investigates the matter, and starts making the inquiry that formed the first event in the development of the case against us as far as we knew at the time. As far as actual facts go, it still is, and I have simply reconstructed a possible sequence of events leading up to this point.

Bearing my theories in mind, let us proceed a little further, and see what light they throw on subsequent facts.

Inspector Bennett gives orders for the Chinese chauffeur to be questioned. The latter believes that the information which has really come from his own conversation in a tea-shop is public knowledge. Whatever confused suspicions he may previously have had, they now congeal in his mind, and with absolute conviction he makes the statement, from which he never wavered, that *he actually saw us throw the beggar into the creek.*

The case against us is now well under way, and nothing can stop it. As one piece of incriminating and circumstantial evidence after another is produced, the charge against us becomes inevitable, and the authorities have no choice in the matter. With the information and evidence in their hands, they were bound to take action.

Events had got out of control, quite beyond the control of any one man or any group of men, and the whole thing went forward of its own accord, carried by its own momentum.

That is how I look on it in my own mind. There are doubtless many other possible explanations, for we shall never know the truth now. But I think what I have put forward above is more than a probable theory of the way things happened. At least, it fills in what my actual knowledge leaves out, and provides a possible sequence of the events that were to bring us such untold and unnecessary suffering.

But I must now return to what happened immediately after our trial and acquittal.

We were both given a couple of days off as soon as the case was over. After that, we were to know our ultimate fate, which I fully expected to be compulsory resignation.

Meanwhile we were kept fairly busy with our private affairs. We had some sleep to make up, for one thing. Then our kit was still at the gaol. Fetching it gave us a glorious sensation. We knew that we should never be behind those bars again.

We were still receiving congratulations on all sides. For the first few days we could hardly go out into the streets without people waving and smiling at us as we passed. But one man's congratulations I shall never forget. The inspector at our station heartily congratulated us. But then he added with a smile, "Although, Peters, I went all out to fix you." Somehow it made me shudder. The contrast between the present and the past was too great.

Knowing that my career with the Police Force was over, I immediately made inquiries at the British Consulate with regard to the procedure of marriage. Everything proving satisfactory, I decided to await developments. I saw my Divisional Officer, who began to explain my breaches of police discipline before I had been arrested.

Having fully admitted them already, I should now like to add a few further remarks. First of all, there are not many police officers in Shanghai who stick to the routine as strictly laid down in regulations. If they did, the whole work of the Force could hardly be carried out, and certainly not so smoothly. Slight deviations from the beaten track can save a lot of time and trouble.

If that beggar had not jumped into the creek that morning, as I believe he did, things might have been very different. Even if it had become known that I had left the charge-room and my false statements had come to light, as well as the fact that I had placed a beggar in a district not my own, the only punishment, the heaviest punishment that I should have received, would have been the loss of six months' seniority. I made one of those momentous decisions that have quite unexpected consequences. I left the charge-room for reasons that I have already explained, but such actions take place every day in the Force. But because of circumstances quite outside my control, that little molehill has been made into a mountain.

I soon found that the trial seemed to be influencing the authorities against me, although I had been absolutely acquitted. I had an uneasy feeling that I was going to be tried all over again for these breaches of the regulations, so I decided to see the Commissioner of Police. Here I did receive a few kind words. The Commissioner told me that he knew very little about my case, as he had been on leave at the time, but that he fully understood the strain of the ordeal through which I had passed. He added that he was afraid it would be impossible for me to continue in the Force owing to the probable feeling against me amongst the Chinese. I quite understood that, and replied that I was quite willing to resign. Then I inquired about the money due to me from the Superannuation Fund. He was very dubious as to whether I should receive anything except what I myself had put into the fund, but told to tender my resignation, and that he would see the Council.

Finally we saw in Police Orders that our resignations had been accepted, and found that we had been granted a second-class passage home, but that the Council refused to pay us their share of the money due to us from the Superannuation Fund according to the length of our service.

This was a bitter blow, and seemed more than unjust: it was inexplicable. We had not been dismissed from the Force, we had resigned of our own free will. This was proved by the fact that we were granted a second-class passage home, for men dismissed from the Shanghai Police are given only a third-class passage. And yet they withheld our superannuation money.

We had spent most of our own money – that is to say, what we ourselves had paid into the fund – to pay for our counsel, so all that we drew now was the small remainder and our back pay. I decided to appeal against this and consulted my lawyer. He advised me to let the matter drop, suggesting that I had seen enough of courts for the time being, and that it would probably cost money to appeal, and I had practically none then.

But the fact remains, why didn't they dismiss us if our conduct was such that they considered it deprived us of our full superannuation? On the other hand, if they didn't dismiss us, what right had they to deprive us of our full money? I cannot bear to think that they allowed us to resign and gave us a second-class passage home out of sympathy. But no, it wasn't that; it was because the Shanghai Municipal Council wanted to get rid of us as quietly and with as little bother as possible.

So smash went all the hopes that I had been building, for my position then made everything impossible. I explained the whole matter to my girl, who, although heartbroken, was brave enough to promise to wait until I had found my feet again at home, or until I could meet her again in Japan. This blow was the hardest of all. I could probably have forgotten all the hardships and the bad luck connected with the actual case and trial, but this was my love, my happiness, the thing that I had been building for. This I could not, I cannot forget or forgive.

When I had settled several outstanding accounts, I was left with nothing, so I decided to travel home third class instead of second. The rebate on the ticket would help me on my way. It was, of course, quite impossible to think of getting work in Shanghai. Besides the case, an Englishman in that comparatively small community stands small chance of getting a job if he is stranded. A shark of an agent promised to arrange matters for me, and I finally obtained a third-class passage home via Siberia, but with a rebate of ten pounds instead of the thirty pounds that it should have been. I remained in Shanghai a little over a month after my acquittal, and when my sailing date arrived I was completely broke. A few dollars from some friends, and I actually had exactly three pounds nineteen in my pocket when I stepped on to the boat for the long journey to England.

I had kept silent about my leaving, and there were just my girl, her father and a friend of hers to wish me good-bye.

It was a very sad farewell, and with the shout of "I shall never forget" from my girl, the boat started on the first part of the journey from Shanghai to Vladivostock, leaving behind the person I loved most in the world.

I found I was travelling along with a Danish fellow and also a Dutchman. The latter, who had very Communistic views, was going on a short tour of Russia, but the Dane was going home in much the same financial condition as myself. The other passengers were Russians. After a decent trip of five days, we arrived at Vladivostock. Bad luck still seemed to dog me. I had been told that I should get immediate and direct connection throughout the journey. Instead of that, I found that I had to wait two days there.

The compulsory tourist hotel was quite impossible. I found that a plate of soup cost the equivalent of two shillings and sixpence and a loaf of bread four shillings. The Dutchman proved his worth when he invited us to his room in the hotel and gave us food, of which he had plenty. I am afraid I should have been stranded if it had not been for his generosity. Here at this hotel I had to barter for two suit-cases in place of my trunks, because it was impossible for me to pay the excess baggage fees. Half my belongings went with my trunks, and I generally did a bad exchange.

I got a fairly bad impression of Russia at Vladivostock. Everyone seemed to be poor and emaciated. I saw women sweeping the roads. And yet everywhere there seemed to be a sense of happiness in poverty.

At last we left. I had made friends with the Dane, who spoke excellent English. We found that our fellow-travellers in the compartment were a Russian and his wife returning to their home town. He was very ill, and was always bemoaning his fate to us, telling us that he thought he would die before he reached his home. Having just had so much trouble myself, it certainly did not make the burden any lighter to hear his dismal remarks.

Travelling third class across Siberia is no pleasure. We sat on hard wooden seats and slept on them at night. This we had to endure for ten days. Loud speakers all along the train bellowed forth Russian music from morning till night, originating from a gramophone played in a special compartment.

We halted from time to time, and then we used to alight to take a little exercise. I know I was pleased to get back to the warmth of the train. The cold was intense, the rivers were all frozen over; but this did not seem to make any difference to the old women who waited at the various stations trying to sell their goods.

At last we arrived at Moscow. Here it seemed quite another country, very prosperous and busy. So on through Poland, Germany and finally Belgium. My ticket was to Ostend, and I remember asking a conductor about my destination. He told me that the train went direct to Ostend. I dropped off to sleep, and woke up to find myself at a terminus. On alighting, I found that it was Brussels, and that the train did not go to Ostend. Having no money, I had to wait for six hours in the third-class waiting-room. It was a vast place, cold and cheerless. I should imagine that all the criminals in the city were sitting about there and dozing. I did not sleep, but watched what little remained of my belongings.

I arrived at Ostend at about eight o'clock in the morning, and finally travelled over to Dover with a crowd of holiday-makers returning after their Easter holidays in Belgium.

And so at last I reached England twenty-two days after leaving Shanghai, rather proud of managing it without seeking aid from one of the various British Consuls on the way.

And now I have to start a new life, to regain my happiness. That is my one ambition. I must attain it in the near future.

THE END

Peters and Sumiko

First-Hand Notes on the Trial

The China Daily News, Tuesday, June 2, 1936
"Comment on Judd Letter"
Editor, The China Press

Sir: — The following passages appeared in the letter of Mr. W.A. Judd recently published in some of the local papers:

"Peters and I were shown every consideration while being detained pending our trial in the Civil Wing of Ward Road Gaol away from the prison proper."

"Our legal practitioners called whilst we were being detained...often after 5 p.m. and regardless of regulations they were allowed to see us.

If Mr. Judd's above statement is to be taken as truth then it would appear that not even foreign prisoners are treated alike in the Ward Road Gaol. Prisoners under criminal charges may be lodged in the Civil Wing and prison regulations may be disregarded at will by those in charge.

Mr. Judd's statement must be true for it was based partly on his own testimony that he and his associate were acquitted.

It was pointed out to me by a doubting Thomas friend that the statements of Mr. Judd and Mr. Peters do not seem to agree and it was held that one of them may have even fibbed. It was further argued that if inaccuracies or untruths could have crept in on such a simple matter as prison treatment, etc. how could they be depend upon to give a truthful and accurate account of what actually did happen that wintry night when a poor Chinese beggar received his fatal immersion in the Soochow Creek?

I would attribute the discrepancies to the inaccuracies of the reporters or to cable mutilation and would abide without the slightest doubt by the decision which was so favorably received by some of the British Community where the decision was loudly applauded, creating thereby a precedent in the annals of British jurisprudence.

Moreover, even if our ex-police officers were guilty of the crime they were charged with they did very little harm except to their own conscience and to the prestige of the nation from whence they came. The victim, the poor beggar, was beyond harming. His lot was miserable and his death was his release.

Kao Kwok
Shanghai, June 3, 1936

The China Press, Saturday, May 16, 1936
"Former S.M.P. Sergeant In Dover Talks of Trial Here"
E.W. Peters Says Jail Cell Tiny, Cold and Food Scanty;
Man Freed On Murder Count Declares "I Will Not Whine"

While William Alfred Judd, former probationary sergeant of the Shanghai Municipal Police, is now working in Shanghai as a private detective. Ernest William Peters, former S.M.P. sergeant who was freed with Judd last February of charges of having murdered a beggar, is now back home in England, ready to start life over again and with very little in the way of capital to help him along.

According to a Dover newspaper, Peters reached that city on April 15 with only 11 pence and a half-penny in his pocket. He had returned to England by way of the Trans-Siberian Railway.

Peters and Judd figured prominently in the headlines of local newspapers early this year when they were tried before Judge A. G. Mossop and a jury of 12 men on a charge of having murdered

Mau Teh-piau, a beggar, by throwing him into Hongkew Creek early one morning in December. After a trial lasting more than a week the jury turned in a verdict of "not guilty."

HELD IN DETENTION CELLS

Both men were given their freedom on bail during the preliminary investigation held before Registrar C.H. Haines in H.M. Police Court, but were sent back to a detention cell when charges of murder were preferred against them.

On his arrival in Dover, Peters granted a press interview, the first he gave since his arrest. The interview follows:

"I will not whine," he said, "although I have lost everything. My job has gone. I have forfeited the pension I was looking forward to at the conclusion of my police service.

"I had been promoted sergeant after only six years' service, and I was expecting further promotion. I left the Tank Corps with an exemplary character, and joined the Shanghai police. For a time I was with the riot squad, and took part in many fierce fights."

Referring to the hardships of his journey across Russia and Siberia, he related: "Many days I was hungry, and the hard boards were none too comfortable. And all this was on top of the five weeks I spent in a Shanghai prison. The story really starts in the early hours of the first day of last December. I was on duty in the station which I was attached. Another officer new to the district was with me. News reached us that a Chinese was lying sick near a creek. Night after night we had received similar messages from Chinese anxious to receive attention.

Off we went to see this latest report. Ordinarily the other officer would have gone alone, but as he was new to the district I accompanied him. We found a Chinese named Mau Teh-piau. There seemed little wrong with him, so we carried him to the side of the Hong-kew creek and put him into one of the scores of "beggar boats" that lie close to the bank.

"Bed Hard...Food Scanty"

"We had to lean over a railing and drop him about two feet. He had been taken to the spot in a police car driven by a Chinese police driver, who later made a statement that the other officer and I deliberately threw Piau (Mau) into the creek. Piau (Mau) was fished out of the creek, but evidence was produced at the trial proving that Piau (Mau) was seen after we had left the spot, and that he threw himself into the creek because he was starving and destitute. But Piau (Mau) died in hospital, and I was arrested and put on my trial accused of murder.

"At first I was granted bail, but subsequently, and until I came before the Supreme Court, I spent five weeks in a Shanghai prison. The cell was tiny and cold. The bed was hard and the food was scanty. Everywhere in the prison it was known that we were police, and the warders treated us more strictly than other prisoners, lest it be thought we were receiving favors.

Free—But Ruined

"It was a weary five weeks. I saw that whatever the outcome of the case I could never hope to be reinstated in the police service. I saw the £200 I has paid into the superannuation fund disappear in paying for my defense. The £200 which would have been added to my £200 by the authorities was withheld. I thanked God I was a single man. The case dragged on. Very contradictory evidence was given. Then I was found not guilty. I was free—but ruined. I obtained a third class passage back across Siberia. The little money I had for food was not nearly enough. I missed more meals than I had. I asked the authorities to appeal to the Foreign Office to see what could be done but this request was refused. The other officer who was with me met with the same treatment. He, however, had a good friend out there, who got him a post up country far away from the scene of our trial. Friends have advised me to get the matter brought up n Parliament. Anyhow, at 32, I am facing the world again with a first-class Army character, with an excellent and unblemished record of service in the police—and 11 pence half-penny."

The Shanghai Times, Tuesday, June 2, 1936
"Correcting Statement"
Editor, The Shanghai Times

Sir, — With reference to a statement made by Ernest William Peters at Dover, England, on April 15 and re-published by some papers locally, I would like to bring to your notice one or two errors made by him in that statement.

Firstly, I will quote parts of his statement: — "I spent five weeks in a Shanghai prison. The cell was tiny and cold, the bed was hard and the food was scanty. Everywhere in the prison it was known that we were Police and the warders treated us more strictly than other prisoners lest it be thought we were receiving favours.

"I saw the £200 I has paid into the superannuation fund disappear in paying for my defense. The £200 which would have been added to my £200 by the authorities was withheld. I

"I obtained a third class passage back across Siberia."

The other officer who was with me met with the same treatment. He, however, had a good friend out there, who got him a post up country far away from the scene of our trial.

The following are a few authentic facts from the officer who was with him: Peters and I were shown every consideration whilst being detained pending our trial in the Civil Wing of Ward Road Gaol away from the prison proper. On the third day of our detention the senior Warder came and told us that a number of the foreign members of the Gaol Staff had asked for and received permission to send us three meals a day, from their own mess, for which they themselves would pay. I take this opportunity to thank them again.

Regarding lawyer's fees, Peters paid exactly the same as I, as Peters' fees were paid the same time as mine, which was $250 for six days in the Police Court and $300 for eight days in the Supreme Court, and included outside-of-Court work.

These fees, I think were exceptionally low, and I believe would not even pay overhead expenses for any lawyer. My Father, thinking I would not have enough money for lawyer's fees, cabled £20 to my lawyer, who handed same to me intact. Our legal practitioners called whilst we were being detained, bringing books, newspapers, and periodicals for us to read, often after 5 p.m. and, regardless of regulations, they were allowed to see us.

After our resignations had been accepted we were paid all moneys due to us and we were both granted second-class passages back to England via any route. Peters wishing to return to England, stayed here and am now working in a clerical capacity for Clarke's Inquiry and Protection Agency, and not "far away up country."

W.A. Judd
Shanghai, May 30, 1936

The North-China Daily News, Tuesday, June 2, 1936
"Echo of the Peters-Judd Case"
MR. JUDD CORRECTS STATEMENTS MADE IN ENGLAND

Mr. W.A. Judd wishes to correct certain statements alleged to have been made in England by Mr. E.W. Peters in regard to the treatment received by Mr. Peters and Mr. Judd during their detention for trial in the recent case in the Supreme Court.

The statement in question was not published in the "north-China Daily New" but references to it have been made in other papers and Mr. Judd wishes it to be known that he and Mr. Peters were shown every consideration whilst being detained in the Ward Road Gaol, and Mr. Judd wishes again to thank the Gaol staff for their consideration. He goes on to say:

Regarding lawyer's fees, Peters paid exactly the same as I, as Peters' fees were paid the same time as mine, which was $250.00 for six days in the Police Court and $300.00 for eight days in the Supreme Court, and included outside-of-Court work.

These fees, I think, were exceptionally low, and I believe would not even pay overhead expenses for any lawyer. My father, thinking I would not even pay overhead expenses for enough money for lawyer's fees, cabled £20 to my lawyer, who handed same to me intact. Our legal practitioners called whilst we were being detained, bringing books, newspapers and periodicals for us to read, often after 5 p.m. and they were allowed to see us. After our resignations had been accepted we were paid all the moneys due to us and we were both granted second-class passages back to England via any route. Peters took the Siberian route and I, not wishing to return to England, stayed here and am now working in a clerical capacity for Clarke's Inquiry and Protection Agency, and not "far away up country.

Sources and Further Reading

E.W. Peters, SMP personnel file, Shanghai Municipal Archives, file U102-3-774: this file is now closed again, but contains personal details, information on recruitment, his disciplinary record, and material related to the trial and his resignation from the police.

North China Herald, 12, 19 February, 1936, transcripts of the trial.

US National Archives and Records Administration, Record Group 263, Archives of the Shanghai Municipal Police Special Branch, file D7137, Peters and Judd case. This mostly contains news clippings about the case, and some material on the monitoring of Chinese press comment, and police interaction with Chinese newspapers during the trial.

Robert Bickers, E*mpire Made Me: An Englishman Adrift in Shanghai* (London: Penguin, 2003): the life and times of Maurice Tinkler, who served in the SMP 1919-30.

Ted Quigley, *A Spirit of Adventure: The Memoirs of Ted Quigley* (Lewes: The Book Guild Ltd, 1994): police sergeant's memoir.

Peter Robins with Nicholas Tyler, *The Legend of W.E. Fairbairn: Gentleman and Warrior, The Shanghai Years* (Harlow: CQB Publications, 2006): biography of leading figure in the force.

Maurice Springfield, *Hunting opium and other scents* (Halesworth: Norfolk and Suffolk Publicity, 1966): senior officer's memoir.

Frederic Wakeman Jr, *Policing Shanghai 1927-1937* (Berkeley: University of California Press, 1995): politics and policing across the city.

Frederic Wakeman Jr, *The Shanghai Badlands: Wartime Terrorism and Urban Crime 1937-1941* (Cambridge: Cambridge University Press 1996): violence and politics during the years

Shanghai was surrounded by Japanese forces.

Bernard Wasserstein, *Secret War in Shanghai: Treachery, subversion and collaboration in the Second World War* (London: Profile Books, 1998). Makes extensive use of SMP Special Branch files to explore wartime Shanghai.

Charles A. Willoughby, *Shanghai Conspiracy: The Sorge Spy Ring* (New York: E.P. Dutton & Co., 1952). General Douglas MacArthur's intelligence chief's account of espionage in pre war Shanghai and Japan, based on the SMP Special Branch files which his agency had acquired in 1949.